Life in Stalin's Soviet Union

ALSO AVAILABLE FROM BLOOMSBURY

Life in Stalin's Soviet Union

Edited by
KEES BOTERBLOEM

BLOOMSBURY ACADEMIC
LONDON • NEW YORK • OXFORD • NEW DELHI • SYDNEY

BLOOMSBURY ACADEMIC
Bloomsbury Publishing Plc
50 Bedford Square, London, WC1B 3DP, UK
1385 Broadway, New York, NY 10018, USA

BLOOMSBURY, BLOOMSBURY ACADEMIC and the Diana logo are trademarks of
Bloomsbury Publishing Plc

First published in Great Britain 2019

Cover design by Liron Gilenberg
Cover image: *The Rabochiy i Kolkhoznitsa* (Worker and Kolkhoz Woman) in Moscow,
Russia. Made by Vera Mukhina for the 1937 World's Fair in Paris. (© Yury Gubin/iStock)

A catalogue record for this book is available from the British Library.

A catalog record for this book is available from the Library of Congress.

ISBN: HB: 978-1-4742-8551-3
PB: 978-1-4742-8552-0
ePDF: 978-1-4742-8550-6
eBook: 978-1-4742-8549-0

Typeset by Newgen KnowledgeWorks Pvt. Ltd., Chennai, India
Printed and bound in Great Britain

To find out more about our authors and books visit www.bloomsbury.com
and sign up for our newsletters.

Contents

Illustrations

Figures

Tables

Contributors

Golfo Alexopoulos is professor of history at the University of South Florida and the author of *Illness and Inhumanity in Stalin's Gulag* (2017) and *Stalin's Outcasts: Aliens, Citizens and the Soviet State, 1926–1936* (2003). She is also the founding director of the USF Institute in Russia.

Frances Bernstein is associate professor of history at Drew University, where she teaches courses in Russian history, the history of disability and the body, and the history of medicine. Her most recent publications include "Prosthetic Manhood in the Soviet Union at the End of World War II," *OSIRIS* 30, 1 (2015): 113–33; "Rehabilitation Staged: How Soviet Doctors 'Cured' Disability in the Second World War," in *Disability Histories*. Edited by Susan Burch and Michael A. Rembis (2014, 218–36); and "Prosthetic Promise and Potemkin Limbs in late-Stalinist Russia," in *Disability in Eastern Europe and the Former Soviet Union*. Edited by Michael Rasell and Elena Iarskaia (2013, 42–66). She is currently working on a manuscript on the management of war invalids after the Second World War.

Kees Boterbloem is professor of history at the University of South Florida. He is the author of *A History of Russia and Its Empire: From Mikhail Romanov to Vladimir Putin* (first ed., 2013; second ed., 2018); *Moderniser of Russia: Andrei Vinius, 1641–1716* (2013); *The Fiction and Reality of Jan Struys* (2008); *The Life and Times of Andrei Zhdanov* (2004); *Life and Death under Stalin: The Kalinin Province, 1945–1953* (1999); and three books in Dutch: *Revoljoetsija: De betekenis van de Russische Revolutie in historisch perspectief* (2017); *De Russische Revolutie* (2016); and Jan Struys, *Rampspoedige reizen door Rusland en Perzië in de zeventiende eeuw* (2014). He was the editor of *The Historian* from 2008 to 2018.

Heather D. DeHaan is associate professor of history at the State University of New York at Binghamton. She is the author of *Stalinist City Planning: Professionals, Performance, and Power* (2013). It was based on her doctoral dissertation, "From Nizhnii to Gor'kii: The Reconstruction of a Russian Provincial City in the Stalinist 1930s," which, in 2005, won the Tucker-Cohen prize for best dissertation of the year from the Association for Slavic, East European and Eurasian Studies (ASEEES). A recipient of many other grants, honors, and prizes, she has published several articles and book reviews as well.

Gregory L. Freeze is the Victor and Gwendolyn Beinfeld professor of History at Brandeis University. A recipient of numerous awards and honors, he is author of, among other works, *The Russian Levites: Parish Clergy in the Eighteenth Century* (1977); *Parish Clergy in 19th Century Russia* (1983); *From Supplication to Revolution: A Documentary Social History of Imperial Russia* (1988); *Guide to the Russian State Archive* (1994); *The Special Files for L.P. Beria, from the NKVD-MVD of the USSR* (1996); and the editor of *Russia: A History*, which has undergone several editions, as well as a translator and editor of several other books. He is also the author of dozens of articles in English, Russian, Italian, and German.

James Heinzen is professor of history at Rowan University. A recipient of many grants and awards, he is the author of *The Art of The Bribe: Corruption under Stalin, 1943–1953* (2016) and of *Inventing a Soviet Countryside: State Power and the Transformation of Rural Russia, 1917–1929* (2004).

Larry E. Holmes is professor emeritus of history at the University of South Alabama. He is the author of many scholarly articles and books, including *The Kremlin and the Schoolhouse: Reforming Education in Soviet Russia, 1917-1931*; *Stalin's School: Moscow's Model School No. 25, 1931–1937*; and *Stalin's World War II Evacuations: Triumph and Troubles in Kirov*.

Elena A. Osokina received her PhD from Moscow University, Russia. Currently, she is a professor of Russian history at the University of South Carolina. She is the author of *Hierarchy of Consumption: Life under the Stalinist Rationing System, 1928–1935* (1993, in Russian); *Our Daily Bread: Socialist Distribution and the Art of Survival in Stalin's Russia, 1927–1941*, 2001; *Gold for Industrialization: Torgsin* (2009, in Russian); and *The Heavenly Blue of Angels' Vestments: Soviet Export of Religious Art, 1920s–1930s* (2018, in Russian).

Karen Petrone is an Arts & Sciences Distinguished Professor and Chair of the Department of History at the University of Kentucky. She is the author of *Life Has Become More Joyous, Comrades: Celebrations in the Time of Stalin* (2000) and *The Great War in Russian Memory* (2011), and has coedited three books: *The New Muscovite Cultural History* (2009), *Gender Politics and Mass Dictatorship: Global Perspectives* (2011), and *Everyday Life in Russia Past and Present* (2014). Most recently, she has coauthored a textbook (with Kenneth Slepyan): *The Soviet Union and Russia, 1939–2015: A History in Documents* (2016), and she is currently at work on a book about war memory in Putin's Russia.

Amy E. Randall is associate professor of history at Santa Clara University. Her recent scholarship includes "Gender and the Emergence of the Soviet 'Citizen-Consumer' in Comparative Perspective," in *Material Culture in Russia and the USSR: Things, Values, Identities*. Edited by Graham Roberts (2017,

135–53); editor of and author of "Introduction: Gendering Genocide Studies," *Genocide and Genocide in the Twentieth Century: A Comparative Survey* (2015, 1–34); editor of and author of "Soviet Masculinities: Guest Editor's Introduction" in "Soviet Masculinities," a special issue of *Russian Studies in History: A Journal of Translations* 2 (2012): 3–12; and " 'Abortion Will Deprive You of Happiness!': Soviet Reproductive Politics in the Post-Stalin Era," *The Journal of Women's History* 3 (2011): 13–38. She teaches Soviet history, gender and national identity in twentieth-century Eastern and Western Europe, the Holocaust, ethnic cleansing and genocide in the twentieth century, the history of sexuality, and identity and the "Other" in the shaping of the modern world.

David Shearer is the Thomas Muncy Keith professor of history at the University of Delaware. He is the author of *Stalin and the Lubianka: A Documentary History of the Political Police and Security Organs in the Soviet Union, 1922–1953*, with Vladimir Khaustov (2015); *Stalinskii voennyi sotsializm. Repressii i obshchestvennyi poryadok v Sovetskom Soyuze, 1924–1953* (2014); *Policing Stalin's Socialism: Repression and Social Order in the Soviet Union, 1924–1953* (2009); and *Industry, State, and Society in Stalin's Russia, 1926–1934* (1996).

Kenneth Slepyan is a professor of history at Transylvania University in Lexington, Kentucky. He has written several publications about the USSR in the Second World War, including *Stalin's Guerrillas: Soviet Partisans in World War II* (2006). He has also coauthored a textbook (with Karen Petrone) *The Soviet Union and Russia, 1939–2015: A History in Documents* (2016). He is currently working on a book about daily life in the Axis-occupied territories of the Soviet Union.

Introduction

Kees Boterbloem

Through its constant upheaval, daily life under Stalin was never like daily life anywhere else in a modern or modernizing (industrializing) society. Without exaggeration, it can be said that few complex societies in history have witnessed such turmoil in such a short period. Meanwhile, the Russian Empire had not been exactly quiet in the quarter century realm before in 1929 Stalin established his absolute rule over the Union of Socialist Soviet Republics, known for short as the Soviet Union. Truly bloody episodes of almost unimaginable human suffering alternated whatever routine prevailed for short periods in Stalin's realm. In absolute numbers of people killed, the quarter century of tyranny (1929–53) of Joseph Stalin (1878–1953) over the Soviet Union ranks as the second deadliest regime in history, after that of his disciple Mao Zedong (1893–1976), who was responsible for even more deaths in Communist China between 1949 and 1976.[1] While Stalin oversaw the "unnatural deaths" of some 10–15 million in peacetime (and the Second World War killed another 25 million Soviet citizens), an urbanizing, modern country developed in the same period in northern Eurasia. Even though the number of Soviet people that was killed or maimed beggars belief, Stalin survived in power and his country became the "other" superpower in the Cold War, after it had been mainly responsible for the defeat of Nazi Germany in the Second World War.

Seen in this light, it should not surprise that during the 1960s and 1970s the first critics (the so-called dissidents) of Stalin and the post-Stalinist regime found little support among the Soviet population. Most Soviet citizens did not want to jeopardize the unheard of stability or normalcy of those decades, even if they realized that Stalin's atrocities had not been truly digested. After Stalin, survivors born between approximately 1890 and 1930 in Imperial Russia or the early days of the Soviet Union longed for a quiet life, enjoying private things rather than facing a traumatic reckoning with the absurd regime that had lorded it over them (and that they had both condoned and endured) in their younger years. Before the 1980s, most of the Soviet residents were willing to accept the official discourse about their country's heroic triumph in 1917 and 1945 and to forget the nightmarish hardships they had faced. They tried to cherish their personal contribution (or indeed sacrifice) to the construction of what, they still half believed, would eventually become a society in which full freedom and equality were to reign forever, according to the recipe of the all-seeing and all-knowing Karl Marx (1818–1883) and Vladimir Lenin (1870–1924). Official discourse maintained that the foundations for a future life of happiness, prosperity, and equality had been laid under Stalin as, in the end, he had adhered to the laws of history as discovered by the prophets of communism. Stalin's savagery, however, was largely left out of the story as it was told between 1953 and 1985. This narrative began to change after Mikhail Gorbachev became Soviet leader in 1985. In a paradigmatic shift that unfolded between 1985 and 1992, Stalin and his Soviet project, or experiment, began to be condemned in Soviet public discourse as the darkest of dark chapters in history. Taking up the argument of Western scholars and Soviet dissidents before 1985, Soviet citizens began to recognize that Stalin's subjects had tried to survive in extraordinarily difficult conditions.

Today any serious student will agree that the history of the Soviet Union under Stalin is first and foremost testimony to human resilience. Like other human beings, however, Russians, Ukrainians, Georgians, Uzbeks, or Armenians all tried to carve out as much as a semblance of normalcy in their lives as could be done within a gruesome (and even absurd) context. At times, they succeeded in this effort, but crisis succeeded crisis, and nothing ever became routine in the Soviet Union before March 1953. The cataclysm began with the 1929–32 Great Turn (*Velikii Perelom*), which saw ludicrously fast-paced industrialization imposed on the country accompanied by the destruction of traditional peasant life. A cultural revolution in the towns and the villages overturned time-honored habits and beliefs.

This profound transformation was supposed to be planned and orderly, following the guidelines of the First Five-Year Plan (1928–32). But plan targets were constantly changed, and although the country's industrialization was outlined in some (albeit ever-changing) detail, the collectivization of agriculture was very sketchily conceived. The Russian and non-Russian peasants, probably four-fifths of the total Soviet population in 1929, were herded into collective farms, without anyone truly knowing how collectivized agriculture was supposed to work. It led to a thorough disruption of crop cultivation and profound damage to animal husbandry, which in turn caused a drastic decline in living standards in countryside and cities. Ration cards became the norm in the towns, whereas in the villages people eked out a living from the scant amount of crops, meat, and dairy that was not confiscated by the state's agents. Eventually, as individual farmsteads were stripped of almost anything they produced (by the imposition of absurdly high taxes in kind), most peasants opted for the only slightly less brutal exploitation by the state of the collective farms. From then on, initiative in Soviet agriculture was top-down, with plowing, sowing, haying, milking, or harvesting planned by state authorities and imposed on the collective farm directors, who had to cajole their farmers to meet the targets.

If they could, when confronted with the brutal terms of collectivization, many peasants immediately made off for the city in hopes of finding a better fate. Some of these refugees had been stigmatized in their village by communist officials as *kulaks*, rich peasants who had allegedly engaged in exploiting their neighbors, and who (if they did not flee in time) were deported in the 100,000s to inhospitable areas in the early 1930s. *Kulak* property (houses, equipment, cattle) was surrendered to the collective farms, but with the departure of the better-off, much of the peasantry's initiative and enterprising spirit left the villages. Together with the *kulaks* the clergy was driven out, their churches becoming granaries or cultural centers for the collective farms. Having tolerated religion somewhat in the 1920s, Stalin's new socialist society would no longer abide Christianity or Islam.

As said, urban industrialization was neither a very organized process. In the course of the First Five-Year Plan, production aims were upped to impossible heights. The result was chaotic, and many of the local political leaders, factory bosses, planners, engineers, foremen, and even shop floor workers developed ways to exaggerate their accomplishments. At times, the Soviet authorities threw in tremendous resources to help develop and complete some of the showpieces of their planned economy, which were then displayed with great fanfare in the Soviet press; some herculean efforts made other projects succeed. But this came at the expense of less prestigious ventures. The statistics issued about the stunning production levels of much of the factories and mines of the First Five-Year Plan were fake, and most projects only began to show a significant yield during the Second Five-Year Plan (1933–7). After 1932, priority was often given to the completion of unfinished projects of which the construction had started in the early years of the Great Turn. Nonetheless, the backbreaking efforts yielded some positive results: The industrial infrastructure laid down between 1928 and June 1941 proved (barely) sufficient to sustain the country during the Second World War, but victory came otherwise at a staggering price.

Because all the new enterprises needed workers, throughout most of the 1930s the cities' population rose quickly, nourished by a steady influx of country dwellers. But the daily needs of the urban dwellers were given a low priority, and living (and labor) conditions were spartan before the middle of the decade: Ration cards provided basic foodstuffs, with anything beyond staples such as bread or milk being exorbitantly expensive; housing was abysmal with people living in communal apartments, in which several families shared one kitchen and bathroom, and used one room each, while others slept on bunk beds in factory barracks without adequate heating, electricity, or running water; and public transport and schools functioned haltingly. Meanwhile, the amount of industrial accidents (and the number of people contracting work-related diseases) was staggering.

This brutal transformation of life in the Soviet Union reached its nadir in the famine that swept across Ukraine, southern Russia, and Kazakhstan in 1932 and 1933. Only a brief respite at most (in 1934 and 1935 living standards began to improve slightly, and the collective farms started to produce more, so that rationing of most goods could be abolished) preceded a new episode of baffling atrocity. In 1936, the first rumblings of the Great Terror could be detected, which reached its climax in 1937 and 1938, when 2 million people were arrested by the Soviet secret police (NKVD). Of them, more than one-third would die in a hail of bullets from a firing squad, while many later succumbed in the prison-and-camp system overseen by the main administration of labor camps (*GULAG*). This camp system, even if its origins can be traced to the Russian Civil War and the Solovki camps of the 1920s, emerged as a gigantic complex in the early years of the Great Turn, when it received many of the *kulaks* and others who were scapegoated (rather than Stalin and his cronies, who were really responsible) as the cause of the bedlam that had unfolded from 1929 onward. Millions would end up in the prisons and *GULAG* concentration camps between 1929 and 1953. It is impossible to establish precisely how many people in Stalin's time became inmates of the camps, but by the late 1930s on any given day some two million people could be found in it, with this number reaching three million by 1950. This has got experts now estimating that 15–20 million people spent time in Stalin's concentration camps. Although many were released after serving their time, the death rate in the camps was frightening, and we can only guess the exact number of those who died in them.

A year after Stalin halted the Great Terror's mass waves of arrests, the Winter War with Finland (November 1939–March 1940) may have cost a quarter million Soviet soldiers their lives, while other Red Army troops lost their lives fighting the Japanese in East Asia in an undeclared war in 1938 and 1939. Then the greatest demographic catastrophe of all, the Great Patriotic War, befell the Soviet Union in which in fewer than four years (June 1941–May

1945) perhaps 28 million people died, while millions of others were, physically or psychologically, heavily scarred for life by their wartime experiences.[2]

While this massacre was going on, wartime deportations of entire ethnic groups accused of collaboration with the Germans were conducted on Stalin's orders, probably affecting another million people (Chechens, Ingushetians, Crimean Tatars, and others). Indeed, the deportation of ethnic groups both before and during the war—mainly as a prophylactic measure to prevent them from collaborating with their co-ethnics across the border—affected more than half a million people as well (among them were the so-called Volga Germans).[3]

And even after 1945, large-scale suffering among Stalin's subjects occurred: A famine in 1946 and 1947 in European Russia killed possibly 2 million people, while thousands of others fell victim to a number of postwar purges; Ukrainian and Baltic independence fighters kept up their battle against Soviet rule long after the official end of the Second World War, in which thousands on both sides were killed and tens of thousands of anti-Soviet guerillas ended up in the *GULAG*. Altogether, the lives of Stalin's subjects unfolded against the background of twenty-five years of almost relentless deaths of "unnatural causes"; for most, at some point during this quarter century, this background became foreground, when they themselves or their relatives and friends were swept up in this maelstrom.[4]

The essays in the following pages try to establish how Stalin's subjects lived and died in this baffling environment, and how daily life of particularly the Slavs among them unfolded in a variety of settings. Russians, Ukrainians, and Belarussians formed the great majority of the Soviet population under Stalin, so their story is in some ways the story of the Soviet Union as a whole under Stalin. Still, our portrayal of daily life in the Soviet Union is not comprehensive: Both for reasons of space and otherwise the reader will not find out anything truly substantial about the lives of those who lived in the Caucasus region or Central Asia, as well as the western parts that were annexed in 1939 and 1940 and then again in 1945.[5] This book mainly discusses Russians' lives, rather than that of the more than 140 or so non-Russian peoples living in Stalin's realm.

***

Stalin's regime, of course, did not emerge in a vacuum. Historians have often discussed the question (perhaps following the cue of Lev Trotsky [1879–1940], Stalin's rival for Lenin's mantle) whether or not Stalin was destined to be Lenin's successor. Obviously, he was not, for otherwise he would have immediately succeeded as an unrivaled leader upon Lenin's death in 1924, or even earlier, when Lenin began to ail in 1922.

Ever since the young Marxist leader Lenin in the early 1900s had called for a vanguard party to lead the industrial working class to the promised land of communism, the chance of a dictatorship by a small faction of party leaders was likely, once Lenin's Bolshevik group gained power in Russia in the autumn of 1917. The first to have warned against such a dictatorship seems to have been the German-Polish socialist Rosa Luxemburg (1871–1919); oddly, Trotsky, one of Lenin's closest collaborators in the 1917 October Revolution and after, had echoed Luxemburg's warnings, before he became a Bolshevik himself a few months before the Bolshevik coup d'état.[6]

In 1902, Lenin had explained the need for a vanguard party by arguing that the mindset of factory workers and miners, the blue-collar "proletarians" celebrated as the people of the future by Marx, was insufficiently sophisticated to bargain for more than trade-union type of reforms (health and accident insurance, pensions, etc.).[7] They could not be trusted to do the right thing, and this was still true even after they (or really his party in their name) had taken power, Lenin suggested. In his writings and in his actions, long before the Bolshevik takeover in October 1917, it is evident that Lenin was convinced of being the sole political leader who identified the correct road to communism. Lenin was persuaded to use the word "communist" for his new type of government to distinguish its rule from that of "socialists." Those socialists, or social-democrats, had betrayed the true Marxist cause in 1914 by backing their national governments in the First World War, instead of adhering to the international solidarity of the working class across the industrialized world (and refusing to take up arms fighting workers on the other side). The word "communist" was part of the title of Marx's best known (or read) work, the 1848 *Communist Manifesto*, and its rhetorical use by Lenin's Bolsheviks emphasized their destiny as the true heirs of the German left-wing prophet.

Once Lenin became the head of the new Soviet government in 1917, in practice all decisions of any importance were made in his presence, or with his knowledge, and often enough based on his suggestions. This occurred even if formally it was the Communist Party's Central Committee that rendered the resolutions determining the regime's policies. Undoubtedly, within the Central Committee and the Soviet government (known as Council of People's Commissars or *Sovnarkom* before 1946), Lenin operated largely through persuasion, rather than using coercion or fear, to make those who disagreed with him fall in line. But he did grow increasingly impatient with those who questioned his viewpoint (and realized that, more often than not, there was not enough time for any long-winded political debates in trying to overcome the onslaught of crises that beset early Soviet Russia) and made his Party into an obedient machine (while the government was wholly subordinated to the Party at the same time). As even the Central Committee was too numerous (and its members often were away on duty during the Civil War that raged from the middle of 1918 to the spring of 1921), in 1919 a smaller executive was created, the Politburo, in which only a handful of leaders rendered all the key decisions. These developments explain to a considerable degree Stalin's dictatorial manner, for Stalin was one of the Politburo members from its inception and partially learned how to run the country from watching Lenin.

At the end of the Russian Civil War, the members of the Communist Party had become used to follow the orders from above without demurring. At the Tenth Party Congress in the spring of 1921, the formation of any faction within the Party expressing a dissenting opinion about the policy line was prohibited. Stalin used the majority within the Central Committee that stood behind him to isolate those who themselves aspired to become Lenin's successor after 1922.[8] The ironic endpoint of this strategy was that Stalin did not need the Central Committee anymore to back him up after 1929, and almost anything significant henceforth was decided by him and his acolytes in the Politburo. Ultimately, even those loyal supporters were sidelined, with Stalin becoming a true autocrat by the mid-1930s.

It was, however, not just the evolution of Soviet politics that set the table for the cataclysm of the Stalin era that began in earnest in 1929. The inhabitants of the Soviet Union had been beaten and bruised since at least the early 1890s (when a devastating famine struck the Russian Empire ruled by the tsar, who was then the all-powerful autocrat). Industrialization and rural overpopulation had combined with growing political restlessness in creating a volatile country. Modernization as such is an unsettling phenomenon, but in early-twentieth-century Russia the problems were writ large because the country found itself twice at war within a decade. The first of these wars, with Japan in 1904 and 1905, was localized in East Asia, and the tsar's government extricated itself from it just in time, even if it was forced to make substantial territorial concessions to its foreign foe and equally substantial concessions to its domestic opponents. Political parties became legal, a parliament (*Duma*) with limited powers was established, and censorship decreased, among other things. The most fanatical domestic opponents of the tsar died in clashes with tsarist troops, or ended up in Siberian or foreign exile.

The tsar's regime was thus saved, but found itself anew at war in August 1914, and this time faced a formidable coalition, which eventually included Germany, Austria-Hungary, Ottoman Turkey and Bulgaria. The Russians had allies, but, in 1916, after the Serbian and Romanian collapse in the war, those allies were fighting on fronts far away from Russia. Russia bore the brunt of the Turkish and Habsburg onslaught, and faced a significant part of the German armed forces as well. The military situation was bleak even if it was not entirely hopeless. But the war dragged on too long.

The simmering anger with the tsar boiled over in the fall of 1916, and led to the tsar's abdication in March 1917. The shocking violence of war and revolution undoubtedly reinforced the violence that was endemic in Russian traditional culture (as it was in most pre-modern societies).[9] The year 1917 saw a good deal of killing, although even in that year the number of soldiers' deaths fighting the Central Powers at the front still vastly outstripped that of those who fell in the hinterland during the revolutionary upheaval. But the Rubicon had been crossed: Many people, not in the least a good number of leading politicians—and especially the Bolshevik chiefs—had become inured to killing through witnessing the First World War's rivers of blood. When a civil war broke out in the former tsarist empire soon after Lenin's Communist regime had concluded peace with Germany and its allies at Brest-Litovsk (March 1918), carnage ensued. The death toll of this conflict is difficult to estimate, for no one kept count, but when the dust settled by early 1921 (when Georgia was occupied by the Red Army of the Communists), perhaps 5 million people had died in the civil war, while a famine was still raging, carrying away many millions more and only abating in 1922.

Little had been accomplished by 1922 in terms of the ambitious program the Bolsheviks dreamed about in October 1917. Their country was still far away from modern in technological terms, and, in keeping with their worldview, was therefore far removed from the Marxist ideal of the society of plenty populated by enlightened people who considered each other as equals. In addition, the Communist Soviet Union was an international pariah, with whom few countries traded. It was feared by many as the harbinger of Communist revolutions elsewhere; politicians in Europe and North America used fiery rhetoric that seemed to promise a concerted military invasion by all capitalist countries to slay this Russian monster. Such a threat, which appeared genuine to the Soviet leaders even if it was mostly empty in the reality of the war-weary world of the 1920s, made Lenin's successors decide that within short order their country needed to be transformed into an industrialized country with a mechanized military that could hold its own against any foreign armed forces.

This, however, required a herculean effort from a population that was still in the great majority living in rural locations and engaging in agriculture toward the end of the 1920s. Almost overnight, Soviet peasants needed to be become factory workers and miners. Industrialization was to be largely financed by domestic means, given the absence of any meaningful foreign investments in the country; this meant that the peasantry that did not join the industrial workforce had to foot much of the bill. Herding them into collective farms seemed a promising way to force them to pay this bill. Stalin would state, not long after he unleashed the full brunt of his modernization program, that the Soviet Union was at least half a century behind the industrialized world, and needed to catch up with it within a decade.[10] Every sacrifice toward this goal was justified. This, then, was the broader context in which Soviet daily life played itself out between 1928 and 1953.

**

With one or two exceptions, the scholars who have come together here to sketch daily life under Stalin are of a generation that witnessed the collapse of the Soviet Union in 1991. Although mainly North Americans, all of us spent lengthy periods in Soviet and post-Soviet Russia and observed the hardships with which the local population was confronted. The collapse was swift and until this very day remains puzzling, but many of the following essays seem to hint at an explanation: Much of the Soviet edifice was no more than a façade, which only held up because of the immense fear for (and lingering memory of) a brutal government. It forced its subjects into silent obedience through its excessive use of violence. Yet, the following pages chart many examples of a sullen defiance, in which people created or salvaged some sort of private life, or displayed an individualism that went against the Party line. It took decades, however, before people dared to question in full the manner in which they had been coerced to build a modern society. Even then, it was the Soviet government (and especially Party leader Mikhail Gorbachev [b. 1932]) itself that began this process by signaling to its subjects to be no longer afraid. On its prompting, the Soviet populace dared to become critical of the Communist regime and its past and present missteps. Once fear no longer ruled people's lives, the end came rapidly. Ever since, it has been hard to make sense out of the Soviet experience for those who lived through it. Only those who deliberately shut their eyes even after 1991 maintained that much worthwhile had been accomplished besides the victory over the Nazis in the Second World War. Otherwise the disillusionment was great in the post-Soviet successor states and the belief in the possibility of a collective better life shaken to the core. As a result, it has been very difficult for the various post-Soviet regimes to develop a sense of common purpose that really strikes a chord. Skepticism and often cynicism appears the prevalent mood in much of the post-Soviet world, or at least in Russia and Ukraine.

The essays written by Larry E. Holmes, Amy Randall, Karen Petrone, and Gregory Freeze look at different aspects of culture. Freeze looks at the tenacity of religious belief and the impossible situation in which the Orthodox Church found itself in the Soviet Union. Holmes investigates how general education was organized under Stalin and gradually general literacy was achieved, while children began to spend a longer time in school than previously. He suggests that teachers and pupils established a measure of autonomy that was unexpected in what is seen as a heavily regimented state. Heinzen explores the degree of success of the Soviet attempt at forging articulate and politically conscious (and reliable) citizens of the population. If found wanting, the *GULAG* lurked. Petrone looks at the impression made of the many festivals on the minds of the Soviet people in the annus horribilis of 1937. Meanwhile, from the early days of Soviet Russia there was much hullabaloo about gender equality, but women remained in practice in a disadvantaged social position, and patriarchy survived in practice if not on paper, as Amy Randall suggests.

Elena Osokina, Heather DeHaan, and David Shearer look at the consequences of living in a scarce economy. As Shearer shows, despite the threat of draconian penalties, many committed crimes, often driven to them by necessity. How dire the shortages indeed were is outlined by Osokina. And, despite lip service paid to people's right to decent healthcare and housing, as DeHaan shows, even in the privileged cities both fell far short of the ideal. Golfo Alexopoulos writes about the other world that was created for the trespassers and those not wanted in Soviet society, that of the *GULAG* camps. It was not only (or even primarily) populated by the "social deviants," or "common criminals," about which Shearer writes, but by those whose political loyalty was allegedly dubious and who often had been incarcerated on wholly spurious grounds (and often served much longer terms than criminals).

Finally, Slepyan and Bernstein's essays, as well as my own, look at specific groups in Stalin's realm who especially bore the brunt of a cruel regime: those who had served in the military especially in the hell that was the Second World War for the Soviet population (Slepyan); those who were maimed in that war or as a part of other savage aspects of Soviet life (Bernstein); and the first mass victims of Stalinism, those who were slated to disappear in the era of communism (the peasantry) and indeed eventually did disappear (as the abandoned collective farms of today indicate), albeit for different reasons than Marx had suggested (Boterbloem).

The book has been written with a broad readership in mind; references therefore are few, even if some contributors have chosen to indicate some of the very important primary (archival and otherwise) or secondary sources (works or scholarship) either to strengthen their point or offer an intriguing aside. Jargon has been as much as possible avoided, and wherever necessary a reasonable English translation of Russian-Soviet terminology supplied. A bibliography has been included for those who want to explore Stalin's era further.

Notes

1 The best treatment of Mao's brutality are Frank Dikötter's works. See F. Dikötter, *Mao's Great Famine: The History of China's Most Devastating Catastrophe, 1958–1962*, London: Bloomsbury, 2010; and F. Dikötter, *The Cultural Revolution: A People's History, 1962–1976*, London: Bloomsbury, 2017. Mao ruled China for about the same time (1949–76) as Stalin ruled the Soviet Union.

2 The number of Soviet soldiers who fell in August and September 1945 during the brief Soviet involvement in the war with Japan remained low, especially in comparison with the bloodshed in Europe.

3 And the first ethnic deportations, in fact, occurred during the Great Terror (of Koreans, Poles, and Finns, among others).

4 For this term and an estimate at assessing the damage, see Iosif G. Dyadkin, *Unnatural Deaths in the USSR, 1928–1954*, New Brunswick: Transaction Books, 1983.

5 See, for an impression, J. Sahadeo and R. Zanca, *Everyday Life in Central Asia: Past and Present*, Bloomington: Indiana University Press, 2007.

6 The Russians followed the Julian rather than the Gregorian calendar; thus, the October coup actually unfolded in November 1917.

7 See Vladimir Ilyich Lenin, "What Is to Be Done?: Burning Questions of Our Movement [1902]," available at: https://www.marxists.org/archive/lenin/works/1901/witbd/, accessed July 26, 2018.

8 The many biographies on Stalin discuss his rise to power, but very useful, too, remains R. Daniels, *The Conscience of the Revolution: Communist Opposition in Soviet Russia*, Cambridge, MA: Harvard University Press, 1960.

9 This is most graphically rendered in Olga Semyonova Tian-Shanskaia, *Village Life in Late Tsarist Russia*, ed. David Ransel, Bloomington: Indiana University Press, 1993.

10 See J. V. Stalin, "The Tasks of Business Executives." February 4, 1931, available at: https://www.marxists.org/reference/archive/stalin/works/1931/02/04.htm, accessed July 26, 2018.

1

The End of the Russian Peasants under Stalin

Kees Boterbloem

Because of the deceptive sameness of collective farming the Soviet authorities imposed on all of the country in the early 1930s, our idea of the daily life of Soviet peasants has acquired a uniformity that in many ways belies the great variety of farming ventures that existed in Stalin's time between 1929 and 1953. Indeed, the operation of the collective and state farms (respectively, known in Russian as *kolkhozy*, a contraction of *kollektivnye khoziaistva*, and *sovkhozy*, a contraction of *sovetskie khoziaistva*) of the Caucasus or Central Asia has hardly been researched.[1] This is in part because primary sources on the farms in those regions are not easily accessible for researchers. Language presents a further hurdle not easily cleared: Scholars writing about these regions in English need to master the local language(s) in addition to the Russian. The official (state and Party) documents might be written in either, or both, of these languages, and, ideally, a researcher would compare the official discourse of life on the farm with the actual experience of the Stalin-era *kolkhozniki* and *kolkhoznitsy* (the male and female collective farmworkers, respectively). With the passage of time, the opportunity to interview these people has disappeared.[2]

For the Slavonic-speaking farmers of the European USSR, we have a far broader source base, however, through the existence of oral testimony, official records, memoirs, fiction, and, for example, the Harvard Interview Project of the 1940s and 1950s that saw Soviet refugees in the United States discuss their lives as residents of Stalin's country.[3] Since Western researchers of the Soviet Union tend to master the Eastern Slavonic languages rather than the Baltic languages or those of the Caucasus and Central Asia, the resulting historiography regarding Soviet farming has focused on the Slavic parts of the Soviet Union (Russia, Ukraine, Belarus). There sedentary agriculture (crop cultivation and animal husbandry) was the norm already long before the 1917 Revolution. It is, meanwhile, perhaps puzzling that thorough scholarly accounts in the Russian language remain scarce of daily life (*byt'*) in the Soviet countryside under Stalin.[4]

The following essay will be largely about daily life on the collective farms of the regions of substantial Eastern Slavic settlement in the Soviet Union, and especially in the Tver' region of central European Russia. It will draw on oral history, fiction and official documents.[5] Peasant life in this region in the time of Stalin presents a good case study and starkly displays the key challenges of collective farming in the Soviet Union.

Tver' (*Kalinin*) province is situated northwest of Moscow, its eponymous capital almost 200 kilometers from the Soviet capital. Its territory is somewhat larger than that of the Low Countries.[6] It is here that the mighty Volga River has its source. Since the 1850s, the *October* (previously *Nikolai*) Railroad bisected it. It is the oldest railway in Russia, linking Moscow with St. Petersburg (Leningrad). Despite the occasional textile mill and a few other manufacturing companies in the larger cities of Tver', Rzhev, and Vishnyi Volochek, this was, like most of imperial Russia, a largely rural realm before Stalin's Great Turn in 1929. Prior to the onset of collectivization in the last months of that year, most of its residents lived in villages and for their livelihood engaged in part- or full-time agricultural pursuits. And, ever more pronouncedly, the countryside of Tver' witnessed a concomitant rural exodus after collectivization began: The villages emptied out at a very swift pace after 1929. This migration to urban localities has proceeded across the Russian Federation until this very day. Urbanization is a phenomenon that has accompanied industrialization everywhere in the world, but its scope and speed in the Soviet Union is remarkable. The astounding speed and size of this phenomenon can only attributed to the hostile policies toward the peasantry unleashed by the Communist regime, especially during the quarter century of Stalin's autocracy (1929–53).

European Russia's continental climate makes the winters at times resemble the weather in the Arctic. With the thermometer dipping to thirty degrees Celsius below zero, and, more significant, frost sometimes lasts from mid-September to the first half of May in the Russian heartland to which the Tver' region belongs. This makes for a short growing season and had led, long before the 1917 Revolution, peasants to cultivate hardy grains such as rye or oats, and, eventually, "technical" crops such as flax, the raw material used for linen and sometimes processed into oil. In addition, pre-revolutionary farms engaged in animal husbandry, but the options for this were limited, for grass, too, only grew abundantly for a limited period in spring and summer, making grazing season short and restricting the opportunity for making hay. It is in a way remarkable that, given such limited options, the region had a population upward of 2.5 million in the 1920s (1.5 percent of the total Soviet population), of whom four-fifths were rural dwellers. The large number of country folk of the Tver' area was typical for the early years of the Soviet Union as such (about the same share of the population was living in the countryside in the entire country in 1929), as it had been of late imperial Russia.

This remarkable high number of rural dwellers in these harsh climatic circumstances was made possible by the habit of the local population to perform other work besides farming, a common feature across most of European Russia. This might be a handicraft, but by the 1920s it often entailed work in the larger cities for part of the year. A willingness to move around in search of work predated the railways, but the arrival of the railways stimulated this itinerant way of life in the last decades of tsardom. Out-migration had become more and more the trend in the Russian villages because of the growing employment opportunities in the factories of industrializing St. Petersburg, Moscow, and elsewhere. For Tver', the most famous example of such a migrant was a local boy who became the official Soviet head-of-state in 1919, Mikhail Kalinin (1873–1946). The provincial capital was renamed in his honor in 1931.

Before 1929, though, the move to the cities often occurred gradually, in stages: Many of the locals returned to their villages at harvest time, when as many hands as could be found were needed to bring in the crops. Only slowly did people settle permanently in the city. This seasonal ebb and flow, too, was to be severely curtailed by collectivization, but the need for help with harvesting or haying remained acute after 1929. In the absence of the traditional wave of returnees, it was then provided by army soldiers (in peace time), or people working in offices who were mobilized. For example, in October 1950, when the harvest was unusually chaotic because of an enforced merger of collective farms earlier in the year (in most cases, two or three smaller farms were amalgamated into one larger farm), one-sixth of the population of the town Vyshnii Volochek, the second largest in Tver' province, was dispatched to the fields to haul in the crops.

After the turmoil of the Russian Civil War had died down in the early 1920s, the peasants of Tver' appear to have been able to resume a way of life that was not very different from before 1914, an existence exquisitely well charted by the German historian Helmut Altrichter in the 1980s. Few joined the Communist Party, which remained a predominantly urban organization, true to its calling of being the movement of the industrial working class. In the 1920s, across the province rural soviets (*sovet* is the Russian word for council) existed, which constituted the official government, but even these administrative bodies had few Communists among their staff. Peasants remained rather aloof from the sporadic anti-religious offensives that took aim at the local priests, and happily distilled their own moonshine. They tended to have larger families than city dwellers, as their housing was not constrained by issues of space. Of course, the amount of arable land was limited (regardless of any adherence to the Russian tradition of periodic repartition, which ever so often allotted larger families more land than smaller ones); as we saw, in this region (and this seems to go for much of Russia to the north of the Black Earth Zone—the territory of fertile soil stretching out along the Russian-Ukrainian border), people had been accustomed for generations to seek their livelihood at least in part in nonagricultural jobs. The brief peaceful hiatus from about 1921 to 1929 appears nonetheless as a sort of idyllic intermezzo in the Russian countryside wedged between long periods of massive upheaval.

But the peasants of the European part of the Soviet Union and western Siberia began to withhold grain from the market and reduce their production in 1926 and 1927 because they could not buy consumer goods in exchange for their crops. Grain prices rose in the cities as a result of the declining market supply. In the course of 1927 and 1928, then, grain requisitioning units were sent into the countryside, a return to the Civil War practice of forcing peasants to give up their yield. But this was not a long-term solution and Stalin decided in the course of 1928 that the NEP, the New Economic Policy, introduced under Lenin that allowed peasants to market their production for a profit, needed to end, not just in terms of the state's agricultural policy but also in the cities, where small businesses had been tolerated. Exactly how, after doing away with the vagaries of the market, an adequate agricultural production was to be achieved to supply the cities remained moot for a while, until in the second half of 1929 the Central Committee of the Communist Party, at Stalin's urging, chose for a radical transformation of the Soviet economy. Under socialism, it was argued, the uncertainty of the supply-and-demand capitalist market would disappear. The state (or its planning committee *Gosplan*) would rationally plan the production and distribution of agricultural and industrial goods in order to supply the Soviet population with the products it needed.

In agriculture, this rationalization of production could be best achieved, the theory went, by the organization of collective farms, joining the peasant households of each village and guided by well-thought-out plowing, sowing, harvesting, or dairy-and-meat production plans. This joint effort would lead to far higher yields, in part because socialist agriculture was to have the use of advanced mechanized equipment. These surplus yields would easily feed the cities, and because fewer workhands would be needed in this allegedly superior manner of farming, many people would be able to leave the countryside to join the urban work force. But nothing of the kind materialized once, in the late fall of 1929, serious steps were made toward collectivization. As a stopgap measure to bridge the gap to the moment that advanced mechanized equipment became abundantly available, the farms were at first to improve production with the help of the confiscated property (land, equipment, buildings, animals) of those who had allegedly been sabotaging the grain supplies of the cities earlier, the richer peasants or *kulaks*. Since the meaning of terms such as "capitalist" or "communist" was often vague to the peasants, the Party borrowed a pejorative term about exploitative richer peasants from prerevolutionary peasant speech, condemning them as *kulak* (similar terms were found in non-Russian languages), a word that was in use for prerevolutionary large farmers. Those *kulaks*, indeed, had in the days of the tsars engaged in squeezing their neighbors like lemons by using them as hired hands against a starvation wage. But after the turmoil of world war, revolution, and civil war (in which wealthier villagers had disappeared) few *kulaks* could be found in truth. Those now labelled *kulaks* hardly tended to be better off than their neighbors: More often than not, their household might have a second horse to put in front of the plow or two instead of one dairy cow. But such facts did not stop the Soviet Communists: *Kulaks* needed to be identified and banished from the villages. They were stigmatized as capitalist exploiters, class enemies according to the Marxist worldview.

This persecution of the *kulaks* ("dekulakization," from the Russian *razkulachivanie*) was a key part of the collectivization process. Stalin's Communist Party saw much of life through the stark prism of a Marxist class war. Following a quota system, the Party stigmatized some 3–5 percent of the inhabitants of each village as inveterate capitalist exploiters. The very highest Communist leaders overseeing collectivization in Moscow set these quotas. In the first months of 1930, across the Soviet Union, hundreds of thousands of "*kulaks*" with their families were exiled from their ancestral homes. The luckier ones were merely dispatched to the outskirts of their native region, but most were sent to "special settlements" in remote regions.[7] "Dekulakization" took place in the middle of winter, and in almost all cases no shelter awaited the banished families once they were unloaded from the trains (mostly, boxcars) that brought them there. Those deemed guilty of active resistance were sent off to concentration camps. They were often accompanied by those labeled "kulak-helpers," a large number of whom consisted of village priests.

The abstract concept of class war, more than anything a figment of the fertile imagination of the Communist leadership, thus translated into a brutal reality in the villages. The richer peasants' property and the churches were confiscated by the collective farms. This added perhaps a few heads of cattle or horses to the kolkhoz property and handed the collective some buildings to house the village club or, as was often the case with churches, a storage. It had the additional advantage that it made the villagers complicit in the banishment of their more prosperous neighbors. Although the wave to sign up people for the collective temporarily waned after "Dizzy with Success" (see below), "dekulakization" was never rescinded. Many *kulaks* and their families perished in the remote inhospitable surroundings where they were dumped, while others survived on the margins in these so-called special settlements for years. Of course, the award of kulak property to the collective farms may have been intended by the authorities, too, to make the kolkhozniks complicit in the persecution of their neighbors.

In order to set up the collectivized farms, thousands of factory workers were dispatched into the countryside in the early winter of 1930. Often with the help of police forces or even army units, they did manage, it seems, to exile the *kulaks* and their families, but they were factory workers. They knew little to nothing about how to set up such an untried novelty as a collective farm and make it work. Their efforts do seem to have conveyed to the peasantry that farm animals were to be "socialized," in part perhaps because tractors and combines and other sophisticated equipment were promised that would provide draft power. The result was wholesale slaughter of horses and bovines in the winter of 1930. The Soviet countryside would not recover from this butchery until Stalin's death, and dairy production remained anemic throughout Stalin's years. In addition, acreage undoubtedly shrunk, as in many cases people were forced to put themselves in front of the plow in the absence of horses or oxen. And the lack of horses also inhibited the delivery of crops or dairy and meat to the state collection points from where they were to be transported to the cities.

The effect of Stalin's Great Turn of the early 1930s and the Second World War on Kalinin *oblast'* (*oblast'* is one of several Russian words that means "province," more or less) can be readily seen from its population numbers. In the census of 1926, when the province had more or less the same borders as in the second half of the 1940s, some 2.6 million people resided in it. After the war, however, this number had dwindled to 1.6 million. Even though especially the city of Tver' grew (it was to reach about 500,000 people in the late Soviet era), the population size of the province never reached the number of the 1920s again. There is no doubt that the emptying out of the countryside was in part due to the havoc and dislocation caused by the Nazi-led attack on the Soviet Union: Kalinin fell into German hands in October 1941. The city was recovered by the Soviet army in December of that year and never relinquished to the Germans (and Finns) again, but fighting continued in the region into the first months of 1943, along a frontline that stabilized only thirty to forty miles west of Kalinin. This made it impossible for many who used to till the land in the western half of the province to resume farming. In addition, most adult men were called up for army service, from which (if they had survived the war) they were only released in the first few postwar years.

And the death toll of the war was here, as elsewhere in the Soviet Union, frightening: There is no reason to believe that fewer than one in six inhabitants was killed (which was the rate for the Soviet Union as a whole). But the death of one-sixth of the population of 1926 would still have given Kalinin province some 2.3–2.4 million people (if a sort of normal natural growth rate following previous trends had prevailed between 1926 and 1946) by 1948. Instead, there were probably three-quarter million people fewer living there in that year. The conclusion can only be that, from the moment collectivization was imposed, the countryside emptied out at a stunning rate. Even the introduction of an internal passport (a sort of an identity card that one had to always carry when in public) in the winter of 1932–3 had done little to stop this out-migration. In other words, anyone who could flee the collective farms between 1929 and 1953. Those who stayed did rarely perform their work according to the desired standard, further contributing to the, from the Soviet authorities' viewpoint, continually disappointing agricultural yields. Why was this so? The key reason was that daily life on the collective farm was utter misery.

After the sort of false start of collectivization that occurred in the winter of 1930, by spring-sowing season in 1932 most peasant households joined the collective farms. The first campaign to collectivize the peasants had been halted by Stalin himself in a notorious editorial of March 1930 in the national newspaper, *Pravda* (The Truth). In "Dizzy with Success," as the article was titled, Stalin claimed that some of the Communists and their allies (those earlier mentioned factory workers who were also sent from Tver' and Vyshnii Volochek into the surrounding countryside) who went to the villages had made people sign up for the collectives through bullying and intimidation. Additionally, these enthusiasts had believed that merely having people join the farms without explaining how to organize farming as a collective would be sufficient.

Clearly, confusion was rampant. As we saw, when faced with the requirement to join the farms, most peasants proceeded to slaughter their private cattle. Even more devastating was the slaughter of horses, as the collectivization campaign seemed to promise that mechanized equipment was to replace horse-drawn power. No machinery was distributed in any meaningful number in the Soviet countryside, and plowing and harvesting suffered as a result. Fitful attempts were made to develop organizational blueprints for the collective farms in the months following "Dizzy with Success," which tried to suggest (or, rather, impose) how to conduct plowing, sowing, haying, weeding, milking, or harvesting efficiently together—in 1932 the Communist Party leadership allowed every peasant household to have a dairy cow for its personal use as well—but little progress toward any truly productive operation of the farms was made in practice. Machine Tractor Stations (MTS) were organized that supplied farming districts with mechanized power, but too few appeared, while various farms competed for their services at the same time during the agricultural seasons. The equipment with which the MTS were supplied was standardized, which meant that it was poorly adapted to local peculiarities of the soil; it also was of poor quality, needing frequent repairs.

Ultimately, most peasant households rejoined the collective farms after an initial massive exodus in the spring of 1930 following the publication of "Dizzy with Success." Incentives and fees made such a choice virtually inevitable. Individual farmsteads were faced with the payment of very high taxes in kind (crops, dairy, meat) to the state. They were severely handicapped by the killing of their horses and other cattle in 1930, for which they could not find replacements. At least the collective farms seemed to offer some sort of shelter against the state's absurdly high demands for crops, meat, and dairy for which it paid almost nothing. The possibility of teaming up during the most intensive periods of agricultural work (such as sowing, haying, or harvesting), too, made joining the *kolkhoz* a more promising option than trying to survive on an individual farmstead.

The confiscated *kulak* property initially amounted to almost the only positive material incentive offered to those joining the collective farms. Few rewards were ever added before Stalin's death. From the beginning of collectivization until 1953, the collective farmers' payment for the crops, meat, and dairy delivered to the state remained almost nominal. The overwhelming share of what was produced in the socialized sector of the farms was delivered to state procurement points, with some seed grain staying behind for next year's crop. Although the theory was that surpluses would be so abundant that enough would be produced for the collective farmers to keep for themselves to survive on, this was rarely the case. *Kolkhozniks* survived because they were allowed (which became enshrined in the 1935 *kolkhoz* statute) a small truck (or market) garden, as well as a cow and some smaller animals (chickens, rabbits, goats), to which they could tend after toiling away most of their days in the socialized sector of the collective farms. The potatoes, meat, eggs, and milk they produced on their "private plots" helped the farmers to survive not merely because they consumed much of this produce themselves but also because they were allowed to sell any surplus on the markets of nearby towns.

A high official in Kalinin oblast's government suggested in the summer of 1948 how

> several *kolkhozniks* [have] turned their private plot into their basic income [despite a campaign against this in 1947] ... [this is] clearly illustrated in the grain deliveries by *kolkhoznik* households from their private plots ... [increasing] every year. Thus, in 1945, 28,676 households with a sown area of 2,569 hectares were liable for taxes on grain deliveries; in 1946,

this number increased to 45,361 households with a sown area of 3,657 hectares, and in 1947 the 49,920 households with a sown are of 5,432 hectares of grain crops were taxed.[8]

This amounted to about one in five households in the Kalinin region surviving by working for themselves rather than for a collective farm, more than a dozen years after collectivization had allegedly been completed. There is no reason to believe that the situation was much different anywhere else in the Soviet Union.

Work on the socialized land, or with the socialized cattle herds, was remunerated by an odd accounting system, through which the collective farm chair, or the brigadiers (foremen or women) of the teams that performed the work, awarded "workdays" or "workday credit" (trudodni) to the farmers for their labor. As the name indicates, a workday was supposed to be the equivalent of a day's work, but no one knew what exactly amounted to a day's work. In theory, one could even earn many more than 365 workdays per year, and kolkhozniki were encouraged to overfulfill the plan as much as workers in the factories or miners in the mines were. But most topped out at about 300. The value of each of these workdays was hard to predict, as it was calculated at the end of the fiscal year, after the collective farm had first delivered its crops, dairy, or meat to the state, for which it was paid in money and kind (usually by being allowed to keep some of its production). Before whatever revenue was distributed among the collective farmers according to the workdays each had earned, the farm needed to pay off loans contracted for various purchases, the managerial staff (chairman, accountants, brigadiers), as well as renting equipment and personnel operating it from the MTS. Trudodni, then, yielded little, and were often contemptuously called palochki, or sticks, by the farmers (for the way in which they were written down into the labor books kept for the farmers). Whereas most kolkhozniks earned somewhere around 300 of such workdays per year, even in a good year (such as 1948) in Kalinin province a farmer received 1.5 kilograms of grain and potatoes each and less than a ruble in money per workday (when textile workers made about 700 or 800 rubles per month!). If more than one household member earned workday credits, a household (even with dependents) may have had some surplus crops deriving from workday payment that could be sold on the local kolkhoz market. Two years later, however, the income in kind per workday credit had been halved in Kalinin oblast', and no such option was possible. In this vein, Fyodor Abramov's novella suggests a desperate survival strategy by recounting how "if you worked in a [kolkhoz], you sought a wife who was state employed."[9]

The elimination of the kulaks had another effect on life in the villages that, even if undoubtedly important, is in many ways impossible to assess exactly. At the time of *dekulakization*, the hardest working, inventive, and enterprising villagers were often labeled *kulaks*, because their very diligence and entrepreneurship had allowed them to accumulate some more animals, better housing, tools, and so on than their neighbors. As such, they had set a good example to their fellow villagers of what might be achieved through hard work and ingenuity. But when they disappeared from the villages, peasants were left without those role models, people who often had been community leaders by setting a good example. Those who were left behind, the poor and middle peasants, had frequently been previously mired in poverty because they lacked the right attitude and did not (or did not know how to) apply themselves very well in their efforts to improve their lot. In other words, the villagers were bereft of community leaders who had earned their respect and led by example. Instead, sycophants who knew how to butter up Communist Party and state officials became *kolkhoz* chairmen. They were more often than not bad farmers, who might additionally lack the leadership skills to guide their fellow villagers in establishing and improving a collective farm. Soviet authorities' turnover of collective farm directors was high, for these chiefs were usually singled out as responsible for failing to meet the various procurement plans (that is, meet the target of the state-determined delivery plans). Very few individuals survived for more than a few years as farm directors. In the immediate postwar period, for several years, one-third of *kolkhoz* chairs was dismissed in Kalinin *oblast'* annually. During the Second World War, for the first time on a significant scale, women were appointed *kolkhoz* chairs, but Soviet society's gender bias here too became apparent after the end of the war, when in most farms male veterans replaced women as directors.

In everything the Communist Party did regarding the peasants in Stalin's Soviet Union, the contempt for "the idiocy of rural life," as Marx had called it, is palpable. The collective farms had to produce a maximum amount of foodstuffs and technical crops in exchange for a minimum price in order to feed the workforce of the industrializing cities. Peasants quickly sensed the Party's utter disdain toward them and in some ways even internalized this sentiment; even if in 1932 the regime introduced an internal passport to stop an uncontrollable exodus from the countryside to the towns, many avenues to abandon the villages (or, at least, farming) remained open. Factory bosses (backed by Party and state administrators) periodically were allowed to recruit workers in the countryside, while army service (and the option to learn a skill there) or the completion of advanced schooling was commonly used as a way to acquire a permit to settle permanently in the towns. The Soviet Union, a country consisting of approximately 80 percent rural dwellers in 1928, had fewer than half of its population living in the countryside by 1960. Within a generation, tens of millions of people had migrated toward the cities (even if taking the famine and wartime deaths into account). The process proved unstoppable even when the worst treatment of the collective farmers ended after 1953: Russia today is littered with ghost villages, in which not even one "idiot" is left.

Collectivization was sometimes met with resignation, but in many villages signs of protest and resistance could be encountered. In the first instance, peasants showed their defiance by killing their cattle rather than have it "socialized." After collectivization, the Soviet villlage may have been the first place where the attitude toward "building socialism" was the infamous "we pretend that we work, and they pretend that they pay us." Few gave it their all when working in the socialized branch of the farm business. Abramov's *New Life* depicts this sullen resentment and foot dragging most graphically:

> [Kolkhoz chairman] Anany Yegorovich ... had walked through about a third of the village, had visited alnost every house, had talked incessantly trying to persuade, convince, and shame them ... And what had he achieved? Would the people go out unto the fields tomorrow to work on the silage?[10]

Little was done without drinking vodka, and most men in the villages were either functioning, or dysfunctional, alcoholics. Heavy imbibing predated collectivization, and in the 1920s Soviet authorities had often been on the lookout for moonshine distillery by peasants (*samogon*). Such practices were prohibited throughout Soviet history, but the state itself made significant profits of the sale of alcohol, and, even without homebrew available, vodka rather than money was often used as a currency, so that only in the leanest years the villages went without. Women drank less, in general, but alcoholism was not wholly gender-specific.

Drinking often begot violence. It is not quite clear in how far men's habitual beating of women and children, as was common in prerevolutionary times, declined in the Soviet era. Undoubtedly, a sort of civilization offensive was unleashed by the authorities (which saw an emphasis on "cultured" [*kul'turnyi*] behavior in the cities, especially as exhibited by Party members). Since the Communist Party had a rather thin presence in the countryside, *kolkhozniki* may not have witnessed many people who endeavored to treat their wives and children respectfully. In how far reading material or lectures to which the collective farmers were now and again treated may have improved matters in this respect is moot.

While in Soviet cities adult men and women almost all worked, day-care facilities and schools provided at least for child care; in the villages, mothers, who bore traditionally much of the responsibility for child rearing, called in the assistance of their own mothers, at least if the latter because of advanced age were no longer obliged to work the normal load of workday credits on the farm. But this was not always the case. Illiteracy and semiliteracy even in the countryside of the postwar Kalinin *oblast'* reached well-nigh 10 percent, showing inadequate supervision of children and truancy. Evidently, some women had no relative on whom they could rely to look after their children. Those who went to school usually followed four years of a general curriculum in the 1930s; seven years of schooling became the norm only in 1949 in the villages.[11] The level of instruction may often have been low (with teachers poorly prepared and writing and reading materials scarce), while at various times school children suffered from malnutrition and inadequate clothing or footwear. School buildings were often derelict. Not every village had its school, which meant that children had to travel significant distances to get to their school buildings. Enforcement of school attendance was spotty, as the local soviets lacked the personnel to suppress truancy. Many farms turned to children to help out with some of the work, especially in the busiest times of the year, and education was neglected.

Advances were made in further eradicating infectious diseases between 1929 and 1953, but some regress can be noted for the war period and immediate postwar era in this respect. Eventually, after about 1948, the incidence of malaria began to fall rapidly in Kalinin province, and penicillin treatment or inoculation began to lower the number of people suffering from tuberculosis or diphtheria. The towns, more than the villages, seem to have been plagued by the presence of diseases linked to contaminated water, such as typhoid, spotted fever, or dysentery.

Despite the hardships of the Soviet countryside under Stalin, peasant families remained larger than those of city dwellers, which was in part due to the very cramped housing circumstances in the towns. And while much of the picture of the Soviet countryside under Stalin appears bleak, some improvements are undeniable. Infant deaths (of children up to twelve months) dropped from 20 percent in 1940 to 10 percent of all newborns in Kalinin *oblast'* after the Second World War, the new availability of antibiotics being a likely cause. This was a remarkable drop, for around 1900 more than one-third of babies had died before reaching the age of one. It is difficult to judge whether there was much of a difference in the incidence of infant deaths between town and country; in the cities, births took normally in a hospital or birthing house (*roddom*), which may have had the advantage of more professional care being given to mother and child but may have also exposed them to contagious diseases; in the villages, births often took place at home, with the help of a *feldsher* (practitioner nurse), or *akusherka*, a midwife, who may often have been quite experienced (in some ways an heir to the prerevolutionary wise women, or *baba*s), but hygiene maintenance (not in the least because most villages lacked access to running water or electricity before 1953) may have been worse. And if complications arose, a birth in the village was more likely to end tragically than in a town hospital.

Since many Russians, Belarusians, and Ukrainians identified as religious believers in the 1937 Soviet census (which seems to have annoyed Stalin so much that he had its results suppressed), one might also attribute the larger peasant households in the countryside to a reluctance to have sexual intercourse while using birth-control methods. Obviously, no such thing as the pill was available yet, but it seems as well that condoms (then usually made of scarcely available rubber, which usually was designated for other purposes in a country that lacked rubber trees), or intrauterine devices were rare commodities. In general, then, abortion was the most commonly used method of birth control, but it might only be available in the towns even when it was legal (before 1936). Some data on the rate of abortions in Tver' province appear to indicate that despite the prohibition between 10 and 20 percent of pregnancies was thus terminated during the 1940s. Undoubtedly, this sometimes occurred on grounds that women's health was endangered by the pregnancy, but the high number suggests that abortions were performed for other than strictly medical reasons. Even if their incidence may have been higher than the authorities will have registered because they could not keep track of such operations, the occurrence of abortions, however, was likely to be lower in the countryside. Undoubtedly, a much greater reluctance among village women to undergo an abortion played a role here. Religious objections informed this attitude, one surmises, although having an abortion may have also had a social stigma for unmarried village women, who might have been more inclined to try to marry when they were found they were pregnant rather than seek an abortion.

Weddings even after the war often were held in the winter, the time of least activity on the farms. Registration of marriages was required at the offices of the local soviet, and some sort of a civil ceremony accompanied them, but many may have furtively turned to a priest to receive religious blessing for their union. The lavish celebrations of prerevolutionary times were uncommon because of the grinding poverty of many peasants. Similarly, burials were modest affairs, with the deceased being carried in an open coffin to the graveyard. As in the past, women especially cried and moaned about the dead person during the wake and on the way to the burial; the deceased almost always was carried to the grave with a burning candle placed between the hands, a clear nod to Orthodox practice. Here, too, priests seem often to have been called in to officiate, if they could be found. In some cases, it appears, a lay person filled in performing the religiously mandated last rites. Finally, newborns were still baptized, if such a ceremony was at all possible. Bereft of churches or chapels, as well as the necessary vessels, clothing, and so on, here, too, much was improvised. Births, meanwhile, were registered by the local soviet's population statistics office rather than in the parish register of the past.

While often the local church and *kulak* property were confiscated in 1930 by the collective farms to serve as "cultural amenities," the light of the "Cultural Revolution" that can be discerned in the Soviet cities during the 1930s only dimly flickered in the countryside, as the persistence of excessive drinking habits and violence that noted previously indicate. Indeed, some of those cultural amenities simply did not reach the farmers, because most villages were not hooked up to any electricity grid (and generating electricity through running engines, etc., was rarely possible, as collective farms did not own motorized vehicles), and the more remote settlements were often unreachable during the muddy season (*rasputitsa*) of spring and fall. Even today, in the former Soviet Union, properly paved roads for motorized traffic are relatively few. Railroads (even trunk lines) did not reach the proximity of many villages in the 1930s and 1940s. Villages did not have telephones or radios. Water came from wells, and sewage was at best collected in cesspools. Maybe once a year a traveling band of "cultural workers" came by to show some films. Undoubtedly, some efforts were nonetheless made to improve the quality of life. The local club (located either in a former *kulak* house or in a former church) might have a library with some books and (outdated) newspapers; lectures were sometimes delivered by a local or visiting Party member, and people engaged in performing plays, or played in a music ensemble. Since it is unclear whether people already performed on stage or as musicians before 1930, which seems likely, this may not have constituted much of a change. Perhaps most significant in terms of a cultural sea change was that school attendance was mandated for all children, as we saw, even if most of them attended schools with only a four-year curriculum in the 1930s and 1940s.

In the early 1930s and during and immediately after the war, even the most basic consumer goods were often lacking in the villages, such as salt, sugar, matches, or soap. The farmers were traditionally inventive (many, for example, were quite adept at distilling *samogon*), but, different from earlier centuries, most households had forgotten to be self-sufficient, and relied on raw materials and tools they could only buy on local markets or in village stores to make clothes, footwear, and so on. Most of these goods were only sporadically available, while the peasants often enough could not afford them because of their exceedingly low monetary income. As in the past, access to such scarce goods might be provided by a relative visiting the ancestral village, or by those who received temporary permits to work in the towns. Many left illegally, or found work in nonagricultural occupations, even if they remained on the books as *kolkhozniki*. They often could do so if they offered the *kolkhoz* director a sufficiently high bribe. Whereas the evidence is anecdotal, it appears as if from the very beginning of the regimentation of the villagers a shadow economy developed, in which bold individuals acted as middlemen, supplying the farmers with the goods they so desperately needed, in exchange for high fees. These fees may have been paid in money, but in part vodka (or, rather, moonshine-*samogon*) became an important currency.

It is not coincidental that in the first year, 1932, that the majority of the Soviet peasant households belonged to collective farms, various parts of the country were plagued by a massive famine, which in Ukraine today is seen as deliberately caused by the Russian-Soviet government in Moscow in order to bridle Ukrainians' independent spirit and kill off as many Ukrainians in the process (the *Holodomor*, which according to some Ukrainians amounted to a Russian attempt at genocide). After the war, another famine raged affecting largely European Russia, and costing perhaps 1.5 million people their lives.

Since it actually caused less havoc than in the cities, the Great Terror's imprint on daily life in the countryside was relatively slight. The massive arrest waves of 1937 and 1938 mainly haunted the urban parts of the Soviet Union in 1937 and 1938; certainly, those arrest waves targeted "former *kulaks*," as well as priests, but the roundups of such suspects primarily occurred in the towns and cities. In the countryside, the effect of the Great Terror did not compare to what occurred there between 1929 and 1933 as a result of collectivization, or to the war years from June 1941 to May 1945. Of course, it is difficult to establish in how far people were affected by the detention of urban relatives, friends, or acquaintances.

Although life in the *Gulag*'s camps was certainly worse, life on the collective farm under Stalin was abysmal. The exodus that in a way began with *dekulakization* never stopped and everyone who could seem to have tried to abscond. Sometimes farm work could be left behind by joining the Communist Party or government and finding work in a district office, while at other times education or military service (for men, of course) offered an escape route, as we saw. Although the Soviet authorities, as is evident from the 1932–3 passportization, regularly undertook efforts to tie the labor force to the farms, they were concomitantly faced with an ever-increasing demand for labor from the mushrooming industrial enterprises across the country. Perhaps the Great Terror of 1937–8 did not affect manual laborers as much, but obviously the massive bloodletting of the war caused enormous labor shortages. Of course, food needed to be produced, even if it was often rationed in Stalin's cities. Therefore, the collective farms could not afford to lose all of their workers. In some areas, indeed, the regime organized farms allegedly representing a "higher" form of socialist agricultures, the state farms or *sovkhozy* (*sovetskie*

a finished log hous

FIGURE 1.1 *A typical log cabin, the usual sort of housing of Russians in the villages of European Russia (Library of Congress).*

khoziaistva, soviet farms). Here, workers received a guaranteed wage independent of their farm's production. The *sovkhozy* were at first mainly specialized farms, such as those concentrating on rearing pedigree cattle, but they also seem to have been set up to overcome the worst shortages in basic foodstuffs, because their output was higher, produced by a workforce that was more incentivized. But precisely because they offered a guaranteed wage, they were also more costly, and the state could ill afford to have too many of them before the 1950s.

Immediately in 1953, Stalin's successors decided to offer significantly higher prices for the crops, dairy, and meat the collective farms delivered to the procurement agencies. It allowed for better-stocked shops in the cities and a higher standard of living in the countryside. But in a sense, the damage had been done: Even if life in the countryside became more bearable, few passed up on the possibility to leave their village if it was offered. The Russian peasants (*krest'iane*) had become (collective) farmers (*kolkhozniki*) and then "voted with their feet," to leave their farming life behind altogether.[12] The exodus continued after 1953, and today's Russian countryside is littered with empty villages.

Notes

1 The differences between *sovkhoz* and *kolkhoz* will be discussed below in the text.

2 Or, of course, vice versa for native speakers to master English well enough to report on their findings to the wider world. Apart from documents of the Soviet era (and then mainly those originating in the central Party-and-state apparatus), few Russian-language works of scholarship are translated.

3 See, for example, Alex Inkeles and Raymond Bauer, *The Soviet Citizen: Daily Life in a Totalitarian Society*, Cambridge, MA: Harvard University Press, 1963. See as well, Merle Fainsod, *Smolensk under Soviet Rule*, Boston, MA: Unwin and Hyman, 1958. For a general overview of the 1930s, see S. Fitzpatrick, *Stalin's Peasants:* Resistance and Survival in the Russian Village after Collectivization, Oxford: Oxford University Press, 1994. Perhaps, because Fitzpatrick predominantly looks at the 1930s (perhaps too short a period to identify the trend), she does not emphasize the astonishing long-term exodus of the peasants from the Russian countryside after 1929. Cf. David Shearer's work elsewhere in this collection.

4 Some interesting anthropological fieldwork was conducted in the post-Stalin era by Iu. V. Arutiunian and Anokhina and Shmeleva (Arutiunian's main findings were translated into French: Iu.V. Arutjunjan, *La structure sociale de la population rurale de L'U.R.S.S.*, trans. Yves Perret-Gentil, Paris: I.S.M.E.A., 1979; L. N. Anokhina and M. N. Shmeleva, *Kul'tura i byt' kolkhoznikov Kalininskoi oblasti*, Moscow: Nauka, 1964). But Soviet scholars skirted around the true catastrophe of the Stalin years. The invaluable works by Basile Kerblay in French and by Helmut Altrichter in German predate the fall of the Soviet Union (see Basile Kerblay, *Du mir aux agrovilles*, Paris: Institut d'études slaves, 1985; and Helmut Altrichter, *Die Bauern von Tver: Vom Leben auf dem russischen Dorfe zwischen Revolution und Kollektivierung*, München: Oldenbourg Verlag, 1984).

5 In particular, K. Boterbloem, *Life and Death under Stalin: The Kalinin Province, 1945–1953*, Montreal: McGill-Queen's University Press, 1999; K. Boterbloem, "Communists and the Russians: The Kalinin Province under Stalin," PhD diss., Montreal: McGill University, 1994; F. Abramov, *The New Life: A Day on a Collective Farm*, New York: Grove Press, 1963; and Altrichter, *Die Bauern von Tver*.

6 After a flurry of administrative reorganization, prerevolutionary Tver' province (abolished in early 1929) reappeared in January 1935 in a somewhat larger size than in the 1920s; after its territory was reduced to two-thirds of its previous size in 1944, it was given its current borders in 1957. For the purposes of this essay, these changes make little difference.

7 See Lynne Viola, *The Unknown Gulag: The Lost World of Stalin's Special Settlements*, Oxford: Oxford University Press, 2009.

8 Boterbloem, "Communists," 426.

9 Abramov, *The New Life*, 70.

10 Ibid., 100.

11 For more on the discrepancy between the legally mandated length of compulsory schooling and the actual amount of grade school actually attended, see Larry Holmes' article in this book.

12 Albeit not farming itself, for most Russian families happily, and sometimes out of necessity, dedicate much of their spare time to cultivating a market garden in the vicinity of the cities in which they live today. Their produce is a welcome addition to the foodstuffs they buy in the store.

2

Food Consumption, Diet, and Famines

Elena A. Osokina

The Fragile NEP

Why did the relative well-being of the 1920s, the period known as that of the New Economic Policy (NEP), suddenly turn into a period of acute food shortages, culminating in a mass famine of 1932–3 in Ukraine, parts of Russia, and Kazakhstan? Indeed, until 1927, memoirs describe an abundance of outdoor and indoor markets and a plentitude of food in the Soviet Union. Yet, within a few years, a meager diet, consisting mainly of poor-quality black bread and watery lean cabbage soup, became the norm throughout the country.

Private production and private trade ensured the relative prosperity of the 1920s. Peasants, who constituted more than 80 percent of the population, provided for themselves.[1] They worked on their own individual farms and decided for themselves on how much to produce, how much to keep for family needs, and how much to sell, when, to whom, and at what price.[2] Being their own masters, peasants lived by the principle of self-interest. Their only serious obligation to the state was a fixed agricultural tax which, since 1924, they paid in cash. If peasants went to a shop, it was not for bread or meat but to buy only what they could not produce themselves.

The well-being of the peasant economy safeguarded the survival of the cities. Food markets worked in every city or town and served as a primary source of food for the urban population. Market sellers were the peasants themselves, second-hand dealers (*perekupshchiki*), or private purveyors who bought produce from peasant households. In the NEP years, a complex interregional network based on peasant food production and private food trade emerged.

The relative abundance of food during the 1920s was, to a considerable degree, based on the activities of private procurers of agricultural produce. In the second half of the 1920s, they bought about one-quarter of grain in the grain-producing areas and provided more than 20 percent of the grain to the grain-consuming regions, including one-third of all wheat. Private procurers were especially important in those distant and difficult-to-reach areas where state procurers were absent. They penetrated the far hinterlands of the country, transporting produce to the markets of remote areas and selling grain to small market traders, owners of stalls, kiosks, restaurants, and cafes, as well as accumulating grain stocks for later sales.

Similarly, private entrepreneurs played an important role in the manufacturing of goods, providing, by the end of NEP, one-fifth of the gross industrial output; their role was especially important in retail markets. Private trade (excluding peasant markets) made up a quarter of the country's retail market, but its true importance in supplying the population was much more substantial than that. In 1927, about 75 percent of shops were privately owned (410,700 out of 551,600). Unlike the state and cooperative stores that concentrated mainly in large industrial cities, private trade on a small scale was more evenly scattered, occurring throughout the country at numerous stalls, shops, kiosks, or was conducted by peddlers. Private traders adapted to the market conditions more quickly than the state and were dominant in remote areas where there were no state or cooperative stores. Private traders sold not only privately produced goods but also the products of the state enterprises. Motivated by personal gain, private traders maneuvered supplies faster, more effectively, and with a fewer losses than the state trade organizations.

Based on private initiative, it took only a few years after the destruction and chaos caused by the revolutions of 1917 and the world and civil wars to meet the needs of the population in food and essential goods. Although the NEP had its limits, and the growth of the population's income outpaced production and trade volumes, famine (thanks to the peasant farms and markets, as well as private procurers and trade) did not threaten the country. The Central Statistical Bureau recorded yearly improvement in the population's diet, reaching a high point in 1926.[3]

The importance of private initiative in supplying the population was particularly pronounced in comparison with the weak development of state production and trade. The food processing enterprises that the Soviet state inherited from the tsarist past for the most part consisted of small and primitive mills, creameries, bakeries, confectionaries, and slaughterhouses, operating predominantly with manual labor. A state-mechanized food processing industry had yet to be created. The first bread factory was built only in 1925, while two years later the construction of the first Soviet meat-processing plants began. By the end of the 1920s, the state-owned food industry still lagged behind the pre-First-World-War production of tsarist Russia, annually producing per capita only about 5 kilograms of meat and fish, 8 kilograms of sugar, 12 kilograms of dairy products, one-half kilogram of butter, 3 liters of vegetable oil, and less than one can of tinned goods. The variety of food products was limited, with the staples of grain products and meat making up one-third of assortment.

State-owned trade was as underdeveloped as the state's food production. State stores specialized in wine and spirits, furs and books. The state used consumer-cooperative shops to sell about 80 per cent of goods produced by state enterprises. Together with the state stores, cooperatives provided three-quarters of the country's commodity turnover. However, they owned only one-quarter of the trade network. In other words, the state and cooperatives sold more goods than private shops, but their trade was concentrated only in a few large city stores.

The NEP supply mechanisms prove that the relative affluence of the 1920s rested on private initiative. If one were to remove from this picture peasants' self-sufficiency in food, peasant markets, and private stores that provided for the urban population, what would have been left were underdeveloped state food industries and a meager state and cooperative network concentrated in a few large cities. The destruction of the private sector would therefore spell catastrophe. Such a scenario would force the state to supply millions of consumers who had been self-sufficient before. The destruction of the private producers and markets proved disastrous as well because the creation of food and light industries was not the state's first priority. At the end of the 1920s, the country's leadership set a course for the forced development of heavy and military industries.

The Soviet Union was the first country in history to industrialize not as a market economy but as a state-centralized planned economy. Private production and the markets of the 1920s were destroyed by repression against private entrepreneurs in the cities and violence used in the countryside during the forced state procurements of agricultural products and collectivization of peasant households. In deciding the path and methods of industrialization, Marxist economic ideology with its hostility toward the market and private property played a role. There was also a political factor involved in the leadership's strategy: the Bolsheviks viewed the growth of the private sector in the economy as a resurgence of capitalism and therefore a threat to their power. The destruction of private production and markets for the Bolsheviks was also driven by economic reasons. Expecting a war at any moment, Stalin's leadership strove to industrialize in the shortest time. It did not want to waste any effort or time to tinker with the private entrepreneurs who competed with the state, diverted resources from industrialization projects and profited from the state's failures and miscalculations. It seemed easier and faster to simply eliminate the private sector at one fell swoop, monopolize resources in the hands of the central government, and invest them directly in those industrial projects that the state considered important.

Industrialization Starts

In December 1927, the Fifteenth Communist Party congress reviewed the early drafts of the First Five-Year Plan, which was then formally adopted in its most ambitious version in April 1929. By that time, industrialization was already in full swing. Planning targets continued to be raised throughout the rest of the year.

Bread has always held a central place in the Russian diet; in periods of food shortages, it was the primary and often only food. With the beginning of the industrial boom in 1928, the state's need for grain sharply increased in order to provide for the growing numbers of industrial workers, create food reserves, supply the military, and, most important, increase grain exports. By the beginning of its accelerated industrialization plan, the state had exhausted its gold reserves and viewed grain exports as a major source of foreign currency to pay for the import of machines, blueprints, and raw materials essential for Soviet industrialization.

Industrialization desperately depended on grain, but state procurements did not go well in the later 1920s. Private producers refused to sell to the state, considering its prices to be too low. In response to what the authorities labeled "sabotage," in December 1927, massive repressive measures began, first against the grain private traders and procurers, and then, from the end of January 1928, against peasants who hid their grain. The violent coercion and arrests were the result of both orders from above and the spontaneous actions of local officials who despaired of fulfilling the state grain procurements.[4] By the end of April 1928, the Soviet secret police, then called OGPU, reported that it had arrested 4,930 private grain dealers in the previous months.[5] Expecting new rounds of violence and arrests, peasants saw no point in increasing their production: "Several years went by quietly, but now again they begin to strip us bare until there is nothing left to take ... we will probably have either to abandon the land or sow just enough to feed ourselves."[6]

The result of the state's "battle for grain" was predictable: the private grain market was destroyed. Bread rationing spontaneously spread from below, initiated by local officials, in an attempt to protect primarily those who were directly involved in industrial production. Since local actions were not coordinated, ration norms, at the start, varied depending on local conditions. By the summer of 1928, bread lines and various types of local bread-ration cards had appeared all over the country. Bread shortages spurred rumors about an imminent war, famine and a coup and the OGPU recorded a bevy of anti-Soviet sentiments:

> Communists are hiding bread in anticipation of war ... They themselves are incapable of trading well and they don't let private traders do so but are thinking, nevertheless, about waging war ... The government has lost its mind. If it keeps up this way, it won't last another month ... If it wasn't for private traders, we'd be finished off.[7]

Mass repression continued during the 1928/1929 state procurement campaign, thus further undermining sources of peasant self-supply and private trade.[8] As a result, already in the spring of 1929, the OGPU reported instances of local famine in the villages in the Central Black Earth, Smolensk, and Leningrad regions, the Far East and Ukraine. The poorest peasants were the first to starve.[9] In a leaflet written in a folk-style poem, a peasant complained:

> You get up—wake up, Vladimir, get up—wake up, Ilyich![10]
> Look at the burden that lays,
> That laid on the shoulders of the peasant—*seredniak*[11]
> There are no goods at all for us in cooperative stores
> Other than matches and paper, tobacco and candies,
> No sugar, no butter, no cotton, no chintz, no cloth
> Vodka alone loads the whole of Russia.[12]

On February 14, 1929, the Communist Party's highest body, the Politburo, approved the introduction of an All-Union rationing system for bread. Since local ration cards were already in use in the country, the decree was meant to unify norms and principles of state bread distribution. Only the working urban population and their families were allotted bread rations and norms depended on the industrial importance of a city and one's place of work. Other groups of population still could buy bread in stores, but only what was left after distributing the rationed supply and at double the price.

Bread shortages were the main albeit not the only problem aggravated by the repressions. By the end of the 1920s, the cities experienced acute shortages of all basic foodstuffs. In addition to bread, local officials spontaneously began to introduce ration cards for butter, meat, sugar, cereal, and other products. By the fall of 1929, the OGPU reported to the Politburo that in all industrial regions major foodstuffs were rationed. The situation with meat and fats was especially alarming. In 1929 and 1930, the government issued several decrees that officially established and regulated rations for bread, groats, meat, herring, butter, sugar, tea, and eggs for the population of the leading industrial centers, that is, Moscow, Leningrad, the Donbass along the border of Ukraine and Russia, and the Kuzbass in Siberia.

Forced collectivization of peasant households, which started in the fall of 1929, gave a final and deadly blow to the private producers and markets of the NEP era. By the spring of 1930, the state had forced about a half of the peasant population onto the collective farms, often threatening and sometimes using violent means. By 1933, the major agricultural regions of the USSR were collectivized.[13] Hundreds of thousands of peasant families who resisted collectivization were exiled to remote and inhospitable regions. The consequences proved to be deplorable. Agricultural production fell drastically. An initial abundance of meat in the markets, when peasants were slaughtering and selling their livestock and fowl, unwilling to give their animals over to the collective farms, was short-lived and turned into a long-term acute shortage of meat and dairy products.[14] The state used the collective farms to increase state procurements regardless of the production levels in the countryside, pumping away resources to feed the cities and increase export.

Simultaneously with the onset of collectivization in the countryside, the government eliminated private licensed trade. The Politburo's resolution of August 15, 1929, initiated by Stalin himself, sanctioned a new wave of repression against private procurers and traders. As a result, the share of private trade in the country's retail dropped to 5.6 percent in 1930. The next year, private trade stopped being licensed altogether.

OGPU reports reveal that the food situation further declined after each new wave of repression against the peasants in the course of collectivization and each campaign against private trade.[15] In July 1930, about five months after the introduction of the All-Union rationing system for bread, the Politburo officially introduced the All-Union rationing system for meat. As with bread rationing, the government thereby merely standardized local meat distribution practices already in place throughout the country. According to the new regulations, only 14 million city dwellers out of a total population of about 160 million were to receive meat rations through the state's distribution network.

The destruction of the peasant economy and private trade also created a sharp shortage of vegetables. In 1929, private trade provided about one half of the country's vegetables and potatoes; by 1930 this share dropped to 5 percent. The rationing of potatoes, the second most important food in the Russian diet after bread, was not far away.

By the end of 1930, then, a food crisis reigned in all cities and towns. In addition to bread and meat, which had already been officially rationed by central government, varying local norms established by local officials to provide for workers' needs existed for fish products, groats, vegetable oil, and sugar. Other foods, such as eggs, sausage, cheese, sour cream and other dairy products, candy and the like were absent from store shelves for weeks or months, and, when available, were also rationed by local authorities. The Politburo tried to control the spontaneous spread of rationing from below and stop the chaotic local implementation of purchasing norms and rations. It prohibited the introduction of local rations without the People's Commissariat of Supply's permission. Nonetheless and under pressure of acute food shortages, the illegal rationing practices of the local officials continued.

Workers who complained were rampant:

As they started herding peasants into collective farms, literally nothing is left to eat ... Soon even potatoes will be rationed ... This five-year plan will drive workers into the grave. Life is worse than before the revolution ... Enough with eating good meat, in the thirteenth year of the revolution we have to get used to *konina* (horse meat) ... We are feeding our children bread and salt, and have only bread for ourselves ... Long live the five-year plan of empty stomachs ... The country is falling into an abyss because of repression against peasants ... I bet that people's commissars on their tables have as much good white bread as they want, while there is not even a pound of sodden bread for us.

The OGPU reported on local famines already in the winter of 1929/30 in Bashkiria, Kazakhstan, the North Caucasus, and the middle Volga region. In the course of 1930, conditions further worsened in the countryside. Forced collectivization and state procurements depleted peasants' food reserves.[16] As in the previous year, the famine as of yet only affected poor peasants and some *seredniaks* (middle peasants). This was, however, only a prelude to an impending tragedy.

Food shortages in the cities and countryside in 1930 intensified anti-government sentiments and caused disturbances in store queues, the occurrence of spontaneous meetings and even workers' strikes.[17] The Politburo refused to take responsibility for the deterioration of the food situation. Instead, it searched for scapegoats. In 1930, the OGPU conducted arrests in all major state agencies in charge of food supplies, of "saboteurs of meat, vegetables, canned food, and others."[18] Many of them were executed, but, predictably, the food situation continued to deteriorate and affect industrial production negatively.

To deal with the raging supply crisis, the Politburo, in January 1931, officially instituted nationwide rationing for all major food staples and goods, thus finally streamlining the regional rationing that had spontaneously spread throughout the country from the beginning of industrialization in 1928. This rationing continued until the mid-1930s, representing a rare instance in history of the use of long-term state-regulated consumption during peacetime.

Rations as Carrot and Stick

At the core of the 1931–5 countrywide rationing system was state "industrial pragmatism," that is, a pragmatism defined by the needs of industrialization. The government used rations as "carrot and stick" to force industrialization forward. Under conditions of acute food shortages, it could not feed, or refused to feed, everyone and supplied mainly those who were directly involved in industrial production. The answer to the two questions "Where do you live?" and "Where do you work?" would have been sufficient to reveal the standard of living of a Soviet citizen in the first half of the 1930s.

From the beginning of 1931, there were four major categories eligible for state-rationed supplies. These were called "lists of cities," but, in fact, they were mainly groupings of enterprises (see Table 2.1). The large cities and leading industrial enterprises of Moscow, Leningrad, Baku, the Donbass, Urals, Siberia, and the Far East made up the two top groups.[19]

These consumers were to receive bread, flour, groats, meat, fish, butter, sugar, tea, and eggs from the state, before, and in greater quantities than, others eligible for state supply. Constituting only 40 percent of the total number of people who received state rations, they consumed 70–80 percent of the state-rationed supplies. Small towns and nonindustrial cities as well as nonindustrial enterprises, such as factories making glass and porcelain, matches, paper; municipal services; bakeries; small textile factories; and printing offices, made up the two lower groups and were to receive from the state only bread, sugar, groats, and tea in smaller quantities than the top two groups.[20]

The hierarchy of state rationing was not confined to the industrial importance of cities and enterprises. Within each of the four major groups, various subgroups of consumers existed based on how their jobs ranked in industrial importance. The first category (group A) included factory and transport workers and the second category (group B) consisted of nonindustrial workers.[21] White-collar workers made up the third and lowest group.[22] Children under the age of fourteen comprised a separate group that was supplied with cards

TABLE 2.1 Rations, 1931 (Kilograms per Person)*

	Special List		List I		List II		List III	
Food	1	2	1	2	1	2	1	2
Bread	0.8	0.4	0.8	0.4	0.8	0.4	0.75	0.35
Flour	1	1	1	–	–	–	–	–
Groats	3	1.5	2.5	1.5	1.5	0.85	1	0.5
Meat	4.4	2.2	2.6	1.3	1	1	–	–
Fish	2.5	2	2	1.4	2	1	–	–
Butter	0.4	–	0.2	–	–	–	–	–
Sugar	1.5	1.5	1.5	1.5	1	1	0.8	0.8
Tea	0.3	0.3	0.25	0.25	0.1	0.05	0.1	0.05
Eggs (each)	10	–	–	–	–	–	–	–

*Bread rations are daily, tea is yearly, and the rest is monthly.
1: Workers' rations.
2: Rations of white-collar workers and family members of both workers and white-collar workers.
"–" means no rations.
Source: Russian State Archive of the Economy, Moscow (RGAE), f. 8043, op. 1, d. 2, l. 238.

and had a hierarchy that mirrored the status of their parents (see Table 2.2).[23] In industrial centers, children received higher norms and a richer assortment of foods. In small and nonindustrial cities, children did not receive any meat, fish, butter, or eggs from state supplies.

The same principle of "the closer to the industrial production, the better the provisions" applied to the state-rationed provisioning of intellectuals, state rural employers, students, and even the disenfranchised (sentenced kulaks, *lishentsy*, that is those deprived of the vote before 1936 because they belonged to the privileged classes in tsarist Russia or *NEP*men of the 1920s), if the latter were employed at leading industrial enterprises. In preparation for war, Soviet industrialization was tightly linked to a military buildup, and the "military consumers," which included Red Army and Navy personnel, cadets and professors of military schools, secret-police troops, and militia, were assigned special rations.

TABLE 2.2 Children's Rations, 1931 (Kilograms per Person)

Food	Special List	List I	List II	List III
Bread	0.4	0.4	0.4	0.35
Flour	0.5	0.5	–	–
Groats	1.5	1.5	0.85	0.5
Meat	2.2	1.3	1	–
Fish	2	1.4	1	–
Butter	0.4	0.2	–	–
Vegetable oil	0.2	–	–	–
Sugar	1.5	1.5	1	0.8
Tea	0.3	0.25	0.05	0.05
Eggs (each)	10	–	–	–

*Bread rations are daily, tea is yearly, and the rest is monthly.
"–" means no rations.
Source: RGAE, f. 8043, op. 1, d. 2, l. 238.

FIGURE 2.1 *A hierarchy of consumption. Workers at lunch, the Volga city of Samara, 1932. Courtesy of the Russian State Archive of the Kino-Photo Documents.*

Thus, the state system of rationing generated a very heavily stratified social and geographic hierarchy of consumption.[24] The resultant social stratification differed from the class structure of a socialist society traditionally defined by Marxist analysis (workers and peasants as solid homogenous classes, and white-collar workers and members of the intelligentsia as social layers), as canonically presented by the Soviet authorities. The "blade" that carved out groups of consumers in state supply went not along class lines as defined by Marxism but across them, dividing classes into numerous subgroups whose supplies were strictly differentiated. The Communist Party and state decrees that defined norms of supply shuffled these subgroups and, according to the principle of industrial importance, combined them into new social strata, making the Marxist class boundaries blurry. As a result, only within the same list of supply (either Special list, or List 1, or List II, or List III) workers as a class looked homogenous and privileged compared to the white-collar workers or "Soviet intelligentsia." However, countrywide white-collar workers who were employed at leading industrial enterprises had much better supplies than factory workers in small towns or workers at nonindustrial enterprises, such as, for example, a small textile factory or a bread factory. Even children in the large industrial centers were assigned better rations than workers in small towns. This "disappearance" of Marxist classes in the 1931–5 rationing system became one of the outcomes of state industrial pragmatism in action.

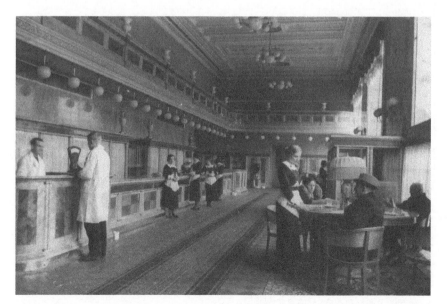

FIGURE 2.2 *A hierarchy of consumption. A restricted access distribution center that supplied the NKVD employees, Moscow, 1936. Courtesy of the Russian State Archive of the Kino-Photo Documents.*

This analysis of the principles of state rationing demonstrates that social stratification in the 1930s was defined by the state as a near-monopolist distributor of supplies and other social benefits. Proximity to power, therefore, along with industrial pragmatism, played a huge role in rationing policy. The highest leadership, such as secretaries of the Party's Central Committee or the *Komsomol* (Communist Youth League) Central Committee, members and their deputies in the Central Executive Committee of the USSR, Council of People's Commissars, the State Planning Committee, the State Bank, as well as heads of the people's commissariats (families included) allocated the best supplies (ration "A") to themselves, reflecting the words of Louis XIV, "The state: it is me." One step down in this elite hierarchy was the ration "B"

TABLE 2.3 Average Food Prices, First Half of 1932 (Rubles per Kilogram)

Food	Prices				
	1	2	3	4	5
Wheat flour	0.44	0. 25–0.28	0.29–0.32	3–5	3–4
Meat	1.45	1.47–2.12	1.46–2.23	4.68–6.84	6–10
Fish	1.10	1.23–1.37	1.53–1.46	2.69–3.14	4–5
Milk (per liter)	0.30	0.42–0.48	0.40–0.50	1.45–1.47	2
Butter	5	6.36–8.47	7–10	19–20	19–21
Sugar	1.25	1.02–1.13	0.96–1.19	4–9	12
Eggs (per dozen)	1	2–3	8	9–10	13–14

Notes
1: Elite rations' prices in the restricted access distribution centers that supplied residents of the House of Government on Bolotnaya square, Moscow (the ration "B" category).
2: Average rations' prices in the restricted access distribution centers of industrial workers across the USSR.
3: Rations' prices in the restricted access distribution centers of industrial workers in Moscow.
4: Average market prices across the USSR.
5: Average market prices in Moscow.
Source: RGAE, f. 8043, op. 1, d. 60, ll. 107–8; and f. 1562, op. 329, d. 62, ll. 17, 18, 133–6.

category, assigned to the leading personnel in the same institutions, but at the lower level of heads and their deputies of departments and sectors.[25]

The state rationing system provided mostly for the urban areas. Peasants who made up more than 80 percent of the USSR's population did not receive rations and rely on themselves, and some of their collective farms' proceeds. Once a year, in the fall, collective farms distributed among their members whatever produce was left after the state procurements and creation of seed funds, in accordance with the alleged number of days worked on the farm (of which was kept track in a labor book).[26] The state sent supplies to the countryside mostly to stimulate state procurements, such as some industrial goods for the grain producers, or flour for the producers of technical raw materials (such as beets, potatoes, jute, cotton, hemp, or flax). The state decreased, or even completely stopped, its supplying of areas that did not fulfill their production quotas. Thus the state turned its distribution system into a powerful weapon of coercion and even repression. In addition to peasants, among those who were denied state rations, there were also *lishentsy* and *NEP*men.

The Hierarchy of Poverty

The state-centralized supply system was not only hierarchical and selective but also quite clearly insufficient. It produced a hierarchy of poverty.

The urban population, including the "privileged" industrial vanguard, teetered on the brink of starvation in the first half of the 1930s. The assigned rations often remained on paper. In 1933, according to budget data, the actual state-provisioned daily ration of an industrial worker's family in Moscow, one of the most privileged categories in the rationing system, consisted (per family member) of about one-half kilogram of bread, 30 grams of groats, 350 grams of potatoes and vegetables, 30 grams of meat or fish, 40 grams of sugar or sweets, and one glass of milk per week. Industrial workers in Moscow were much better off than their non-industrial comrades such as the textile workers in Ivanovo (located northeast of Moscow) who daily received (per family member) only a few grams of meat, but even the industrial workers in Moscow who engaged in hard physical labor received utterly insufficient norms.[27] The white-collar workers' actual rations consisted mainly of bread, some groats, and sugar.

Peasants were at the bottom in this hierarchy of poverty. In the years from 1931 to 1933, urban inhabitants, constituting about 20 percent of the population, received the lion's share of state supplies, including close to 80 percent of the flour, groats, butter, fish, and sugar; 94 percent of meat products; all the margarine; over half of vegetable oil; and one-third of the state supply of salt

TABLE 2.4 Domestic Consumption of Industrial Workers' Families Provided by State Rations, 1933 (Grams per Day per Person)

Food	Across USSR	Moscow	Ivanovo Region
Rye bread	286	308	207
Wheat bread	166	248	9
Groats/beans	34	27	12
Potatoes	182	241	221
Vegetables	106	106	101
Fruits/berries	4	9	2
Meat	17	35	6
Fish	21	31	13
Milk	31	41	41
Butter	2	4	1
Vegetable oil	1	1	1
Sugar/sweets	26	40	17
Tea	0.2	0.3	0.2

Source: RGAE, f. 1562, op. 329, d. 62, ll. 20–3, 25, 27, 29, 84.

and tea. The state supply system operated from the premise that the rural population would take care of itself. However, state procurements aimed at providing for Soviet export and urban supplies, as well as violence committed against peasants in the course of collectivization, undermined the countryside's ability to support itself. As a result, those collective farmers (*kolkhozniks*) who produced grain did not have enough bread to eat themselves, or those who raised cattle did not eat meat or drink milk. Under conditions of ever-increasing state procurement quotas and grossly inadequate state provisioning, the two successive poor harvests of 1931 and 1932 spelled disaster. In the fall and winter of 1932 and 1933, millions of peasants died from starvation in major agricultural regions of the USSR, first, and most of all, in Ukraine, but also in large parts of the Northern Caucasus and the middle and lower Volga regions, Kazakhstan, the Russian Black Earth region, and parts of the Urals. Cases of cannibalism were numerous. From 3 to 7 million are estimated to have died during this famine.[28]

In the entire country, only the highest elite received sufficient state supplies. In 1932, for example, the monthly ration of the residents of the famous House of Government on Bolotnaya square near the Kremlin in Moscow included 4 kilograms each of meat and sausage, one and one-half kilogram of butter, two liters of vegetable oil, 6 kilograms of fresh fish, 2 kilograms of pickled herring, 3 kilograms each of sugar and flour (not counting a daily ration of 800 grams of baked bread), 3 kilograms of various groats, eight jars of canned goods, two dozen of eggs, 2 kilograms of cheese, 50 grams of tea, 1,200 cigarettes, two bars of soap, and 1 kilogram of black caviar (!).[29] These families also received a liter of milk a day and an assortment of vegetables, fruits, and confectionary.[30]

The number of those who received the best elite ration "A" by the mid-1930s reached only 4,500 people. If we include 41,500 of the lower-rank elite receiving ration "B," as well as 1,900 of the highest segment of the intellectual elite and a number of retired Bolsheviks who were recipients of exceptional state privileges, the total number of people who received special rations reaches only 55,500 (without family members), of whom 45,000 lived in Moscow. In other words, a fraction of 1 percent of the country's population received sufficient supplies from the state.

During the famine of the first half of the 1930s, stable and sufficient food provision was probably the most important privilege enjoyed by the elite. However, only one person in the country did not live "on the ration and by coupon," Stalin. All other high-ranking officials were assigned rations. They were cheap and plentiful, but rations all the same. An analysis of other material conditions (salary, housing, wardrobe, medical care, leisure activities, etc.) allows us to say that an assessment of the hierarchy in poverty must include the material wealth of the Soviet elite, which in the 1930s hardly exceeded the living standards of the Western upper-middle class.[31]

How did people exposed to such hierarchical, selective and clearly insufficient state provisions survive? They "took care of themselves." Factories, cooperatives, schools, hospitals, unions of scientists and artists and even the highest levels of state and Party institutions built their own poultry incubators; pigsties; rabbit, milk, and fish farms; and planted vegetable gardens. The organizations bartered with the collective and state farms and conducted their own procurements in the countryside. All of these took an enormous amount of time and energy away from manufacturing or professional labor. The food from this supplementary economy went to feed workers and employees in the institutional canteens and buffets. According to budget data, in 1932 and 1933, factory canteens provided up to one-third of the groats, potatoes, and vegetables; 30–40 percent of the meat, fish, and milk products; and half of the fat in workers' diets.

Not only organizations but every urban family had its garden. Either with or without official permission, each piece of suitable land around the city or within the city limits was planted, usually with potatoes. Townsfolks also raised cattle, pigs, and poultry in sheds near the gardens or even in their apartments. In this regard, an interesting order was issued by a dorm's overseer in Tashkent (Uzbekistan): "It is also prohibited to have in the rooms chickens, dogs, pigs and any animals, including bears, as was noticed." In 1932–3, this people's supplementary economy provided up to a third of the milk and eggs and about 10 percent of the potatoes, vegetables, fruit, and fat in the diet of an urban worker.

In feeding the population during the 1930s, peasant individual plots (that is the land adjacent to their house, *uchastki*) played an even more significant role than the urban kitchen gardens. Allowed by the 1930 Collective Farm Statute, these plots could not exceed 0.5–1 hectare (about 1.2–2.5 acres). Though small, they became the main source of peasants' self-supply and the basis of the legal peasant markets, which officially and, quite often undeservedly, were called the collective farm markets. Budgetary data show that these markets supplied 50–80 percent of the potatoes, milk, eggs, fats, and butter, and 20–30 percent of the meat, groats, vegetables, fruits, vegetable oil, and flour in the urban diet. Prices, however, were exorbitant. The market price for wheat bread in 1932 was 3–5 rubles per kilogram, in comparison with about 25–30 kopecks if bought on a ration card (a ruble is 100 kopecks); the market price for meat was 5–10 rubles per kilogram, while on ration (if available) it cost only 1.50–2 rubles; butter cost 6–10 rubles per kilogram on ration and about 20 rubles at the market.

People developed other sources of supply. They sold or traded personal belongings for food at the markets and bazaars, engaged in speculation on the black markets, and stole from work. In the summer of 1929, the government opened state commercial stores in the cities. Anyone could buy there. Despite the prohibitive prices, lines and purchasing norms were common even in commercial stores.[32] In 1931, the government allowed Soviet people to purchase in the currency stores called *Torgsin*, which only served foreigners before.[33] People could buy in *Torgsin* shops paying with foreign currency, gold, silver, and other valuables. Hunger and deprivation drove people to *Torgsin*, and, consequently, its network grew in proportion to the worsening food situation. During the mass famine of 1933, sales in *Torgsin* increased by more than 200 percent in comparison with 1932. More than 80 percent of the goods sold by *Torgsin* in 1933 were foodstuffs, and bread constituted more than 60 percent of that. Starving people were exchanging their heirlooms for bread.[34]

Using all available sources of supply, from rations, peasant and black markets, commercial stores, to *Torgsin*, the daily menu of a member of a worker's family in 1932–3 consisted of one-third of a loaf of black bread, two or three slices of white bread, a plate of groats with a little dab of vegetable oil, a watery soup with a tiny piece of fish, two or three potatoes with a small piece of meat, weak tea, a few pieces of sugar or cheap candy, and a glass of milk for the children every fourth or fifth day. A comparison of food consumption of industrial workers at the peak of NEP in 1926 with their consumption during the period of 1932–5 reveals the quantitative decline and qualitative deterioration in diet. Cheaper and coarser black bread replaced more expensive and high-calorie white bread. The consumption of meat, dairy products, and fats drastically dropped. Instead of 150 grams of meat per day as in 1926, workers on average ate 40 grams in 1933. Butter, eggs, and milk virtually disappeared from the diet. Only the consumption of bread, potatoes,

TABLE 2.5 Consumption of Industrial Workers' Families in 1926, 1933, and 1934 (All Sources of Supply, Grams per Person per Day)

Food	February	First Quarter	First Half Year
	1926	1933	1934
Rye flour	1	40	32
Wheat flour	46	12	35
Rye bread	222	315	359
Wheat bread	325	158	194
Groats/beans	46	36	33
Potatoes	243	228	262
Vegetables	99	89	104
Fruits/berries	18	3	5
Meat	150	40	34
Fish	28	24	28
Milk	199	52	98
Butter	9	1	4
Vegetable oil	12	3	2
Sugar/sweets	36	35	40
Tea	2	0.2	No data

Source: Trudy TsSU 30:5 (1927): 76–7, 84–5; and RGAE, f. 1562, op. 329, d. 62, ll. 2, 86.

groats, and fish remained approximately at the 1926 level. By the mid-1930s, workers' diet improved, but the consumption of meat and milk products still did not reach the 1926 level.[35]

Food shortages spurred people to protest. The secret police documented disturbances in store lines, demonstrations, and strikes. One of the largest protests occurred in the textile enterprises of Teikov and Vychuga in the Ivanovo region in April 1932 and February 1933.[36] In the first quarter of 1932, the lack of supplies caused ten strikes in the Urals, and seven more took place there in April alone. The largest of these involved 580 people at a factory in Votkinsk. Food shortages also led to disturbances in Donbass, the Nizhnii Novgorod region, along the Black Sea area, and in other places.[37]

After Rationing: Life Became Better?

By the mid-1930s, due to the end of mass repression in the countryside and a few good harvests, the food situation in the USSR stabilized. Bread rations were abolished in January 1935, followed by the end of rationing of other foodstuffs in October 1935. The government proclaimed a new era of "free trade" (*svobodnaia torgovlia*). Tired of hardship, people looked to the future with hope.

Life became easier indeed. Access to stores was no longer restricted to specific groups of consumers or regulated by rations. People could buy goods in any store available. Although the government continued to prioritize heavy industries and military production, during the Second Five-Year Plan (1933–7), it increased investments in consumer industries. As a result, many new food industries appeared, among them a production of Soviet champagne and ice cream. Moreover, the state substantially decreased industrial imports and the export of foods and raw materials, which also contributed to the improvements in population's supply.

However, the foundation of the Soviet economy did not change. Private production and trade remained as limited as before and the deficient state-centralized distribution system, with its social and geographic hierarchies, still dominated the supply system. As war approached the Soviet borders at the end of the 1930s, investments in defense increased, resulting in a sharp decline in the production of consumer goods. Even by 1940, state food industries produced (annually per person) only 13 kilograms of sugar, 8–9 kilograms of meat and fish, about 40 kilograms of dairy products, about 5 liters of vegetable oil, seven tins of canned goods, 5 kilograms of confectionary products, and 4 kilograms of soap. A significant share of even this rather limited production did not go to stores. It went to so-called off-market consumption to supply state institutions, was used in food processing, or was added to the strategic food reserves. In 1939, for instance, the state retail trade in total provided for (annually per person) about 1.5 kilogram of meat, 2 kilograms of sausage, 1 kilogram of butter, and 5 kilograms of groats. One-third of all sugar went to the off-market consumption sector. The state fund of flour available for sale constituted a relatively large amount, 108 kilograms per person per year, but this translates into a mere 300 grams per person per day.

Insufficient state production and other factors such as the rapid growth of the population's cash income and an underdeveloped and uneven distribution of a network of state stores that remained concentrated in large cities perpetuated food shortage in the country.[38] Although the extremes of the geographic and social hierarchy of rationing did not return, permanent shortages made the government prioritize supplies. The redistribution of resources in favor of industrial cities at the expense of nonindustrial towns and the countryside persisted. Moscow and Leningrad remained the most privileged, and alone these consumed more than half of the state supplies of meat, fats, and eggs, although their residents constituted only a small percent of the country's population. The administration of factories continued to use supplies as carrot and stick to stimulate production. Shock-workers (from late 1935 called Stakhanovites, after the miner Alexsei Stakhanov, 1906–1977) were not only better paid but also received special "orders" of food (so-called *zakazy*).

By the end of the 1930s, the countryside received from the state less than a third of the goods allocated for sale, even though the rural areas still accounted for almost 70 percent of the country's population and held nearly 40 percent of its purchasing power. At the same time, state procurements took from the countryside more than 90 percent of grain; up to 70 percent of potatoes; half the meat, fats, and eggs; and about 60 percent of the milk produced. As before, the peasant subsidiary economy served as the main source for self-provision and the peasant markets, where urban dwellers continued to buy a substantial part of their food. State procurements, in combination with a crop failure in 1937, caused local famines in the rural areas of the Volga River (the Saratov and Kuibyshev regions, the Republic of the Volga Germans) and also in the Voronezh and Cheliabinsk regions. During the winter and spring of 1937, several thousands of families were starving and bloated from hunger in these areas and dozens died from starvation. Peasants complained in those days how *"I have been working on a collective farm for five years and have never had enough food to eat;" "Blue and white collar workers have protection but we are discriminated."*

The highest party, state, military, cultural, and scientific elites continued to hold the top position in the hierarchy of state supply after the abolition of rationing. They took advantage of better salaries to buy food in open state trade

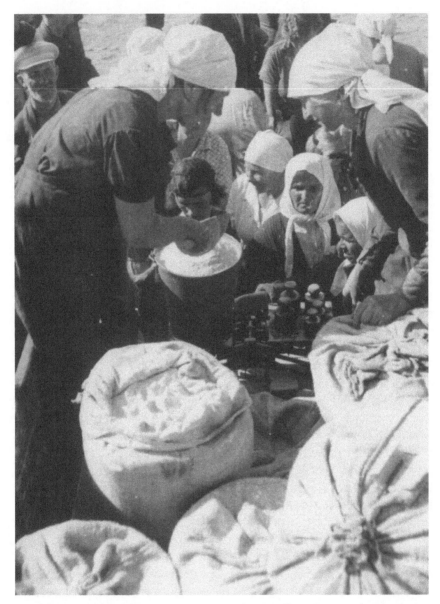

FIGURE 2.3 *"Life became better, comrades!" Selling flour at the peasant market, Ukraine, 1938. Courtesy of the Russian State Archive of the Kino-Photo Documents).*

and at peasant markets, but they also could buy at their institutional buffets, dining rooms, and received weekly a selection of foods (*zakaz*) to take home.

In comparison with the previous period of rationing, the material situation of all the groups of the population improved in the second half of the 1930s,

FIGURE 2.4 *"Life became better, comrades!" The first year without bread rations. A bread store at the Molotov Automobile Plant, The city of Gor'kii, 1935. Courtesy of the Russian State Archive of the Kino-Photo Documents.*

but progress was slow. By 1940, the level of consumption reached at the height of NEP was not yet matched. The hierarchy of poverty persisted.

The Soviet people entered the 1930s on rations, and exited the decade on rations. The Soviet-Finnish war and the military conflict with Japan in the Far East aggravated the existing economic disproportions. From December of 1939, bread and flour disappeared from stores, followed by acute shortages of other goods. Food prices at the peasant markets skyrocketed. Not being able to afford to buy by kilograms, people bought milk by the cup, potatoes by the piece, and flour by the saucer. Even the privileged capital encountered difficulties. The country returned to queuing, restricted access distribution centers to provide for selected groups of consumers (the military, enterprises and transport working for war), and a spontaneous revival of rationing from below on the initiative of the local leaders who tried to protect the population involved in industrial production, while a sharp decrease of the state supply of rural areas caused thousands of peasants to flee to the cities. On the eve of 1941, the government had to admit that "free trade," introduced in 1935, had ceased to exit.

The supply system began to fall apart under the pressure of the relatively minor military conflicts of the late 1930s, but its major trial was ahead. On June 22, 1941, Nazi Germany invaded the USSR.

Notes

1 According to the 1926 All-Union census, only about 26.3 million people in the total population of about 147 million lived in the cities.

2 Peasants also provided for themselves with homemade clothes, shoes, simple furniture, and other household items.

3 Carr and Davies assert that by 1926 workers and peasants in the USSR had better diets than in tsarist times, see E. H. Carr and R. W. Davies, *Foundations of a Planned Economy, 1926–1929*, New York: Macmillan, 1971, 697.

4 The mass repression against peasants were sanctioned by the Politburo telegram from January 14, 1928. Members of the Politburo, Stalin included, went to the regions to speed up the state grain procurements.

5 Central Archive of the Federal Security Service of the Russian Federation, Moscow, [from here: *TsA FSB*], *fond* [f.] 2, *opis'* [op.] 6, *delo* [d.] 567, list [l.] 466. This is the Russian (or Soviet) style of filing archival documents, *fond* meaning – more or less – collection; *opis'*, series or subdivision; *delo*, file; and *list*, sheet or page (plural *listy*, abbreviated as "ll." with sometimes *oborot* for verso on two-sided pages).

6 *TsA FSB*, f. 2, op. 6, d. 85, l. 227.

7 *TsA FSB*, f. 2, op. 5, d. 385, ll. 428–42; ibid., d. 386, ll. 45–84; and op. 7, d. 599, ll. 76, 237, 244, 272.

8 Here I mean a financial year of 1928/29. Calendar years started on January 1, financial years on October 1.

9 *TsA FSB*, f. 2, op. 7, d. 527, ll. 15–56; ibid., d. 65, ll. 266–72; and ibid., d. 605, ll. 31–5.

10 Vladimir Ilyich Ulianov (Lenin), leader of the Bolsheviks and the founder of the Soviet state died in January 1924.

11 *Seredniak*: Middle peasant, belonging to a group the Communists identified as positioned in socioeconomic terms within the villages as between the *bedniak* (poor) and *kulak* (wealthy) peasants.

12 *TsA FSB*, f. 2, op. 6, d. 605, l. 130.

13 For more on this process, see Boterbloem's essay on the peasantry in this collection.

14 As a result of peasants' slaughtering of livestock in resistance to collectivization, the total number of cattle dropped from 6 million heads in 1928 to 3.3 million heads in 1934: Even by 1940 it stood below 5 million heads. The number of horses dropped from 3.2 million heads in 1928 to 1.5 million in 1934, rising only to 1.7 million heads by 1940.

15 There were other factors that aggravated food shortages at the end of the 1920s and beginning of the 1930s in the USSR, such as the building up of state food reserves for an anticipated war and, most important, an inflation caused by state's constant mass emission of paper money. In less than two years, from the end of 1928 to July 1930, the state issued 1,556 million rubles, while it planned to issue only 1,250 million within the entire Five-Year Plan; while the trade volumes decreased the amount of money in population's possession increased.

16 Economic historians estimate that the 1929/30 state grain procurements left the countryside with 6 million tons less grain than the previous year (see R. W. Davies, Mark Harrison, and S. G. Wheatcroft, *The Economic Transformation of the Soviet Union, 1913–1945*, Cambridge: Cambridge University Press, 1994, 290).

17 For instance, the first quarter of 1930 witnessed ninety-two strikes (sixty-six in 1929) at the female-dominated textile mills, of which nine were caused by the poor food provisions. Male-"cadre" blue-collar workers kept calmer. In the first half of 1930, only four of twenty-two strikes in the metal industries were in protest of food shortages (numbers based on *TsA FSB*, f. 2, op. 8, d. 655, ll. 137–49, 466, 764–70).

18 The Soviet press reported an execution of forty-eight "saboteurs of provisions" on September 25, 1930; Stalin personally insisted on the execution of the arrested and publication of their "confessions" (*Pis'ma I.V. Stalina V.M. Molotovu, 1925–1936 gg.*, ed. L. Kosheleva, et al., Moscow: Rossiia Molodaia, 1996, 185–6, 216–18).

19 See Table 2.1, Special list and List 1.

20 See Table 2.1, List II and List III.

21 Same norms applied to craftsmen in cooperatives, public health and trade employees, retired people with the state privileges, old Bolsheviks, rural workers at *sovkhozy* (state farms), and others.

22 These norms also applied to family members of workers, craftsmen who were not members of cooperatives, retired people, and invalids.

23 See Table 2.2.

24 With time, the rationing system became even more stratified as, in 1932, the managers of the leading industrial enterprises received the right to define groups and norms of provision (within the limits established by the state). To stimulate production they established new gradations of supply, such as blue-collar "shock workers," white-collar "shock workers," workers with a certificate of honor (*pochyotnaia gramota*), and so on.

25 See Table 2.3.

26 See Chapter 1, Boterbloem's essay, in this collection for more on this.

27 See Table 2.4.

28 On the famine and its deathtoll, see Davies, Harrison, and Wheatcroft, eds., *Economic Transformation*, 16–17, 58, 68, 74–7.

29 Commemorated in Yuri Trifonov's famous novel *House on the Embankment* (see Yuri Trifonov, *Another Life and the House on the Embankment*, Evanston, IL: Northwesten University Press, 1999). See for more on the history of this apartment building, Yuri Slezkine, *The House of Government: A Saga of the Russian Revolution*, Princeton, NJ: Princeton University Press, 2017.

30 See Table 2.3.

31 For more on this, see Elena Osokina, *Our Daily Bread: Socialist Distribution and the Art of Survival in Stalin's Russia, 1927–1941*, Armonk, NY: M. E. Sharpe, 2001, 94–8; M. Matthews, *Privilege in the Soviet Union*, London: Routledge, 1978.

32 In 1933, for example, sugar, which cost 92 kopecks per kilogram when rationed, cost 8 rubles in commercial stores; the price of cheese was, 5–7 rubles on rations versus 13–24 rubles in commercial shops, and price of butter 4–5 rubles versus 20–26 rubles (respectively).

33 *Torgsin* is a Russian abbreviation for The All-Union Organization for Trade with Foreigners. It served Soviet customers from June 1931 until February 1936.

34 The government was able to accumulate a substantial amount of people's wealth through *Torgsin*. Its total income, about 300 million rubles, equaled the cost of the foreign equipment imported by the Soviet government for ten giant industrial enterprises, such as the Gor'kii Automobile Plant, the Stalingrad Tractor Factory, the Ural Mechanical Engineering Plant, Magnitka and Kuznetsk, and other enterprises. Less than one-third of *Torgsin*'s income was received from sales to foreigners. The rest, more than 70 percent, consisted of the proceeds from the receipt of Soviet people's heirlooms.

35 See Table 2.5.

36 See J. J. Rossman, *Worker Resistance under Stalin: Class and Revolution on the Shop Floor*, Cambridge, MA: Harvard University Press, 2005.

37 *RGAE*, f. 8043, op. 11, d. 56, l. 51; and *TsA FSB*, f. 2, op. 10, d. 116, l. 69, 172–4.

38 On average, by the end of the 1930s, there were twenty-one shops per each 10,000 people. Most of them were small, selling goods only between 100 and 200 rubles per day.

3

The Cities: Urbanization and Modern Life

Heather D. DeHaan

The Russian Revolution provoked a new form of urban politics, not only as a direct result of Marxist ideology, but also indirectly, due to the form of governance that developed in the Stalin period. Soviet authorities sought modernization—that is, roads to support rail movement and motorized transportation; sanitary technologies such as running water and sewers; an electric grid and a network of schools, factories, and other institutions important for both industrial production; as well as the social reproduction of an educated, Communist Party-minded workforce. The early Soviet period of the 1920s, as Stalin consolidated his power, was thus a period of experimentation with new types of cities and new living spaces, with attempts to develop new scientific systems of social regulation. These experiments failed, and the Stalin-era cityscape remained one marked by distinctly spatialized inequality, with a highly uneven provision of basic city services both within urban space and across the Soviet Union.

In the immediate wake of the 1917 revolution and subsequent Civil War, urban change was rather limited and strategic, centering on symbolic changes rather than systemic, fundamental improvements to urban life. The private gardens of religious institutions (such as monasteries or convents) and of the estates of the imperial Russian elite were democratized. Streets were renamed, substituting references to revolutionary heroes for those celebrating tsarist rulers and generals. Old statues were torn down and new ones erected in their place. To meet peasants' demand for land, the Bolsheviks followed their seizure of power with the abolition of private property, allowing for both the seizure of noble estates by peasants and also the new practice of *uplotnenie*, or "compression," whereby members of the former elite and others deemed to have a surplus of "living space" were required to allocate room within their homes and apartments to house their less fortunate neighbors. The concept of "living space," which assessed the volume of housing in terms of square meters, reinforced this intrusive form of politics, which penetrated deep into the home in the name of equity and justice. It also ushered in one of the most enduring housing forms of the Soviet era, the communal apartment (*kommunal'ka*). In these apartments, kin groupings resided in a single room or a portion of a room in a large home, sharing kitchen and bathroom with other occupants of the building.

Although revolutionary, these changes inserted themselves into an urban landscape that itself remained largely unchanged. Quality brick or stone housing, usually in traditional classical, gothic, or baroque architectural styles, dominated the center of Soviet cities, clustering around central administrative and cultural institutions. In historic cities with an ancient fortress (Kremlin), leading administrative institutions could generally be found inside the Kremlin's walls, which were long emptied of the residential construction that they had originally been designed to protect. Outside, a boulevard might follow the lines of an old moat or since-removed outer fortification, and other major streets would jut outward from this central point, creating the radial-ring road structure for which many historic Russian cities were known. Tramlines, streetlights, electricity, running water, and both public and private parks and gardens were generally concentrated in these central areas, where the elite lived in tsarist days. More fire-prone, low-rise wooden construction, unpaved streets, outdoor toilets, and well water prevailed on the outskirts of town, where municipal services did not reach. To the extent that such suburban housing had modern conveniences—these were generally supplied by local factories, and then only in limited quantity—usually just water through a street pump, and perhaps some electricity. Long traditions of *zemliachestvo* (the cohabitation in cities of peasant migrants from the same village) ensured that village sociability and custom also prevailed in these lower-class areas.

More recently colonized regions of the former Russian empire had a slightly different urban profile. Except for a handful of major economic and administrative centers such as Baku (an oil-boom city on the Caspian Sea) or Tbilisi (an administrative center for the southern Caucasus), imperial cities located on the Asian continent were fairly small, lacking in the economic growth that had proliferated in places such as Warsaw, St. Petersburg, and smaller industrialized towns of European Russia. In Central Asia and the Caucasus, flat roofs, earthen or limestone construction, walled courtyards, and female seclusion defined many urban spaces, particularly in areas with large Islamic

FIGURE 3.1 *Factory town of Sormovo, located near Nizhnii Novgorod. Late nineteenth century.*

populations. In the imperial outpost of Tashkent, prerevolutionary Russian authorities had sponsored the construction of a European quarter meant to stand as a beacon of civilization in a region of supposed backwardness. Carrying forward this ideology of progress, Soviet authorities set for themselves the goal of eliminating the divide between such Russian urban development and native urban life, largely through the universal imposition of "Soviet" housing and infrastructure, which admittedly also privileged European housing ideas and practices.

Such transformation seemed possible with the launching of the cultural revolution (as part of the Great Turn), when Soviet architects and designers proposed to dramatically restructure these cities, stamping out the inequities that distinguished cities from villages and centers from peripheries. Many Soviet architects at the time were inspired by the garden city, as theorized by Great Britain's Ebenezer Howard (1850–1928). He proposed to dispose of large metropolises, dispersing large urban populations into smaller suburban settlements that were integrated into rural agricultural and recreational environments. Another idea for eliminating the rural–urban divide came from well-known Soviet urban planner and architect Nikolai Miliutin (1889–1942) who proposed the creation of linear cities in which parallel strips of residential, recreational, and industrial development stretched side by side, without a clear outer boundary. His plan allowed for broad industrial expansion, while ensuring a green buffer between manufacturing and residential zones. In the spirit of the time, it was anti-hierarchical and articulated no particular center for economic or political power.

Such radically democratic sentiments, fueled as well by faith in scientific modernization, also shaped debates about the appearance of Soviet architecture. Given the formal abolition of private property and "bourgeois" taste, architects expected rationality, functionality, and anti-traditionalism to become firm principles of urban design—something to be led by experts no longer restricted by private property rights. To them, this heralded an era in which science and reason, not privilege, would define not only the placement of architecture but also its aesthetic and appearance. After the 1917 revolution, a new avant-garde school of modernist architecture emerged to advance the principles of constructivist design, in which a building's form reflected its purpose and its construction materials and technique. Members of the constructivist school rejected classical facades, which they regarded as a political mask, in favor of buildings using iron girders and flat, glass-filled facades that, to the Soviet and international avant-garde, represented transparency and authenticity. These ideas were both challenged and extended by another modernist group, which advocated rationalism. Unlike constructivists, who focused on architectural form and function, this cohort experimented with the impact of architectural shape and color on the human psyche. These two leading modernist groups fought over the appropriate architecture of the future, a debate in which groups with more traditionalist leanings also played a role. For instance, many architects in the former capital of St. Petersburg (known as Leningrad in the Soviet period) were keen to preserve the imperial city's classicist grandeur.

To understand this debate, it might be helpful to compare architecture, a type of urban skin, to clothing, an extension of human skin. Like clothing, cities express values and identities by enabling, enhancing, or restricting particular movements or postures. Their architecture reflects new design technologies and capabilities, as well as news ideals for human lives and relationships. It should therefore come as no surprise that both clothing and architecture underwent radical experimentation, often with similar goals of advancing science and reason, social innovation, industrial production, and women's liberation. Women's garb in particular captured the radical politics of the era: constrictive bodices that highlighted small waists and full figures ceded to designs that flattered slim athletic bodies and drew attention to bodily movement through the hips. In Islamic countries and in the Soviet Union in the interwar era, there were campaigns to remove the veil. In both cases, changes in clothing were meant to represent and facilitate the rise of a "modern" woman who could participate in production, and not just reproduction. Geometric designs on free-flowing clothing embodied the ideas inherent in functionalist, minimalist architecture. Both clothing and building design aimed to liberate from tradition and hierarchy.

DER GEIST
DER NEUEN
MODE

ENTSPRICHT DEM GEIST
DER NEUEN ARCHITEKTUR

Figure 14. "The spirit of the new fashion corresponds to the spirit of the new architecture." Cover for the *Lette-Haus* fashion magazine (1929).

FIGURE 3.2 *Weimar-era magazine cover that identifies women's liberation and new fashion with new functionalist housing designs.*

For those attuned to Friedrich Engels' theories, the emancipation of women required the abolition of the family, regarded by leading Marxist theorists as a bourgeois institution in which males exploited the unpaid domestic and reproductive labor power of women.[1] With this in mind, the well-known urban planner and economist Leonid Sabsovich (d. 1938) designed the housing combine, which was a residential complex that rendered the family obsolete as an economic and reproductive unit. Not unlike the assembly-line system in which each worker focused on one narrow aspect of the production process, the housing combine assigned each of the duties traditionally assumed by housewives to specialized institutions. Professionally staffed nurseries were to answer for childcare, while factory kitchens were to provide meals, and state laundries eviscerated women's responsibility for hand-scrubbing dirty clothing over a sink or washbasin. Women were thus free to reproduce without bearing any responsibility for childcare or family needs.

The housing combine was designed to foster Soviet selfhood, which was not quite the equivalent of Western, liberal selfhood. In the predominant Western conceptualization, "insight" was to come through withdrawal from societal engagement, thus making space for personal reflection, thought, contemplation, and discovery. By contrast, Soviet knowledge was to be fostered through integration into "the collective," or through interpersonal interaction in shared spaces. Thus, each Soviet housing combine included a library, theater, sports gym, reading rooms, and Lenin corners, which were small interior nooks featuring the latest Soviet news, iconic images of Soviet leaders, and educational pamphlets. The housing combine's small sleeping cells were not supposed to be sites for individualized leisure or self-reflection; residents were supposed to read, listen to music, and spend leisure hours in the shared spaces of the combine or in the House of Culture that served the entire settlement.

For the Soviet state, this model also ensured that experts would play a leading role in shaping future Soviet generations. Expert childcare by professionals would help prevent the transmission of outmoded values and ideas by parents. Factory laundries and kitchens promised better hygiene in laundering and in food preparation. The overall structure compelled members of a family unit to merge into the world beyond hearth and home. By liberating women's hands for use in factory labor, the housing combine also limited the number of dependents per factory laborer, thus reducing the population required to support a factory. Besides, a healthier and more educated workforce raised by experts would, in theory, overcome labor problems associated with putative old peasant mores, including absenteeism, a lack of respect for punctuality, a tendency toward drunkenness (particularly during religious festivals), and a disregard for both personal hygiene and the careful maintenance of equipment. Given the influx of "uncouth" peasants into Soviet cities and the desperate need for industrial labor, the Sabsovich program had ready appeal.

Ironically, foreign expertise from capitalist countries was crucial to realizing this plan, despite the Soviet rejection of both private property and the bourgeois family. To facilitate the Soviet leap into industrial modernity during the First Five-Year Plan, Soviet authorities avidly recruited technologies and experts from abroad, particularly from more highly industrialized countries in Europe and North America. "American tempo" and efficiency held great allure for the new regime. To some degree, such cooperation was based on shared values. Like their Western capitalist opponents, Soviet leaders had a linear view of societal progress and sought universal education, efficient and large-scale production, expert-managed public health, and sanitary infrastructure, the end to the caste or estate system (in which people were born to their station), and broad public participation in political life, as well as the cultivation of sport, culture, and other leisure activities conducive to the development of physically healthy and productive bodies and minds. They also believed in science, but differed from nonsocialist governments in their conviction that Marxism, too, was a science. Henry Ford therefore exported production technologies to the Soviet Union—admittedly, also to compensate for his declining global competitiveness with Chevrolet.

Such partnerships foundered on ideological and cultural differences. For instance, the Soviet Ford Factory in Nizhnii Novgorod (known as Gor'kii from 1932 to 1991, through which the company is even today known as *Gor'kii Avtozavod* or GAZ) included a model settlement, the design of which was initially contracted to the Austin Company, operating out of Cleveland, Ohio. Its owners were Baptists, not socialists, and its planners regarded the family unit as the natural focal point of democratic, working-class housing. Troubled by the Austin Company's plans for garages, nurseries, and apartments designed for nuclear families, local Soviet architects and experts quickly intervened to assert ideological control. Problems with the lack of Soviet access to supplies that conformed to standard American measurements and parts lists additionally complicated the partnership.[2]

Such misunderstanding was hardly the only challenge standing in the way of building such housing combines. From 1928 to 1932, the Soviet state poured its resources into building factories, not into providing shelter for workers, thereby compelling newly recruited factory workers—many fleeing the violence of collectivization—to find their own housing. As a result, entire families took residence in sleeping cells in housing combines, though these were designed for individuals and lacked plumbing, domestic furnishings, and cooking facilities. Unfinished boiler rooms and factory kitchens in these same combines became private living spaces, as did laundries, firmly putting an end to the Soviet experiment in fully collective living.

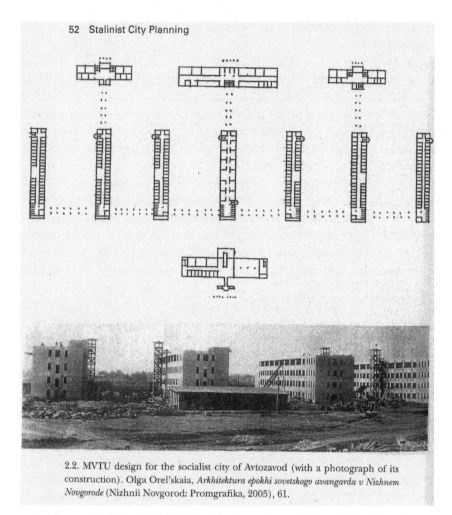

52 Stalinist City Planning

2.2. MVTU design for the socialist city of Avtozavod (with a photograph of its construction). Olga Orel'skaia, *Arkhitektura epokhi sovetskogo avangarda v Nizhnem Novgorode* (Nizhnii Novgorod: Promgrafika, 2005), 61.

FIGURE 3.3 *Housing combine buildings, Avtozavod District of Gor'kii, c. 1931.*

Elsewhere in the Soviet Union, local denizens made homes of mud huts and dugouts, as well as barracks, dormitories, and tents. Some workers slept in the factory building where they worked, shared a cot in the barracks with other workers, or rented the corner of a room. Communal apartments became a permanent institution, not because these were regarded as the ideal but because housing shortages provided few alternatives. If workers were lucky, a local factory provided either housing or the supplies with which to build it. The most unfortunate were forced laborers who were deported to remote regions of the Far East and Far North for the purposes of resource extraction; they often had neither shelter nor supplies with which to construct it. Overcrowding and subpar shelter were widespread and lingering problems. Urbanization drove the number of occupants per room upward from 2.71 in 1926 to 3.91 in 1940.[3]

The very idea of the socialist city clearly went through dramatic political reinvention in the last years of the First Five-Year Plan (in the early 1930s). Ideas once lauded as revolutionary were now denounced as "bourgeois" or "formalist." Radical avant-garde design ceded to so-called Socialist Realism, a stylistic mishmash that incorporated classical, gothic, and imperial styles without marking a complete return to any of them. Perhaps most notably embodied by Stalin-era high rises such as Moscow State University, Stalin's Socialist Realistic architecture tended to be ornate, mixing classical symmetry with gothic detail and massive bulk. The socialist future was no longer minimalist and functionalist, but grand and larger than life, something perhaps most strongly represented by the winning design of the 1930s for the House of Soviets. It was so immense that it was unrealizable from an engineering perspective. Images of it circulated abroad, often with small planes inserted into the frame to help articulate the massive height and size of the promised edifice.

With Stalin's consolidation of power around 1930, the Soviet state came to embrace social and spatial hierarchy, something echoed in the spatial structure of cities and in the emergence of models of home design that architects of the 1920s would have regarded as "bourgeois." Stalin's leadership praised "cultured" (kul'turnyi) living, something to be achieved through education, self-discipline, and exemplary service to the state. Soviet workers were no longer to seek living spaces with sleek, modern lines and facilities, but rather high-ceilinged, largish single-family apartments with curtains, all the modern conveniences of indoor plumbing and electric lighting, fine china, and a location near the city center, with its paved boulevards and public transportation. In the Stalin era, such privilege was enjoyed by only a select group of Party and cultural workers, along with hero workers known after 1935 as Stakhanovites. These groups were most likely to enjoy indoor plumbing, attractive furnishings and tableware, space for books, and the incredible privilege of having the resources to be clean and comfortable. Perhaps most important, their enjoyment of privilege was publicly celebrated as something they earned and deserved, and something to which other citizens could aspire.

In this world of hierarchy, Moscow enjoyed a level of investment unparalleled elsewhere and became a model toward which provincial towns aspired, with its architecture defining what was socialist and what was also advanced and privileged. Its new city plan of 1935 featured wide, straight downtown streets, which were supposed to be widened to 40 meters to allow for political demonstrations and higher levels of traffic. Such vastness, seen as a symbol of the people's greatness, also allowed for a rise in building heights without resulting in narrow, dark streets. The plan did not foresee the full destruction of historic Moscow, instead fitting itself into the radial-ring structure typical of many old Russian cities. Elements of historic Russian classical symmetry and baroque ornamentation appeared in new Soviet design, which appropriated these motifs as a way to signify its status as the vanguard of human development and the culmination of human history. The incorporation of such palatial grandeur into Soviet design also evoked the idea of a "palace for the peoples," something perhaps best exemplified by the elaborate decoration inside the Moscow metro system, a palatial world whose aura was in many ways attached to its daring gift of starry brightness to the depth beneath the city of Moscow.

Gone were aspirations for an end to the urban–rural divide, and the defeat of spatial and social hierarchies. The new verticality and hierarchy served to bolster the rise of Stalin as sole leader of the Soviet Union, the authoritarian *vozhd'* who stood at the top of the political hierarchy. Soviet iconography juxtaposed Stalin's image with that of the Kremlin towers, cementing the association of Moscow as place with Stalin as leader. Such symbolic and real power was routinely performed on the anniversaries of the Revolution, as Stalin stood on Lenin's tomb, immediately adjacent to the Kremlin wall, surveying the grand parade of people and military hardware across Red Square. Such parades were echoed at a smaller scale throughout the Soviet Union, offering ritual unity that also reinforced the symbolic centrality of Stalin, the Revolution, and Moscow.[4]

Throughout the Stalin era and after, spatialized inequality was part of the structure of Soviet life. Multistory buildings with amenities such as running water could be found in city centers and along major boulevards, which were often strategically lined with multistory stone, cement, or brick construction, all designed to give an appropriately modern face to the Soviet city. These areas also tended to have parkland, much of which continued to consist of appropriated gardens of now vanquished nobles, merchants, and religious institutions, though the Soviet state did invest in the broad expansion of such green areas. There were pockets of fully serviced housing around factories. For the most part, however, the areas far from the city center suffered from the same spatial disadvantages that plagued outlying areas prior to the Great Turn and Cultural Revolution. Running water, sewers, electricity, parks, and other services were in short supply. More remote regions of the Soviet Union suffered a particular shortage of infrastructure and services, because insufficient transportation systems made the delivery of construction materials and equipment extremely difficult.

Dysfunction turned less-than-ideal urban structures and systems into permanent realities. For instance, in theory, the Soviet state, or at least urban planners, despised low-rise construction because it tended to be substandard and sprawled over wide swaths of territory, requiring a greater investment into roads and services than did multi-story construction. However, Soviet housing as a whole was substandard and in short supply. Further, Soviet public transportation systems were notoriously inefficient, underserviced, and overcrowded. Factory managers solved both shelter and mobility problems for their workers by distributing building supplies to workers, enabling them to erect housing near the factory. Though planners warned against the negative health ramifications of situating housing next to industry and insisted that all such construction be designated "temporary," with an eye to moving workers to better housing and better locations, such low-rise homes assumed a permanency that planners did not intend. Often, planners found themselves compelled to make room for such districts in official plans—again, a concession to the reality that Soviet building materials, construction trusts, and transportation infrastructure were all incapable of meeting demand.

Wherever it was located, Soviet construction tended to be of very poor quality. Construction workers were inexperienced, as were foremen, who were often unable to read or interpret official architectural plans. Construction crews suffered atrocious working conditions, often working without proper mechanization and in cold temperatures that made it difficult to hammer nails or pour concrete. Paint and other construction materials were chronically in short supply, compelling foremen to ignore approved plans and make ad hoc adjustments, often to the detriment of the building's structural or aesthetic integrity. Urban planners and architects might wish to object, but any such objection put them at risk of being denounced as "enemies of the people," standing in the way of meeting workers' needs. Besides which, municipal planning offices lacked the staffing, transportation, political clout, survey maps, and surveyors required to ensure expert-managed, controlled urban development.

Sanitary provisions were also subpar, even in relatively privileged cities such as Moscow. Less than a third of residents of Moscow enjoyed running water in their apartments; elsewhere, numbers were still lower. A small number of prerevolutionary buildings had sewers and water lines, as did many of the best Soviet residential buildings of the 1920s to the 1930s. Even housing with water lines might not have running water, however, while demands on the municipal system were so powerful that pressure was perpetually low. Many fifth-floor apartments had running water only in the evening hours, a problem exacerbated by industrial expansion and the growing claim on municipal water systems with limited capacity. Sewerage was also sparse. For instance, though 80 percent of towns in Moscow province had sewerage of some sort in 1947, 70–90 percent of housing lacked it. Soviet people generally relied on outhouses, cesspits, and crude holes in the ground, and even these were often in short supply. As a result, human waste was not uncommonly dumped in the courtyard. Where cesspits were available but overflowing or frozen, waste tended to be thrown around the pit. Given resource shortages, most municipalities cleansed such pits twice a year, in spring and fall, and then only in central streets and squares. Horses and carts, as well as mechanized garbage trucks, were all in short supply, and the latter were, somewhat disturbingly, often put to alternative uses such as transporting food goods. Regular waste removal began only in the very late Stalin period, in the 1950s, and even then only in select major cities, such as Gor'kii.

The lack of waste collection systems and the limited number of treatment facilities made water contamination a public health issue. Municipal water supplies were increasingly polluted, and Stalin-era municipal treatment facilities could not cope with the volume or range of waste. For instance, though 90 percent of Moscow's waste was treated in 1946, it remained impure: not a single treatment plant in the Soviet Union under Stalin could carry out a full cycle of treatment, with sedimentation, filtering, and chlorination. Untreated or inadequately treated industrial and human waste was often released into local waterways or festered in pits, fields, and dumping areas, contaminating ground and river water, including water intake sources for cities and towns. Because of the public health hazard, the state instructed citizens to boil drinking water to kill pathogens. Even this did not remove chemical waste, of course.[5]

Such systemic problems marked another failure of the utopian hopes of the Cultural Revolution, namely, the idea of scientific governance, through which rationally designed systems structured society, so that sanitary infrastructures took the place of social controls. Paved roads, street lighting, and sewer systems and indoor running water theoretically allowed for governance through technological systems, bypassing the need to police where and how fecal waste was dumped, for instance. In the absence of such technological infrastructures, education, public approbation or sanction, and sanitary inspections necessarily played an important role in securing public health.

In such an environment, the burden of ensuring a healthy, well-fed, and orderly society fell disproportionately on Soviet women, whose unpaid domestic labor compensated for the failures of the state. Simply keeping home and family clean and sanitary was a struggle, given the lack of indoor plumbing, state laundries that catered to the public, and, until after the Second World War, gas stoves. Water had to be pumped on the street, hauled indoors (perhaps up several flights of stairs), and heated on a small portable stove for washing. Many lacked places to dry clothes, or even a second set of clothes to wear during laundering. Shortages of soap complicated the washing of bodies, clothing, dishes, and homes, making its procurement one of life's fundamental challenges. Less fortunate individuals living in barracks, dugouts, communal apartments, tents, and other such substandard housing did not have a space to bathe, making public bathhouses a public health necessity, even though bathhouses were too few in number and often inadequately supplied with towels, soap, and water, let alone hot, clean water.

The Great Patriotic War exacerbated shortages of housing and services, further straining an already inadequate infrastructure. In cities occupied by Nazi armies, it was not uncommon to report a loss of 80 percent of the prewar housing stock, something that had already been insufficient in supply and quality before June 1941. Elsewhere, as evacuees from more western areas were relocated to the interior, wartime urban populations rose by as much as 50–100 percent. With all resources focused on military production, educational institutions and other facilities were turned into industrial facilities or dormitories. Infrastructure fell into disrepair, and housing stocks were neither increased in number nor maintained. Replacement parts for sanitary systems were neither manufactured nor available, and municipalities found themselves without the experts to manage or repair treatment systems and housing. Horses, carts, and trucks were sent to the front, and many sanitation fields for human waste were plowed and used for producing scarce food goods. Running water supplies were further strained and ever more polluted, and bathhouses often ceased to operate. To fight epidemics the Soviet regime screened children, hairdressers, and evacuees and deportees for typhus-spreading lice. In places such as Tashkent, Soviet planners developed a new respect for local building and sanitary technology, which had developed in conjunction with local resource and environmental challenges and were thus more available, as well as effective, in a period of extreme crisis and shortage.

To compensate for such shortages before and after the war, the Soviet state frequently organized competitions and mass volunteer days, or *subbotniki*.[6] On these days, thousands of citizens in a district or city could be recruited to help lay water lines, repair homes, plant trees, or complete the landscaping that construction trusts left unfinished. They were also mobilized for biannual garbage and waste removal. With the encouragement (or demand) of a local party organization, a residential building, district body, or factory might "invite" a similar organization elsewhere in the city or country to compete in winterizing homes, repairing apartments, or cleaning up debris. Awards and prizes were generally granted to the most active and successful group, which often seems to have been to the group whose members had the requisite supplies—white paint, nails, water hoses, horses and carts, or whatever the requisite equipment might be. Such campaigns in no way compensated for the shortfall in services. It was common for garbage piled in vast heaps by mobilized citizens to be scattered by the wind, as no one came to remove it. Housing repairs were shoddy and inadequate. Planted trees died from neglect. Success was hardly universal.

The campaigns nonetheless scripted a form of urban engagement that could, in some cases, help facilitate the delivery of needed goods to local residents, though their primary importance seems to have been symbolic, scripting the city as the people's own. As Stephen Kotkin has noted, these mobilizations engaged citizens in building socialism.[7] That gathered garbage fluttered away in the breeze was perhaps irrelevant to the symbolic function of the campaign. They were part of fostering an identification with the city as a "cultured" space that was clean and neat. Of course, in Stalin's Soviet Union, being "cultured," that is, clean, comfortable, educated, and civilized, was a largely aspirational thing, something exceptionally difficult to achieve for all but the favored few. Still, given the degree to which public health depended on the personal and collective appreciation for order and cleanliness, the campaigns served an important social function.

The state also accepted and promoted the perpetuation of *personal* property, whereby individuals could effectively own housing, apartments, and personal goods (if not the land on which these stood). This reality, too, was produced by the failures of the Soviet state to develop a sizable, effective building industry that could meet ever-growing need. After all, in Moscow in 1946, living space amounted to just 4.4 square meters (about 38 square feet). Elsewhere, particularly in formerly occupied zones, living space was still more limited. To enable citizens to overcome shortages, the state set aside both land and resources, encouraging citizens to gather in collectives to finance and build their own homes.[8] This echoed older traditions: in the 1920s, almost 50 percent of property was personally owned, and already in the 1930s the Soviet state formally allowed for limited free trade through the *kolkhoz* markets, and government agencies themselves relied on the black market to offset the deficiencies in the state distribution system.[9]

The form of social reproduction facilitated by the Stalin-era cityscape was thus something quite distinct from the utopian ideals of the First Five-Year Plan. It officially endorsed the family unit, never again promoting housing combines that would obliterate family life. It allowed for hierarchy, encouraging the construction of monumental city centers while proving unable to provide equitable, high-quality state housing to all workers. As a social form, the Stalin-era city relied a great deal on ritualized participation in collective life, on personalized networks of distribution, and on personal initiative, particularly in sustaining healthy and clean cities and homes. Assembly-line production not only failed to result in assembly-line reproduction, but actually consumed the resources needed to sustain municipal infrastructure. In Stalin's Soviet Union, social reproduction, that is, raising children, sustaining a sanitary home, and procuring food, required exceptional effort, innovation, and a great deal of "making do."

The Stalin era nonetheless paved the way for systematic changes to municipal design and governance. Experts began to develop cities built around a hierarchy of services, with local food stores and hair salons serving small groups of housing, with local district services such as libraries and government facilities marking the next level of services, with the House of Soviets and universities belonging to the city center. Usage of cars was highly limited. Green cities, areas with facilities for leisure and recreation in the outdoors, also proliferated along with parklands and greenery. Urban planning, as a profession, was supported. Private housing, something that exploded in the Khrushchev period, was already entrenched in local practice, as was a commitment to family-based apartments. As Khrushchev's successors switched to prefabricated construction soaring beyond five floors, they pushed further outward, leaving Stalin-era apartment complexes largely intact.

The Soviet Union as a distinct civilization would be thus marked not only by paved roads, new cities, and the explosion of heavy industry and scientific technologies but also by urban societies where local "making do" was part of the fabric of social life. Five-story ornate housing with full servicing became the image of Soviet modernization, behind which more village-like partnerships and workplace cooperatives necessarily remained, as social and economic structures that allowed citizens of the Soviet Union to compensate for the limits of Soviet state power. In the Stalin era, at least, cities governed by technological systems were more an aspiration and an image than a lived reality.

Notes

1   Friedrich Engels (1820–1895) was Marx's faithful companion and sponsor, and was his executor (in intellectual terms) after his death. He did cowrite several key treatises with Marx, and wrote several influential works on his own, including *The Origins of the Family, Private Property and the State* (1884). This work argued for the inevitability of gender (or sex) equality.
2   Heather DeHaan, *Stalinist City Planning: Professionals, Performance, and Power*, Toronto: University of Toronto Press, 2013, 53–7.
3   Mark Smith, *Property of Communists: The Urban Housing Program from Stalin to Khrushchev*, DeKalb: Northern Illinois University Press, 2010, 8.
4   See, for more, Karen Petrone's contribution to this book.
5   Donald Filtzer, *Hazards of Urban Life in Late Stalinist Russia: Health, Hygiene and Living Standards, 1943–1954*, Cambridge: Cambridge University Press, 2010, 34, 45–55, 75.

6   *Subbotniki* was derived from the word *subbota* (Saturday), because in the early postrevolutionary years people "volunteered" for these tasks on Saturday, then often a rest day.

7   Stephen Kotkin, *Magnetic Mountain: Stalinism as Civilization*, Berkeley: University of California Press, 1997.

8   Filtzer, *Hazards of Urban Life*, 32.

9   See, as well, Elena Osokina's Chapter 2 in this book.

4

On the Margins: Social Dislocation and Criminality in the Soviet Union from the 1930s to the 1950s

David Shearer

In January 1933, Joseph Stalin, supreme leader of the Soviet Union, gave a speech to a gathering of the ruling Communist Party elite.[1] Stalin praised the Party for its success in defeating the enemies of socialism that threatened development of the country. In the same speech, however, Stalin delivered a stern warning. Organized internal enemies had been defeated, and the Soviet military and economy were strong enough to deter hostile foreign powers from openly attacking the country, but crime and lawlessness threatened the great task before the Party and the Soviet people to construct socialism. Criminality, Stalin declared, had become so widespread that it posed a danger to the very foundations of the state. In his remarks, the Soviet dictator made it clear that crime and lawlessness were not only the central problem of social order, but that social order was the central problem of state security.

How could that be? Joseph Stalin's Soviet Union epitomized twentieth-century totalitarianism. Millions of people passed through harsh labor camps and penal colonies, sometimes for even minor infractions. Political police held the population in thrall, and often in fear, of their supposed omnipresence and omniscient power. Strict residence and internal passport laws supposedly allowed the regime and its authorities to track people wherever they were and to fix populations to their place of work and residence. Given the regime's pretensions to total social control, could crime have been as rampant as Stalin declared? Did criminality really pose a threat to the state, and to the regime? Who committed crimes, what motivated criminals in their activities, and what kinds of crimes were most prevalent? What kinds of crimes most worried the regime's leaders, and did those crimes reflect a real state of social breakdown or deep-seated anti-Soviet opposition?

Crime did, indeed, pose a threat to the Soviet state, mainly as a result of Stalin's revolution from above. The regime's rapid and forced industrialization program, combined with the collectivization of agriculture, created widespread scarcities and massive social dislocation. Peasant resistance to collectivization led to a veritable war in the countryside, the dispossession of millions of peasant farmers, and eventually to famine that killed 5–6 million people. Scarcities of daily commodities left many in the population in destitute circumstances. Widespread dispossession of property, wholesale deportations, and forced population migration characterized the early years of the 1930s. Scarcities, hunger, and land confiscation set millions of people in motion, migrating across the continent on a near-biblical scale. Millions of peasants and other rural inhabitants, as well as those in prerevolutionary propertied and professional classes (so-called former people, or *lishentsy*), streamed into and through the cities and industrial sites. They took to the rail lines and roads. Famine conditions in the early 1930s and severe shortages of all goods, due to Stalin's industrial priorities, exacerbated the movement of masses of people—to escape famine-stricken areas, to find goods, to seek a better life, even just to survive. This unorganized movement of people drained economic resources and threatened to overwhelm the underdeveloped infrastructure of the cities and the social stability of the country. Large numbers of indigents and itinerants, criminals, unemployed youth, gypsies, orphans, the disenfranchised, and a range of other groups added to these mass migrations. During the early 1930s, millions of people fell into the margins of Soviet society.

Social displacement on such a scale formed the background of Stalin's remarks in 1933 about the rising threat of criminality and social disorder. Stalin, of course, cast the problem of social breakdown in the language of class war, and no official acknowledged publicly that widespread social dislocation was more the result of the regime's policies than of conscious social opposition. Regardless of the causes—state policies or a new kind of class war—leaders understood that rising crime rates and other social problems posed an imminent danger to the state and the establishment of Soviet order. Disorder posed such a danger because Soviet social agencies were underdeveloped and quickly overwhelmed, and the state's policing agencies also experienced difficulty coping with the problems that suddenly confronted them. Stalin's socialist offensive extended the power of the state into every area of the economy and society, and the Party's leaders marshaled extraordinary resources, both financial and human, to achieve this victory—to subdue the peasantry, to defeat opposition to collectivization, and to press large-scale industrialization. The battle for Soviet power had been won in the countryside and in the cities. Maintaining Soviet order was another matter, however. The Party's central institutions of power were secure, but asserting civil and political authority in rural and even in many urban areas was difficult in the early 1930s. Apart from local Party authorities, the task of imposing some kind of civil order in the wake of Stalin's socialist offensive fell largely to a social infrastructure and police force that were woefully inadequate to the task put upon them. This chapter explores social marginality and criminality in the Soviet Union during the era of Stalin's rule, from the 1930s through the 1950s.

Embezzlement of money or goods from the state-owned economy comprised the most common of crimes in the Soviet Union of the 1930s. Most of these crimes were committed by individuals in financial or administrative positions in state and cooperative organizations, especially cashiers and financial workers in cooperative organizations, state trade organs, collective and state farms, banks and post offices, or machine tractor stations (MTS) in the countryside. Understandably, areas undergoing intensive industrial or economic development reported the greatest number of cases. These included the Urals region, Western Siberia, the central industrial region, the Western (border) district, and the Ivanovo industrial region north of Moscow. All of these areas experienced new construction on a large scale, and, as a result, money and goods flowed into the regions through cooperatives and construction offices, often with few or no safeguards. Rural trade cooperatives and collective and state farm (*sovkhoz*) administrative organizations also became a focus for criminal activity, since they functioned as funnels for money and goods coming into the countryside. Even in major population centers, organized rings of criminals targeted financial departments for hiring themselves into positions ripe for easy corruption. Insinuating themselves in this way was not difficult. Organizations were desperate for any kind of financially literate workers and rarely gave more than a cursory screening to new employees, if even that. Background checks were primitive even in those enterprises that bothered with them. Employers had to rely, ultimately, on the word of the employee about his or her background. In the socially chaotic period of the early 1930s, it was relatively simple for a person to hide an unsavory past. As a result, police noted, "many" of those arrested and indicted for occupational and economic crimes were repeat offenders, some with numerous convictions already, and for serious crimes.

Miganov crimes

not hidden

The organized character of embezzlement schemes was a key to their success and to their scale. When one member of a gang found employment, he or she would find employment in the same office for his or her confederates. The size of some operations was truly audacious. B. D. Miganov, who had been a Communist Party member since 1918, headed the office that administered all railroad car and train station buffets for the Moscow railroad line. Following the pattern described above, Miganov staffed his office with comrades in crime from his previous positions in the Moscow-area restaurant administration and agricultural sector. He gathered around him a group that systematically embezzled over 500,000 rubles in a two-year period from 1932 to 1934, when an average administrator's salary amounted to about 200 rubles a month. Miganov's gang hid its dealings mainly through the use of fictitious accounts, receipts, and purchase orders. "Hid" is not exactly the appropriate word, since their activities were well known to others in the administration. A police investigation uncovered that, in addition to Miganov's group, several other individuals were siphoning off money, as much as 17,000 rubles in one case, and 11,000 in another, all with Miganov's tacit knowledge, and with the requisite kickbacks. The administration's Communist Party committee knew about these activities but reported nothing. They, too, were being bought off by Miganov and his gang. The chief accountant of the buffet administration was in on the deal and regularly underreported the organization's balances to higher financial and administrative authorities. When it was finally uncovered, thirty-one people were taken into custody.

Ivanov

The Miganov ring was a large one, but not unusually so. Police files contain reports about many similar kinds of operations. Embezzlement and bribery were commonplace practices. In particular, the practice of bribery (*vziatochnichestvo*) was just as devastating economically as and even more insidious than crimes such as embezzlement and state property theft. Just as important to note, practices of bribery and embezzlement all too often shaded over into areas of accepted and even necessary administrative practice. It was the way things got done. The department head of a Moscow produce trust, a certain Ivanov, understood this. Ivanov was a "pusher" (*tolkach*), the person who was sent on business trips (*komandirovki*) to clear administrative logjams and get delayed goods moving, or secure smooth cooperation with other officials. Ivanov was good at his job. In his routine circuits of vegetable markets and farms of Moscow area, he established good working relationships that resulted in timely deliveries and even in overfulfillment of produce delivery plans, but his working relations also included a widespread system of bribery and kickbacks—to local farm officials, to train station depot managers, and, of course, to local Party, police, and state officials to sign needed release papers and to expedite bureaucratic matters. Bribes ranging from several hundred to several thousands of rubles per person also included prolonged drinking bouts, paid for by produce trust funds, whenever Ivanov was in a region.

Bribery and embezzlement were as corrosive as they were widespread, and they continued to plague the state throughout the 1930s and well beyond. Speculation—trading privately to make a profit—was illegal within the state-owned economy, but it posed a major problem for the regime, too. By definition, such activities were regarded as exploitative and, more to the point, they threatened the state monopoly on profit and taxes. Genrikh Yagoda (1891–1938), chief of both the civil and political police until 1936, claimed that the police investigated about 10,000 cases of speculation each month, and these cases did not include large-scale crimes handled by the Economic Crimes Department of the political police, the OGPU (as it was called in the early 1930s). One report declared that, in the country's "several" major cities, the police arrested 58,314 people for speculation during the first half of 1934. Police expelled from these cities another 53,000 people for speculation. Even these numbers, however, give only a moderate impression of the scale of the problem that faced Soviet authorities.

Most crimes of speculation were connected with buying and selling in commission stores, secondhand shops, and especially in public marketplaces and secondhand bazaars. According to an October 1935 report, speculators "of all sorts" inundated market places. Yagoda, the police chief, hated markets as focal points for all sorts of activities by private traders, so-called socially dangerous elements, and peasants. They were points of exchange that were almost impossible to control, but which were also vital to the country's economy. Banned entirely for a period at the beginning of the 1930s, private trade in public markets and bazaars had not only revived by 1934 and 1935 but also flourished. So, grudgingly, conceded an October 1935 government report. In Rostov-on-the-Don, for example, ten thousand people thronged through the central marketplace on any given Sunday afternoon, although the city had licensed only one hundred selling booths there. In October 1935, Moscow's Iaroslavskii market regularly registered 2,000 sellers to fill its 100 sales' stalls. On any given Sunday, over 300,000 people swarmed through the market buying and selling goods regardless of licensing procedures. The crowds of hawkers and buyers turned and twisted "without order" through the streets bordering the legal confines of the market.

Illegal trade took many and often ingenious forms. The simplest kind involved the resale at high prices of scarce commodities purchased at state stores, or pilfered from factories, warehouses, trains, or other facilities that made up the state's production and distribution system, one of the most common practices involved sellers who met trains from the countryside as they arrived in the cities in the morning. There, on the platforms and out of the train windows, peasants did a brisk and furtive business selling farm products and commodities to urban middlemen. They, in turn, went straight to the urban markets and resold the goods at higher prices. In these cases, the traders were usually individuals working for themselves. But not always. Many entrepreneurs set up networks of middlemen and conducted illegal selling on a bulk scale. These "big speculators" (*krupnye spekulanty*) went so far as to establish direct contact with collective farm officials, with urban workshops and factories, or with bandit gangs seeking to sell stolen goods. Big speculators often gave themselves a thin legal cover by purchasing a license (*patent*) to set up as a private craft worker. A private craft worker (*kustar'*) could, legally, manufacture and sell items on a small scale, supposedly through the state's cooperative system. In fact, many *kustary* did not work but acted as suppliers and purchasing agents for networks of small craft shops or domestic manufacturers, or as urban fences for rural bandit gangs. These networks dealt in scarce commodities, often in clothing or food items, and often operated in large volumes. The speculators Il'evskii, Shedrovskii, and Fel'tshtein, for example, were licensed legally to operate an artisan shop in Moscow. Instead, they put out materials to as many as twelve artisan manufacturers to make and sell women's berets and men's fedoras.

Some speculators operated over long distances. A group of Kiev artisans contracted with a network of artisan workers in small villages to produce women's shoes. Using the name and legal transport license of a local Kiev city cooperative, the entrepreneurs shipped the finished products in batches of one to two hundred to Leningrad where they kept them "warehoused" in borrowed apartments. At certain intervals during the year, the entrepreneurs traveled to Leningrad. By prior arrangement, they paid the administrators of several markets to rent them sellers' stalls for two to three days. They also paid off local police to turn a blind eye to their activities. They would sell out their products and then "disappear" back to Kiev.

Illegal and semilegal craft manufacture abounded and, in the eyes of at least some officials, a craft or artisan's license amounted to a legal license to speculate. A 1934 report surmised that only 4–5 percent of the 8,000 artisans registered with Moscow municipal authorities in fact sold their products to the state at legal prices. The rest, the report declared, took their goods to Moscow's private markets, where "they can sell them at speculative prices." Yet to distinguish between profiteering and legal trade and manufacture often proved a difficult task, especially for items that were used. Who was to determine the fair price for an old pair of boots, or a used tool or piece of machinery, or for goods in general, when state prices varied from month to month and region to region? Procuracy officials often accused police officials either of overzealousness, arresting innocent workers for trying to sell a pair of pants, or for collusion in lucrative illegal activities. Police, in turn, accused procuracy officials of laxness, turning a blind eye to all sorts of dubious *banditry*

practices. Exploitation of the state system was relatively easy, and exploitation abounded in a system designed to eliminate exploitation.

No type of crime alarmed Soviet authorities more than banditry. Although authorities had made a concerted effort in the late 1920s to rid the country of the last of its bandit gangs, the upheavals of the early 1930s, especially in the countryside, brought about a resurgence of such activities. Some bandit gangs ranged across relatively large areas, but most operated in specific territories. Some bands comprised as many as fifty to sixty individuals, but most numbered no more than ten to twelve members. It is difficult to determine how widespread bandit activity was, but it existed in nearly every area of the country. In 1932, thirty-five bandit gangs operated in the Urals region alone. Mounted, armed, and mobile, the most dangerous bandit gangs lived in sparsely populated and relatively inaccessible areas, such as forests or rugged hills. Bandit gangs could be surprisingly well armed, at times with weapons that allowed them to outgun local police authorities. The Fedoseev gang, for example, operated throughout the Urals regions. The gang numbered about fifty members, and carried, in addition to individual revolvers and hunting rifles, three American Winchester repeating rifles, two bombs, and twenty grenades. Bandit gangs usually refrained from attacking individuals, except for sporadic robberies of travelers whom they happened to encounter on the road. At times, bands raided individual farms, but most targeted collective farm villages and Soviet institutions and facilities: trains, warehouses, especially grain warehouses during the planting and harvesting seasons, postal depots, police armories, and other such facilities.

Gang members in the 1930s generally came from one of the several backgrounds. Many, of course, were petty criminals by choice or "profession," but many others were dispossessed peasants, or "*kulaks*" (supposedly rich peasant farmers), who had escaped deportation. Because of the social backgrounds of bandits, instructions to local police authorities warned that bandit gangs were to be regarded not just as criminal elements but as counterrevolutionary insurgents against Soviet power. There was some truth to this assessment, if only because state institutions (collective farms, mail cars, storage facilities, etc.) provided the most lucrative targets for bandit activities. Because of the supposedly counterrevolutionary character of banditry, organizers and gang leaders were subject to the most extreme measures of "social defense," which meant shooting. Because of the political status accorded to bandit gangs, campaigns against them often involved OGPU troops, in addition to local police authorities. The other reason for OGPU involvement was that local authorities often did not have the resources to pursue and eliminate bandit gangs in their territories.

Bandit gangs drew heavily from non-Russian ethnic populations. According to one police report from the Urals in 1932, non-Russian gangs were especially difficult to trace and eliminate. Their members often had family ties and resided in the areas where they operated. As a result, local non-Russian populations not only protected the identities of bandit gangs from officials but also provided bandits with information about police movements. Information was also difficult to obtain because of ethnic and language barriers. Police authorities found it difficult to establish informant networks in non-Russian areas and required translators to interrogate local inhabitants about bandit activities.

Homeless children (*besprizorniki*) and unsupervised children (*beznadzorniki*) constituted one of the most serious problems of social disorder connected to criminality. The sheer numbers of orphaned and unsupervised youth created problems of social stability, as did the threat to order that resulted from the connections between homelessness and crime. The homeless and unsupervised population of children and underage youth acted as a major source for recruitment into the Soviet Union's criminal class. Because of the social upheavals of the early 1930s, the population of such children in the Russian republic alone jumped dramatically from a low of 129,000 in 1929 to a peak of 400,000 in the late months of 1933, and these were only the children who were counted as they passed through children's homes, or temporary gathering centers or points (*priemnye punkty*). These centers experienced a "massive" influx of children during 1933. The former Danilov Monastery in Moscow was one of the largest of these points. Soviet Kazakhstan had a population of around 43,000 homeless children in 1933 and 68,000 in 1934. And in Ukraine, where, according to a report, children's homes counted about 228,000 children in 1933. In the whole of the USSR, then, well over half a million homeless children were counted during the mid-1930s.

Many of these children were orphaned, abandoned, or separated from home during the collectivization campaigns and famine of 1932 and 1933. Other reasons included poverty (18 percent), children fleeing home because of the "influence of the street and friends" (18 percent), and abandonment or "an unpleasant home situation" (29 percent). Police made monthly sweeps of urban areas to round up homeless children and place them in state institutions for adoption, but the police, the courts, and the social welfare organs that ran children's homes were overwhelmed by the epidemic of homeless children. In Moscow, police sweeps netted about 28,000 children in all of 1933, yet conditions in homes were so abysmal that "well over 50 percent" of children ran away. As of May 1934, officials estimated that about 45,000 boys and 15,000 girls between the ages of twelve and seventeen still lived on the streets throughout urban areas of Russia. This included about 2,000–3,000 in Moscow at any given time. Children and youth were highly mobile—a 1933 sweep of ten railroad lines in western Russia brought in 4,000 unsupervised children riding illegally on trains. Moscow was, by far, the preferred destination for homeless and unsupervised children. In 1933 and 1934, well over half of all children who passed through the Danilov Monastery sorting point had come from outside of Moscow. In 1933, 27 percent of them had arrived from Ukraine.

youth crime

Having no home and no work, socially alienated because of their background and the violence that had made them homeless, many youth turned to crime. In 1932, police in the capital detained or arrested 15,648 underage criminals between the ages of twelve and seventeen. Most of the criminal youths were apprehended for theft (87 percent in 1931, 27 percent in 1932, and 41 percent in 1933), and most came from what officials described as socially dangerous classes, that is, families of noncollective farmers, or families of urban nonworker or nonprofessional backgrounds. According to a government report, criminal youth gangs "terrorized" patrons and sellers at public markets and bazaars; they swarmed onto tram and train cars and systematically robbed passengers. In some cities, youth gangs controlled whole blocks and quarters, extorting protection money from both small businesses and residents.

In the spring of 1935, the Soviet regime passed a series of draconian laws against hooliganism, which also dealt with the related problem of homeless and unsupervised children and young people. These laws gave police broad powers to pick up street children and to convict underage criminals under both judicial and non-judicial, or administrative, sentencing powers. Despite such measures, underage crime and hooliganism continued to be a serious problem. Even more ominous, the laws that criminalized homeless and unsupervised children also linked youth crimes increasingly to anti-Soviet intent. Hooliganism especially, noted a 1935 Supreme Court report, no longer involved just insults and "rambunctious" (*beschintsvakh*) behavior, for acts of hooliganism increasingly involved organized social violence by youth and assaults with weapons resulting in serious injury and even murder. In some localities, cautioned the report, youthful hooliganism crossed the boundary into forms of banditry and other counterrevolutionary crimes. Worst of all, even women were participating in hooligan gangs in increasing numbers. The report offered no explanation for this observation, but saw it as a worrisome trend, and as a direct threat to social and socialist order.

laws

One of the most serious crimes in the view of Soviet leaders and police officials was that of being "socially harmful." Social harmfulness was different from other types of criminality, since the designation "socially harmful element" (*sotsial'no-vrednyi element*) or "socially dangerous element" (*sotsial'no-opasnyi element*) constituted a social identity, not so much a statutory category of criminality. Until 1935, there was no specific criminal statute that covered this category, but throughout much of the 1930s, leaders enacted decrees and engaged in numerous policing campaigns against social harmfuls as being among the most threatening to the regime and the

social harm

construction of socialist order. Because of this ambiguity, this category is one of the most difficult to define, both as a marginal social stratum and as a type of criminal.

The category of "socially harmful element" had existed since at least the 1920s, but, during the 1920s, police and other officials attached this label to a specific population of people. People who fell into this category included those with at least two previous court convictions or four police detentions (*privody*). During the 1930s, police began to apply this category more broadly to a range of socially marginal or deviant groups of people. These socially harmful or "alien" elements (*chuzhie elementy*) included itinerants, the unemployed, actual or suspected petty criminals, and those found in violation of residence registration laws. A joint police and procuracy circular from 1935 included in this category not only those in the "criminal world," "but anyone who maintained ties with known criminals," or who was not gainfully employed. The category also listed "professional" beggars, violators of passport and residence laws, and unsupervised or orphan youth picked up for crimes. In fact, those included in this category need not have committed a crime. The category of socially harmful became a catchall category for many kinds of persons. Also included in this category were religious sectarians, those who had been dispossessed of property, and "former people." If caught in the wrong place at the wrong time, such as during a police raid to check identity papers, such people became subject to summary arrest and sentencing by extrajudicial police sentencing boards for up to five years in corrective labor camps or deportation colonies.

The category of socially harmful element (*sotsvredelement*, in the Newspeakian parlance of the day) made policing much easier for authorities. This category amalgamated a complex mass of people into the same undifferentiated category of social danger, and all who fell into this category could be disposed of by nonjudicial sentencing boards rather than through lengthy and individual court proceedings. *Sotsvredelement* lumped together prostitutes and petty criminals; religious sectarians and itinerant beggars; hooligans as well as the déclassé nobles; the dispossessed and the disenfranchised; and the unemployed and violators of residence and passport laws. These were the disobedient, or anarchic (*stikhinyie*) and "unorganized" (*neorganizovannye*) segments of the population. These unorganized segments of the population did not fit into one of the neatly defined social ranks, those of workers (*rabochie*), collective farmers (*kolkhozniki*), or white-collar employees (*slushashchie*), as created by the regime. Like dirt or trash, unorganized populations were "matter out of place." They were unproductive, in the perception of officials, "filth on the face of the cities," as one police report described them. They siphoned off state resources and overwhelmed the fragile infrastructure of both urban and rural networks. Unorganized segments of the population were regarded as carriers of pollution and social contamination, both political and physical. They not only carried the "virus" of anti-Soviet attitudes but were the primary cause, or so officials claimed, of the spread of epidemic diseases, especially typhus and tuberculosis, the great killers of the 1930s. Authorities contrasted "mobile and unorganized" groups within the population—"nomads, wanderers (otkochevnikov), orphans"—to "local core populations (mestnogo korennogo naseleniia)." The latter were good, the former, bad.

In the 1930s, attitudes of officials hardened toward deviant and marginal populations, now deemed not only alien, but dangerous. What had happened to precipitate such a dramatic change in tone and definition was Stalin's speech in January 1933, in which he identified crime as a new form of class war and criminals as the new class enemy. This speech politicized the campaigns against socially marginal groups, turning "unorganized" populations into "socially dangerous elements," and then into anti-Soviet counterrevolutionaries. Stalin's speech crystallized the growing concern among leaders about the threat of public disorder to the regime's policies and its very stability. Stalin's pronouncements allowed lower officials to declare, without irony, that beggars, prostitutes, and the unemployed were counterrevolutionaries and a danger to the regime. Stalin's speech made public order equivalent to state security (which it was, given the circumstances), and turned the campaign for public order into a new phase of class struggle.

Policies to deal with these groups came increasingly under the purview of the police, both political (OGPU/NKVD) and civil (militsiia), rather than the state's social agencies. Policies of social amelioration which, in the 1920s, involved local communities and were centered in civil government became militarized in the 1930s within a system of centrally controlled policing. In the 1930s, it fell increasingly to the police rather than to civil authorities to define who was "near" (blizko) and who was "alien" (chuzhoi), who was a loyal citizen and who a socially dangerous "element." The curtailment of civil jurisdiction in favor of central police authority was characteristic of the Stalinist "revolution from above."

The Second World War, or the Great Fatherland War as it was called in the Soviet Union, gripped the country from June 1941 until May 1945. The Soviet–German conflict was fought mostly on Soviet territory, from the German invasion in June 1941 until the spring of 1944, when Soviet forces pushed German troops into Eastern Europe, and lasted until the final collapse of Germany in May 1945. The war caused indescribable destruction in the USSR. It left 25–28 million people dead, most major cities leveled, and millions upon millions of people displaced due to destruction or evacuation. Understrength, underequipped, and underqualified, police and civil authorities had difficulty coping with the massive dislocation and social disorder created by the chaos of the war and its aftermath. The problems police authorities faced were as overwhelming, even more so, than those they had faced in the early 1930s, during the chaos of rapid industrialization and collectivization. After the war, social displacement and mass migration, criminality, unemployment, and even starvation were exacerbated by the destruction of the cities and their infrastructure, and by the collapse of the trade and distribution systems. Masses of people moved across the landscape through cities and villages singly and in groups. People ignored passport and residency laws. In 1946 alone, police registered over 1.26 million passport violations, and these were only the number of violations that actually came to their attention. In 1946, police expelled a quarter of a million people from major cities who were "looking for food," but had no registration papers. That number reached over half a million in 1947. In just the four years between 1948 and 1952, police charged some 5.5 million people with passport infractions. The majority of these people received fines, but 127,000 were charged with criminal violations and sentenced to some sort of prison or labor camp punishment.

To police authorities, the increase in numbers of passport violators in the late 1940s and early 1950s was a sign that the police was beginning to enforce residency laws more effectively than in the chaos immediately following the war. This was no doubt true, but the figures also testified to the scale of social calamity that had befallen the country. In 1947, in Vilnius, the capital of the newly formed Lithuanian Soviet Republic, over 30,000 people a day arrived in the city's train stations during the first months. According to police, these people were looking for food, as well as shelter, or loved ones. Few, if any, of them possessed passports or other officially recognized identity documents. Authorities in the Krasnoiarsk District, in central Siberia, pleaded to have the city of Norilsk placed under special residence restrictions to stop the inundation of the town by itinerants, former convicts, and outright criminals. Between 1940 and 1946, the population of Sverdlovsk, the administrative center of the Urals region, more than doubled, in large part as a result of the arrival of evacuees from more western cities, but also with a significant "contingent" of ex-convicts from nearby political police (*Gulag*) labor camps. The latter accounted for some 4,000 in-migrants in 1946. In border areas, especially in the still unfenced border reaches of Central Asia and the Caucasus, contraband activities went nearly unchecked. Goods and people moved with little interference across the borders with Turkey, Iran, or Afghanistan. In Sukhumi, the Black Sea port city in the Georgian Soviet Republic, the city government estimated that in 1946 over 1,000 foreign nationals and individuals with no clear citizenship status lived in the city without proper residence papers. Similarly, in the nearby Georgian border port of Batumi, crime rates rose dramatically, according to local officials, due to the unchecked influx of undocumented itinerants and foreign smugglers.

The close proximity of the Turkish border, the mild climate, and the presence of military and naval stores and import and export facilities, made the city a prime target for large-scale in-migration and crime.

If the war brought mass dislocation and migration, it also brought a change in the nature of criminality. Before the war, according to police assessments, the most common form of theft was that of money in the form of embezzlement, and of industrial goods and finished products from enterprises. With the breakdown of the trade and distribution system during and after the war, the most common kind of theft became that of agricultural and prepared food products, and especially of the ration cards and coupons needed for purchase of scarce goods. Relatedly, crimes of speculation also focused on the sale of services and access to food. This stood in contrast to the main focus of speculation during the middle and later years of the 1930s on resale of industrial goods, raw materials, and manufactured commodities. The shift in criminal activity toward services, and toward food and access to it, repeated a similar pattern that prevailed during the early 1930s. During the harsh period of collectivization, famine, and rapid industrialization, outright theft of grain and other food products had ranked high in the registry of serious crimes against the state. After the relative stabilization of the mid-1930s, crimes of theft against the state focused on commodities and money. In the immediate postwar period, as in the early 1930s, theft of food commodities and crimes of bribery, graft, and other forms of bureaucratic corruption were not just crimes of greed and venality; these were often crimes of necessity for survival in a system of scarce commodities, services, and even basic shelter. In these circumstances, it is not surprising that, in the late 1940s and into the 1950s, theft of state property and crimes of bureaucratic corruption soared to levels unseen even during the first years of state collectivization.

Stalin's stress on industrial and military recovery after the war kept much of the Soviet population impoverished well into the 1950s. It was not until after the dictator's death, on March 5, 1953, that a more moderate group of leaders turned attention to basic social needs such as housing, commodities, and higher standards of living. Crime continued, of course, as in any society, especially crimes of corruption and bribery involving state resources, but police, Party, and government officials no longer perceived this kind of criminality as a sign of anti-Soviet subversion. Gone was the rhetoric of the 1930s about internal class enemies and spies working through criminals to undermine the regime. No policeman viewed itinerants, prostitutes, or beggars as counterrevolutionary threats to the state. Police continued to harass and repress those who expressed anti-Soviet views, or who spoke out against human rights' abuses, but regular crime became depoliticized. Criminal (as opposed to political) policing focused on traditional categories of statutory law breakers, and these kinds of criminals fell within the purview of courts and the due process of civil law. Post-Stalinist discourse about criminality was cast in the language of social and economic discipline but not political insurgency. Crime and deviancy became, once again, a social anomaly, not a political battleground.

Note

1 Research for this essay is based on materials in the State Archive of the Russian Federation (GARF, Moscow); the Russian State Archive of Contemporary Social and Political History (RGASPI, Moscow), which contain the former archives of the Communist Party's Central Committee; and regional archives in Western Siberia and the Urals regions.

5

The *Gulag* under Stalin

Golfo Alexopoulos

Penal labor had a long history in the Russian empire. Peter the Great (1672–1725), whom Joseph Stalin admired for modernizing Russia, used prisoners and serfs to build his European city of St. Petersburg. On the eve of the 1917 October Revolution, roughly one quarter of inmates in the Russian empire had been sentenced to penal servitude. Vladimir Lenin established "concentration camps" for political opponents at the start of the Civil War in 1918, just months after the Bolshevik seizure of power. Lenin's concentration camps detained political opponents or so-called class enemies of the new regime, such as former aristocrats and White Army officers, merchants, traders, and priests. The majority of camp prisoners were identified as counterrevolutionary offenders and sentenced either by the security police (which, between 1917 and 1953, was periodically renamed, from *Cheka* to (O)GPU, NKVD, and, from 1946 onward, MVD), or by so-called revolutionary tribunals. At the Soviet regime's first concentration camp, the Solovetsky Camp of Special Significance (SLON), prisoners were initially not obligated to work except in the basic maintenance of the camp. However, in 1926, Stalin began to use prison labor more widely, initially in forestry and fisheries. Three years later, Stalin's penal-industrial complex emerged with his First Five-Year Plan of rapid industrialization. In 1929, he rebranded and renamed Lenin's "concentration camps," calling them "corrective-labor camps."

Stalin employed convict labor on an unprecedented scale. In certain ways, Stalin's *Gulag* resembled New World slavery, with its routine dehumanization and institutionalized physical violence. Stalin's slave labor system appears analogous to slavery in Brazil and Cuba, where mortality rates were high and planters saw value in working slaves to death. Stalin's *Gulag* was above all else a hierarchical system of violent human exploitation. In the eyes of the regime, prisoners were workhorses, mere inputs in an industrial process. Under Stalin, most of these workhorses were not political prisoners but petty criminal offenders convicted by a civilian court rather than the security police. The ordinary Soviet courts that sentenced speculators, thieves, hooligans, and other minor offenders condemned more people to *Gulag* detention than did the notorious Soviet security police. Many of those convicted by the courts for criminal offenses must be understood as political prisoners as well, since they fell victim to Stalin's draconian criminal legislation. Such laws condemned millions of ordinary workers and peasants for infractions such as minor theft and absenteeism.

Under Stalin, the forced-labor camp system reached its apex in brutality, scale, and function. The *Gulag* era emerged in 1929–30, when an enormous influx of prisoners, largely dekulakized peasants, became Stalin's first mass penal labor force. In 1930–1, the original OGPU Camp Administration (ULAG) was renamed the Chief Administration of Camps of the OGPU (GULAG). The Soviet bureaucratic acronym GULAG, roughly translated as "Main Administration of Camps," entered the popular lexicon in the mid-1970s following the publication of Alexander Solzhenitsyn's multivolume work *The Gulag Archipelago* in English. In the Stalin years, hundreds of labor camps and colonies would stretch across the twelve time zones of the Soviet Union's enormous landmass, from the Baltic Sea to the Pacific, forming a "country of *Gulag*," according to Solzhenitsyn. The writer described "the islands of the Archipelago" as scattered geographically, yet

> in the psychological sense, fused into a continent – an almost invisible, almost imperceptible country ... And this Archipelago crisscrossed and patterned that other country within which it was located, like a gigantic patchwork, cutting into its cities, hovering over its streets.[1]

As historians and *Gulag* survivors have noted, this "country of *Gulag*" was not separate but an integral part of the Stalinist state. Prisoners experienced the effects of famine and wartime together with the rest of the Soviet population. The camps displayed the same shortages and inefficiencies that were present in all sectors of the centrally planned Soviet economy.

The Stalinist *Gulag* represented a vast commercial enterprise tasked with generating economic profit for the state. The regime viewed all prisoners, criminal and political, as "human raw material," a commodity to be exploited to the maximum degree possible, and then discarded, like waste. Many memoirs of camp survivors underscore the degrading commodification of *Gulag* inmates. *Gulag* officials spoke of inmates as "useful" or "defective," depending on their productivity and health, and routinely discarded the dying beyond the camp gates as "ballast." *Gulag* inmates were fed according to whether their brigade had achieved its production output: less output meant less food, which reduced labor productivity even more. In this way, prisoners were systematically starved to death. Moreover, the regime concealed the *Gulag*'s destructive capacity, keeping mortality rates low by releasing millions of prisoners on the verge of death. Stalin's labor-camp system worked prisoners to the point of near-death, denied them adequate food, criminalized them for their illnesses, and then discarded its emaciated workforce en masse.[2]

The Stalinist leadership created the camps as a way to mobilize labor for its industrialization drive or "the building of socialism." Socialist construction involved the rapid industrialization of the country and the collectivization of agriculture. To finance the economic transformation of the country, the party pursued the country's rich natural resources, located as they were in the most remote regions of the country. The Soviet Union possessed tremendous material reserves beyond the Arctic Circle. Party leaders sought to exploit these materials for industrial expansion, to profit from gold, copper, platinum, nickel, timber, and coal reserves. Prisoners worked in high-priority sectors of the national economy such as mining and forestry, while the Party valued hard-currency exports to meet its industrialization plans. Researchers have identified 476 distinct camps and colonies that operated in the Stalin years, yet this figure is likely understated. Camps represented complexes or clusters of smaller camp divisions and sections, with often hundreds of prisoners. Moreover, many of these smaller camp units were temporary, hastily installed along a road or railroad track or section of a quarry or forest, then dismantled when the work was completed. For this reason, the magnitude and population of Stalin's forced-labor camp system is probably much greater than our current estimates based on archival or documentary evidence that has been unearthed.

Civilian laborers could not be expected to willingly move to remote and inhospitable resource-rich regions, but the Communist Party could forcibly transport prisoners to do the work it demanded anywhere in the country. For example, the Norilsk metallurgical complex became a *Gulag* venture because the NKVD was willing to take it on. This high-priority economic project proved less feasible for a civilian ministry, such as the ministry of heavy industry that lacked an army of prison laborers which could be dispatched at will to remote and inhospitable regions and forced to perform brutal labor. Prisoners built railroads, highways, airfields, dams, shipyards, and canals. They mined coal and oil, gold, tin, copper, and nickel and extracted timber from Russia's dense forests. They worked in chemical factories, docks, fisheries, and dairy farms. During the war, they produced ammunition, designed planes, and sewed uniforms. The more physically capable prisoners did mining and construction and the weakest (who could not be released) worked in agriculture and light manufacturing, making toys, shoes, and baskets. All prisoners had to work. According to Solzhenitsyn,

> The labor of the *zeks* was needed for degrading and particularly heavy work, which no one, under socialism, would wish to do ... Who, except prisoners, would have worked at logging ten hours a day ... And who other than the Archipelago natives would have grubbed out stumps in winter? ... And who could be sent down into the Dzhezkazgan mines for a twelve-hour workday of dry drilling?[3]

With the Party's economic ambitions and the number of arrests constantly on the rise, the OGPU–NKVD–MVD grew to become one of the country's largest economic ministries. The *Gulag* focused on infrastructure projects and the extraction of natural resources, tasks that involved millions of prisoners in heavy physical labor. Many of these prisoners labored in the harshest climate of Siberia and the Far North. The *Gulag*'s first major construction project was the White Sea–Baltic Canal (Belomor canal or BBK), and its swift completion inspired similar projects, including *Dalstroi* (the Far Northern Construction Trust) and the Moscow–Volga Canal. Belomor canal represented a formative experience for the *Gulag*, as it demonstrated that the state could rapidly deploy workers on demand and physically exploit them to the maximum degree. The gold mining camp of *Dalstroi* represented the *Gulag*'s largest single camp complex, and it was highly valued by Stalin because gold represented a key hard-currency export that helped fuel the country's rapid industrialization. Given the importance placed on rapid industrial development, the ends justified the means. Viewed by Stalin as profitable and essential, the *Gulag* system steadily increased in the course of the 1930s, as the number of prisoners grew nearly tenfold, from 179,000 in 1930 to 1,672,438 in 1939. New camps emerged, and old camps expanded and diversified their production capabilities.

Stalin's *Gulag* was a complex and heterogeneous institution, tasked with isolating, punishing, as well as physically exploiting and even "reforging" prisoners. For less dangerous criminal offenders, penal labor was supposed to "reeducate" and "rehabilitate," thus the *Gulag* leadership considered prisoners' "honest labor" as a means of atonement for their crimes before Soviet power. The goals of reeducating and reforging prisoners were publicly touted by the regime when the system was erected, and the message remained significant throughout the Stalin years. However, rehabilitation did not exist apart from labor, but emerged as part of the process of physical exploitation. The standard phrase was "re-education through socially usefully labor." The *Gulag*'s Cultural-Education Department touted work as honorable and promised the best workers early release. Following Stalin's purges in the Great Terror of 1936–8, a famous book of Maxim Gorky (1868–1936) on the White Sea Canal, which touted the rehabilitation of prisoners through penal labor, was banned, and the rhetoric of reeducation sharply diminished. This rhetoric continued to be used to motivate prisoners and increase labor productivity, but it also helped to recruit skilled civilian laborers to *Gulag* enterprises. A *Gulag* boss at the *Pechorlag* camp was initially inspired by the regime's declared interest in rehabilitating criminals through honest labor. Yet, he describes leaving the camp "a completely different person," who no longer "believed the myth" that punitive "agencies were supposedly helping out people who had stumbled, or who had committed crimes, by using work to reeducate them," explaining how, "Little by little I began to see with my own eyes the inhumanity and basic criminal character of the Soviet leadership's policies in this area."[4]

Human exploitation constituted the defining feature of Stalin's *Gulag*. Under Stalin, camp prisoners had to be maximally "utilized" and worked to the point of utter depletion. The Stalinist leadership may not have planned to exterminate its camp prisoners, but it intended to extract all available energy, to physically exploit prisoners to the maximum degree possible. Naftaly Frenkel (1883–1960), the chief of the *Gulag*'s production department in the early 1930s, said, "We have to squeeze everything out of a prisoner in the first three months – after that we don't need him anymore."[5] The system of extreme physical exploitation and systemic starvation reveals itself especially in the documents of the *Gulag* medical-sanitation department or health service. There were chronic and severe shortages of doctors, medicines, instruments, and rations for sick prisoners. The *Gulag* medical establishment functioned in a highly constrained environment. Many healthcare workers who treated inmates were prisoners themselves, and all were under intense pressure to keep everyone working. The camps had to comply with unrealistic quotas for sick and nonworking prisoners. Doctors were required to place their fellow inmates in the most strenuous form of work, to keep everyone maximally "utilized." The NKVD–*Gulag* leadership expected "labor utilization" rates in the basic work of the camp at no less than 70 percent of the prisoners. Although there were camp officials who tried to save the lives of prisoners, there were rules governing the "maximum utilization of prisoners" that even the benevolent were constrained to follow. Regardless of their health, most prisoners had to work in heavy physical labor.

The Soviet security police managed the labor of prisoners in camps and colonies, and carefully tracked the identities of their inmates, including class background, alleged crime, length of sentence, ethnicity, age, gender, and health or "physical labor capability." Once in the camps, a prisoner's health status often mattered more than other markers of identity, as all prisoners were subjected to harsh physical exploitation. *Gulag* administrators needed people who could perform hard manual labor in logging, mining, and construction, so they examined and documented the bodies of prisoners to determine who was "fit for physical labor." Inmates underwent routine evaluations to determine their physical labor capability. Inside the barbed wire, individuals constituted simply bodies, either "fit" or "weakened." Nonetheless, quotas on working and nonworking prisoners, together with high production targets, forced doctors to assign weak and emaciated prisoners to perform difficult physical labor that only caused their conditions to worsen. Pressure was built into the system to place weaker prisoners in more strenuous work. As Oleg Khlevniuk explains, "[e]xploitation of prisoners was a natural element of an economic system aimed at extensive growth at any cost."[6]

The goal of the Stalinist state was to catch up with and overtake the capitalist West, both economically and militarily. Many defended the violence of the *Gulag* system on national security grounds, and viewed the economic achievements of the camps as tantamount to political and military achievements. Viktor Nasedkin, the longest-running *Gulag* chief, touted the *Gulag*'s wartime contribution. He described how prisoners made ammunition and gas masks, sewed Red Army uniforms, constructed airfields and roads, and produced significant quantities of gold, silver, and precious stones, which generated money for the country's defense. Wartime conditions prompted the expansion and brutalization of the *Gulag* system in the early 1940s. In 1941, the *Gulag*'s penal labor system was divided into several economic branches or administrations (called *glavki*), including a Main Administration for Railroad Construction Camps (GULZhDS) and a Main Administration for Forestry (GULLP). In 1947, these *glavki* held roughly 37 percent of all prisoners. Following the Nazi invasion of the Soviet Union, three quarters of a million prisoners were hastily and brutally evacuated from camps and colonies close to the front, and many would die in transit. Food supplies were interrupted, and illness and mortality rates soared. According to official *Gulag* statistics, over 2 million people died in the camps and colonies during the war years, but the actual death toll is probably much greater.

In the postwar years, Stalin reorganized his security apparatus and expanded the Gulag economy to assist the goal of reconstruction. In March 1946, the NKVD was divided into two ministries. The MVD or Ministry of Internal Affairs managed the camps, while the MGB or Ministry of State Security (later renamed the KGB) was in charge of foreign intelligence. The MVD took on an ever-larger role in the Soviet economy in the late Stalin years. *Gulag* labor accounted for about 40 percent of laborers in nickel and copper mining, roughly 70 percent in tin mining, and over 80 percent of labor in gold, diamond, and platinum mining. Roughly one in five construction workers in the Soviet Union in 1940s were *Gulag* prisoners. As the Soviet economy became ever more dependent on penal labor, the MVD doubled capital construction between

1949 and 1952 alone. Stalin viewed camp prisoners as cheap and expendable labor, so he was easily convinced when the NKVD–MVD lobbied heavily for greater economic responsibilities. In the course of the 1940s and until his death in 1953, Stalin increased the MVD's role in the national economy, and even planned to double the ministry's capital investment in the Fifth Five-Year Plan that ran from 1951 to 1955. In the year before the dictator's death, the MVD controlled more capital investment in Russia than any other ministry.

The *Gulag* system became increasingly violent from the 1930s to the 1950s. There were two periods of profound change in these years, and each resulted in a harsher camp regime. The first occurred in 1938–9, with the end of Stalin's purges and the appointment of Lavrentiy Beria (1899–1953) as NKVD chief. During the purges, the Communist Party blamed the NKVD–*Gulag* leadership and many camp directors for economic failures of the system, accusing them of "sabotage-wrecking activities" and being too easy on prisoners. The first leaders of the *Gulag* administration—Lazar Kogan, Matvei Berman, and Izrail Pliner—were tried and executed, in addition to their NKVD boss, Genrikh Yagoda. Among the many charges against these men was the accusation that they were too soft on prisoners. Matvei Berman, the Gulag chief from 1932 to 1937, as well as Isaak Ginzburg, the chief of the Gulag's medical-sanitation department in the 1930s, were attacked for creating "privileged conditions" for prisoners, and others were accused of "leniency" toward prisoners.[7] The new NKVD chief, Beria, sought to address inefficiency and low productivity in the camps. This involved a brutal redistribution: greater incentives for the healthier and more productive prisoners and harsher punishments for the weakest and less productive. Beria proposed higher food rations but also more severely punished so-called labor resisters and shirkers. Prosecutors went after anyone suspected of refusing to work or encouraging others to refuse work, and these prisoners could face the death penalty. Beria's new rules intensified the practice of redistribution in the camps, from the sick and weak (who were often attacked for willfully shirking or faking their illnesses) to the healthy and strong inmates. This redistributive system would remain a principal feature of *Gulag* operations for the remainder of the Stalin era.

The other period of profound change in the history of Stalin's *Gulag* were the years 1947–9. The inmate population sharply increased with Stalin's draconian theft decrees of 1947, and reached over 2.5 million prisoners on the eve of Stalin's death in 1953. Stalin's excessively harsh decrees of June 4, 1947 concerning the theft of state and personal property condemned ordinary peasants and workers to camp sentences of up to twenty-five years. Largely as a result of Stalin's theft decrees, new prisoners flooded into the *Gulag* in the late 1940s, resulting in severe overcrowding, deteriorating living conditions (malnutrition, poor sanitation), and staffing shortages, all of which worsened prisoners' health. In 1948, a new system of rations reduced the center's obligation to supply food to the camps and placed greater responsibility on the camps themselves to feed prisoners using local resources. That same year, a system of severely exploitative and brutal "special camps" was created. Sentences grew longer for both political and criminal offenses, and the twenty-five year sentence became common. In 1949, new instructions on the "utilization of prisoners' labor" forced weaker inmates to perform heavy physical labor. The physical exploitation of prisoners intensified. Memoirists described how the camps in the 1940s "began to take on a mass character ... things became harsher ... as the camps grew bigger, the regime grew crueler."[8]

Since the opening of the archives around 1990, the official Gulag data on camp mortality has come to light, and it appears lower than expected. Mortality rates were generated as monthly or yearly averages, and typically camp officials reported that roughly 1–5 percent of the total inmate population died on their watch, although the figures reached as high as 15 percent following the 1932–3 famine and 25 percent during the Second World War. Scholars have been justifiably cautious when using this data. Not only did Gulag bosses require camps to keep mortality rates within established target figures, but higher rates of mortality were consistently interpreted as the fault of camp administrators. Given the pressures they faced, camp officials developed ways to keep their mortality rates low, just as they exaggerated production output through padding or deception. Yet, suppressed mortality rates in the context of brutal physical exploitation was entirely planned. The Gulag had a system, conceived and designed at the highest levels, to maximally utilize prisoners at each stage of their physical capacity, and then to release inmates when they were no longer useful. Gulag officials isolated their least productive or unproductive contingent in invalid camps or camp sections, but they preferred to release them. Periodic releases of invalid prisoners took place throughout the Gulag's existence. Inmates who regularly benefited from early release included invalids, the elderly, minors, pregnant women, and the mothers of small children. Gulag officials most valued inmates who could be classified as capable of heavy physical labor.

As Stalin expanded the Gulag economy in the postwar years, the system experienced a general crisis. The Gulag economy became overextended in capital construction projects, particularly in the defense industries, and countless tasks failed to be completed on schedule. The MVD–Gulag leadership and many party leaders recognized the inefficiency of the forced-labor economy. The costs of operating the vast network of camps and colonies had increased over time, as prisoners became increasingly unable to meet official targets for economic output. From the 1930s to the 1950s, camp administrators complained to their superiors in the Gulag administration about the lack of equipment and technology, shortages of labor and supplies, and excessively high work norms. The Stalinist system of forced labor was inefficient, disorganized, and ineffective. Notwithstanding MVD slogans, the *Gulag*'s contribution to industrialization remained unimpressive. Many *Gulag* projects (including the White Sea–Baltic Sea canal, the Baikal–Amur Mainline railroad, and the Kuibyshev hydroelectric system) proved largely worthless. Even prisoners described their work at times as unproductive and senseless.

The *Gulag* moved and managed an enormous labor force but not efficiently. The *Gulag* supplied penal labor to various sectors of the Soviet economy, from construction to mining. In the postwar years, the MVD constituted the largest construction ministry, as roughly two-thirds of its economic activities centered on heavy construction, largely in remote and inhospitable regions. At the same time, it contracted out over half a million prisoners to civilian Soviet enterprises, largely in construction. Nonetheless, the Stalinist leadership largely overlooked the system's profound inefficiency and waste. It calculated, for example, how many prisoners produced how many kilograms of gold, and assumed that more inputs of labor would produce greater output in gold. In fact, more inmates often had the opposite effect. Inmate overcrowding and poor living conditions resulted in reduced productivity, as happened during the mass arrests in the late 1930s and late 1940s. Typically, sudden expansion in the camp population resulted in chaos: fewer resources per prisoner, sharp declines in health, overcrowding in the barracks, and corresponding decrease in productivity.

Despite efforts to squeeze out more from prisoners while supplying less, the forced-labor camp system remained grossly inefficient. Like other sectors of the Soviet centrally planned economy, the *Gulag* system was plagued by enormous material losses. Many of Stalin's closest associates recognized that the economic returns did not exceed the system's increasing costs. A number of the *Gulag*'s vast projects proved unnecessary or unusable, and penal labor productivity was only 50–60 percent of comparable non-convict or civilian labor. Among the factors that contributed to *Gulag* inefficiencies were the lack of technology and machinery and the poor work conditions. Declining productivity was no less a consequence of the system's violent exploitation, as sick and emaciated prisoners could not do physical labor. Poor labor productivity in the *Gulag* resulted from the system's destructive capacity. Emaciated and exhausted prisoners could hardly do the work assigned to them. The Party leadership constantly discussed the low productivity of penal labor and sought ways to improve the economic efficiency of the *Gulag* economy. The Stalinist leadership pursued material and other incentives for prisoners who exceeded their production norms and outperformed others. It did not improve the quantity or quality of food, as prisoners continued to receive starvation rations. It did not abandon the fundamental rule in the camps that only those prisoners who met their output norms would be fed at subsistence. It did not modify its view that all prisoners must be maximally "utilized." In fact, in the late 1940s and early 1950s, the Stalinist leadership implemented policies that made the system even more brutal. It forced even greater numbers of weakened prisoners into heavy physical labor and provided fewer resources for their survival.

And yet the economic landscape was changing. It became increasingly apparent that the Soviet Union did not need physical laborers so much as skilled laborers. In many ways, prison laborers became displaced by new technology. After the war, the MVD chief insisted that the Gulag economy required high quality machinery and technology. Yet the OGPU–NKVD–MVD economy was based on heavy physical labor. In the postwar period, unskilled manual labor was becoming less important in the key industries in which the *Gulag* was most engaged. The Soviet timber, mining, and construction sectors were being changed by new technologies. By the 1950s, the MVD economy required permanent skilled workers to operate machinery. As the Soviet economy evolved and modernized, the need for heavy physical labor diminished. The MVD could no longer simply arrest a peasant and hand him a saw. The use of power saws for timber cutting had doubled from 1939 to 1950, and timber haulage had become increasingly mechanized as well. From 1940 to 1952, the use of mechanized excavators at NKVD–MVD construction projects increased sixfold. By 1952, over 87 percent of earth-moving operations employed machinery.[9] The nature of work in the USSR transitioned rather naturally toward skilled salaried laborers. The *Gulag* model was built for the mobilization of heavy physical labor for primitive production and not for the recruitment of skilled labor for a mechanized industrial operation. Eventually, MVD production officials preferred to work with relatively free workers who delivered higher labor productivity and did not require expenditures on armed guards and barbed wire fences. The old model of relying on heavy physical labor grew increasingly outdated and obsolete for an industrial economy. In the postwar years, the MVD economy gradually reoriented toward skilled free workers.

Moreover, the *Gulag* system was dismantled because it was so violently destructive that it undermined its economic function. During the Second World War, the *Gulag* leadership argued for a smaller system because it confronted an enormous population of weakened prisoners. It made no sense to maintain a *Gulag* population in which over a third were incapable of work, due to illness and emaciation. The *Gulag* faced a similar crisis at the end of the 1940s when large numbers of prisoners entered the system. Stalinist violence undermined the productive capacity of the camps. The system was dismantled because extreme violence proved economically inefficient.

Stalin's closest associates eventually recognized the inefficiencies of the slave-labor system, yet they feared him, especially in his later years. The dictator had become increasingly erratic and paranoid, and many close to him anticipated another great purge of the party elite. Beria himself, who supervised the enormous MVD economy, was kept in check through a purge of many of his closest comrades. The *Gulag*'s problems were not openly discussed with the architect and defender of the system. But after Stalin died, his entourage acted quickly. Grandiose construction projects were scrapped, such as new hydroelectric power stations and a tunnel connecting Sakhalin Island to the mainland. In a draft resolution to the Council of Ministers on March 21, 1953, Beria urged his colleagues to terminate "the construction of a number of hydrotechnical installations, railroads, highways, and factories mandated by previously adopted government resolutions" on the grounds that these projects were "not justified by the needs of the economy."[10] From March 18 to 28, 1953, the government either abandoned or sharply reduced MVD capital projects, reassigned responsibility for camps and colonies to the Ministry of Justice, and transferred MVD economic functions to the appropriate civilian economic ministries. The Party reassigned control over the labor-camp system from the MVD to the Ministry of Justice. Camps engaged in agriculture, mining, forestry, or railroad construction now came under the authority of the relevant economic ministries. The MVD retained control over the high security and brutal special camps, designed in 1948 for the state's most dangerous enemies.

The *Gulag* coincided with Stalinism and reflected the violent economic logic of the Stalinist system. The vast forced-labor camp system emerged with Stalin's consolidation of power and ended abruptly after the dictator's death. Stalin's *Gulag* became an enormous production system with the arrest of dekulakized peasants, and it ended with the mass release of a similar demographic, the petty criminal offenders. As soon as Stalin died, the government swiftly approved the largest single release of *Gulag* prisoners. Over the next three months, roughly 1.5 million prisoners or 60 percent of all *Gulag* inmates were freed from detention. In a memo to the Presidium of the Central Committee (which for a dozen years or so after 1952 was the name for Politburo), Beria defended this mass release, stating openly that "dangerous state criminals" made up fewer than 10 percent of the *Gulag* population. These prisoners were largely confined in the special camps, but the others, who constituted the *Gulag*'s key demographic, were released. The gates of the camps finally opened for the millions of ordinary workers and peasants who were swept up on petty criminal charges. This destructive system of human exploitation began with their detention in 1929–30 and ended with their mass release shortly after Stalin's death.

Notes

1   Alexander I. Solzhenitsyn, *The Gulag Archipelago, 1918–1956: An Experiment in Literary Investigation*, vols. I–II, New York: Harper & Row, 1973, x.

2   See Golfo Alexopoulos, *Illness and Inhumanity in Stalin's Gulag*, New Haven, CT: Yale University Press, 2017.

3   Alexander I. Solzhenitsyn, *The Gulag Archipelago, 1918–1956: An Experiment in Literary Investigation*, vols. III–IV, New York: Harper & Row, 579–80. *Zek* is short for *zakliuchennye*, or inmates.

4   Fyodor Vasilevich Mochulsky, *Gulag Boss: A Soviet Memoir*, trans. and ed. Deborah Kaple, New York: Oxford University Press, 2011, 168–9.

5   Solzhenitsyn, *Gulag Archipelago*, vols. III–IV, 49.

6   Oleg V. Khlevniuk, *History of the Gulag: From Collectivization to the Great Terror*, New Haven, CT: Yale University Press, 2004, 337.

7   Anne Applebaum, *Gulag: A History*, New York: Doubleday, 2003, 96–7, 270.

8   The words of Olga Vasileevna, an engineer and inspector for the *Gulag*, quoted in Applebaum, *Gulag*, 113.

9   O. Khlevniuk, "The Economy of the GPU, NKVD, and MVD of the USSR, 1930–1953: Scale, Structure and Trends of Development," in P. Gregory and V. Lazarev, eds, *The Economics of Forced Labor: The Soviet Gulag*, Stanford, CA: Hoover Press, 2004, 56–7.

10   Galina Mikhailovna Ivanova, *Labor Camp Socialism: The Gulag in the Soviet Totalitarian System*, New York: M. E. Sharpe, 2000, 124.

6

Private Ivan's Life and Fate: Daily Life in Stalin's Red Army during the "Great Patriotic War"

Kenneth Slepyan

On June 25, 1945, at a banquet celebrating the Soviet Union's triumph over Nazi Germany, Joseph Stalin toasted the Soviet citizens who had made this victory possible:

> I would like to drink to the health of the people of low and unenviable rank. To the people who are considered the 'little cogs' of the government mechanism, but without whom we the marshals and commanders of the fronts and armies, speaking plainly, aren't worth a damn.[1]

Despite his condescending tone, Stalin was right that the so-called little cogs, the ordinary men and women who fought in the ranks of the Soviet military, had indeed played a preeminent—perhaps *the* preeminent—role in the most defining moment in Soviet history, the defeat of Nazi Germany, in what was known to Soviets as "The Great Patriotic War."

Thirty-five million people, including over 1 million women, served in the Soviet military during the war, and the war experience helped forge a powerful Soviet identity for ordinary citizens. Of these, between 8 and 11 million soldiers were killed or reported missing and at least another 22 million were wounded.[2]

Shockingly, only 3 percent of the Red Army recruits born in 1923 survived the war.[3] In addition, over 20 million civilians lost their lives. The war was thus both a triumph and a catastrophe for the Soviet people. The war experience also fundamentally shaped individual and collective values and attitudes. For many, defending and sacrificing for their country brought them closer to the regime's goals and values. For others, the war experience fostered a sense of independence and personal autonomy that enabled them to envision a state more responsive to its society.

No discussion of the daily life of the Soviet soldier in the Second World War can take place without understanding the extraordinary violence of the Nazi–Soviet war. As Michael Geyer and Mark Edele note, it was a war, initiated by Nazi Germany, which was fought without restraint, a war of annihilation. The racialized goals of Operation Barbarossa, displaying "an utter disregard for Soviet life," called for the complete colonization of Soviet land and the targeted killings of Jews and Communists, all aided and abetted by the German army. Red Army soldiers, themselves subjected at times to extreme coercion from their own government, responded to German brutality with their own. As Geyer and Edele put it, "What we see in the Nazi-Soviet war is a liberation of violence, and thus, a savage dynamic of cruelty—that even soldiers, observing themselves, noted with a great deal of astonishment."[4] The constant presence of this violence (or its threat) framed the everyday life of Soviet soldiers.

This chapter examines the daily lives and experiences of Soviet military personnel during this defining period in the history of USSR. As the fortunes of the war swung wildly, Red Army *frontoviki* (as combat soldiers were called) went through an extraordinary range of events, from the catastrophic defeats and mass encirclements of 1941 to the dramatic advances of 1944 and 1945. In truth, however, relatively very few soldiers underwent all these experiences since, as Catherine Merridale notes, "In all, the Red Army was destroyed and renewed at least twice in the course of this war," as "another generation was called up, crammed into uniform, and killed, captured, or wounded beyond recovery."[5] Yet, as we will see below, while Soviet soldiers in 1941 and 1942 when compared to the years 1943–5 experienced very different circumstances in the conditions associated with defeat and victory, the constants of recruitment, training, logistics, casualties, and the exigencies of daily life transcended this admittedly crude divide.

Since its founding in February 1918, the Red Army's role in the Soviet Union was much larger than providing national defense. The military was charged with transforming the largely peasant recruits into ideologically reliable citizens, teaching the largely illiterate peasant soldiers not only basic literacy and mathematical skills but also rudimentary Marxism. Demobilized soldiers brought their education back to their villages, thus influencing a wider circle of family members and fellow citizens.[6]

The Soviet public was also exposed to militarization through the government's civil defense organization, "The Society for the Promotion of Defense, Aviation, and Chemical Industries" (known by its Soviet acronym as *Osoaviakhim*). Established in 1927, *Osoaviakhim* provided instruction for shooting, parachute jumping, and flying to Soviet citizens and promoted military values such as adherence to discipline and duty, and an appreciation of technology. Many future snipers and air force pilots, especially women, credited their prewar *Osoaviakhim* training for their later success on the battlefield.

Yet the military was not immune to the political turmoil of Stalin's Soviet Union. The collectivization and dekulakization policies of the late 1920s and early 1930s shook the army as the mainly peasant soldiers were sometimes called in to suppress demonstrations and riots, leading to internal opposition to Soviet policies and possibly even local mutinies.[7] The Great Terror of the 1936–8 were an even greater shock to the armed forces. The NKVD (the Soviet secret police) removed, imprisoned, or shot 45 percent of the senior military and political officers, including some of the Red Army's foremost military thinkers and innovators. In all, over 34,000 officers were "purged" from the military between 1937 and 1940, even if some 11,500 were later reinstated.[8] The wholesale replacement of senior commanders with inexperienced junior officers lowered unit training and competency. The simultaneous expansion of the Red Army from 1.5 million to 5 million men meant that by 1940, approximately 70 percent of regimental and divisional commanders had held their post for only one year.[9] Although ordinary rank-and-file soldiers generally remained unaffected by the purges, their discipline and morale was undermined by their belief that their officers were corrupt and treasonous.

On the eve of the Second World War, the Red Army, on the surface, appeared to be ready for war. Its 5 million men possessed between 15,000 and 20,000 tanks, more than the rest of the armies of the world combined. Many Soviets were confident that the popular film of 1938, *If War Comes Tomorrow,* which predicted an easy defeat of any foe who dared to attack the USSR, was proclaiming fact rather than wishful fantasy. As one former Soviet citizen recalled in the 1950s, people believed that the country had been preparing for war decades and "would do quite well" if war came about.[10] The Soviet leadership's claims of and popular belief in the Red Army's invincibility, however, belied deeper realities of inadequate training of individuals and units, inexperienced commanders, and an enormous weapons stockpile composed of mostly obsolete and shoddy equipment.

The events between the start of the war in 1939 and the invasion of the USSR in 1941 further sapped the morale and fighting spirit of Soviet military personnel. The German armed forces' extraordinary successes in overrunning most of Europe, especially the surprising and rapid conquest of France in 1940, led many soldiers to believe in the "invincibility myth" of the *Wehrmacht*. In contrast, the Red Army's poor performance in the "Winter War" of 1939–40 against Finland, in which Soviet forces suffered almost 550,000 casualties including over 131,000 killed, exposed the USSR's seeming incapacity to fight a modern war.[11] Even the Soviet seizure of the eastern Polish provinces (now part of Ukraine and Belarus) in September 1939 contributed to this loss of self-confidence as soldiers saw with their own eyes that ordinary Polish peasants and workers fared better under seemingly oppressive capitalism than they did living in Stalin's socialist paradise.[12]

Operation Barbarossa, the German invasion of the Soviet Union, caught virtually everyone, from Stalin to the lowest Red Army soldier, by surprise. German and allied forces, numbering over 3.5 million men supported by 3,300 tanks and over 2,000 aircraft, broke through Soviet defenses, encircling hundreds of thousands of Soviet soldiers in enormous "pockets," and capturing major cities within the opening weeks of the campaign. Soviet forces fought back fiercely, launching hasty and poorly planned counterattacks, in the vain hope of stopping the German advance. Nevertheless, while the Germans penetrated deep into Soviet territory along a broad front, reaching the gates of Moscow by December 1941, and inflicted almost 4.5 million casualties, including over 3.1 million dead, captured, and missing in the first six months of the war, they failed in their attempt to destroy the Soviet Union with a single knockout punch.[13] Despite their vaunted reputations, the German generals overestimated the *Wehrmacht*'s abilities and underestimated the Red Army's. They neglected to adjust blitzkrieg operations, well suited for the smaller theaters of western and southern Europe, to the Soviet Union's wide open spaces. They assumed that the Red Army would collapse under the shock of the German attack, grossly miscalculating Soviet resilience. The existence of unknown Soviet reserves caught German military intelligence by surprise. Finally, the Red Army's counterattacks wore down the German forces, which, by December, had lost over a quarter of their fighting strength, even though they cost Soviets dearly.[14]

The combination of the speedy German advance and Stalin's unwillingness to authorize needed strategic retreats produced one of the most striking phenomena of the years 1941 and 1942: the encirclement and subsequent mass surrender of Soviet soldiers. A total of between 5.3 and 5.7 million Soviets became Axis prisoners during the war, of which over 3.8 million surrendered in 1941 and 1942.[15] These mass surrenders have generated fierce debate about the loyalty of Red Army soldiers to the Soviet Union, with some historians, particularly during the Cold War, arguing that they indicated widespread disaffection with the Soviet regime. Recent studies based on archival sources have demonstrated that the mass surrenders were less an indicator of political loyalty to the regime than a reflection of the tactical situation, unit commanders' leadership, and the troops' physical condition and morale. Soviet soldiers fought tenaciously, so long as their units maintained physical cohesion and their officers exercised effective command and control. Soldiers usually capitulated only when their units broke down and they sensed that their tactical situation was hopeless.[16]

Germany's political and military leadership planned the invasion of the USSR as a war of racialized colonial conquest. In order to feed the *Wehrmacht* and German civilian back home, the German command argued that, since the Soviet Union was not a signatory to the Hague and Geneva conventions, its captured soldiers did not merit humanitarian considerations and therefore were deliberately starved. The POWs' plight was exacerbated by Stalin's order in August 1941 that declared captured Soviet soldiers to be "traitors to the motherland" and decreed that their families could be arrested. POWs were often held in open fields without shelter. The hellish conditions in the POW camps were described by one survivor:

> There was real famine in the camp. The POWs rooted around about 40 centimeters deep into the ground and ate all the worms and roots they could find. Finally, they began to strip the bark off the trees and eat it. They devoured needles on the branches too. It reached the point where there was nothing left, in the trees, on the ground, or in the earth. In the beginning, the soldiers shot anyone who climbed into the trees, but after about 200 people had been shot and the POWs still did not stop climbing the trees to get the green twigs, they stopped shooting, as it was too much even for the soldiers.[17]

In all, approximately 3.3 million Soviet prisoners died in German captivity; by comparison, Mark Mazower calculates, "as many British and American soldiers died in German captivity during the whole war as died in these camps in one day."[18]

The cavalier attitude of Soviet generals toward their men's lives was another reason for the extraordinary combat losses suffered in the first two years of the war. A product of the Soviet tendency in the 1930s to solve difficult problems through the indiscriminate use of human resources, and of the generals' inexperience and lack of military sophistication, commanders frequently resorted to 'human-wave' attacks in the hope of overwhelming the enemy with superior numbers. Boris Gorbachevsky, a survivor of one of these attacks, described such an assault in the Rzhev sector in August 1942:

> Together with everyone else, tipping my helmet-covered head forward. . . . I hurry quickly, trying not to lag behind those running beside me . . . I'm crazily yelling . . . 'Ura-a! Ura-a' and this unifying cry brings with it some

new mysterious strength, muffles my hearing and stifles my fear. We're attacking head on, in echelons, and my company is advancing in the second line ... [at about 300 meters], the German trenches speak up. A growing, destructive fire sweeps up and down the attacking lines with a storm of machine-gun fire. The hoarse coughing of mortars follows the machine guns. Artillery starts to roar. Enormous geysers of earth toss the living and the dead high into the air. Thousands of shell splinters, like poisonous hornets, rip into men, tearing bodies and the earth ... 'Forward! Forward!' shout officers who are still alive, many just before dropping dead among their own soldiers. The men are mechanically moving forward, and many are dying – but we no longer belong to ourselves; we have all been seized by the incomprehensibly savage element of battle ... How can people withstand such a thing? Where can one protect oneself in such a hell?[19]

The Soviets lost heavily in these attacks, yet they still managed to push the Germans from the outskirts of Moscow. However, beginning in late June 1942, the Germans once again went on the offensive, although they were so weakened by the previous year's fighting that they were able to attack only along the southern sector. As in 1941, the panzers broke through Soviet lines causing panicked retreats. As the triumphant German advance continued, Stalin issued his infamous "Not One Step Back" order, which forbade unauthorized retreats, gave officers the right to shoot fleeing soldiers on the spot, and established "blocking units" to bolster the Soviet defenses. By late August 1942, the German Sixth Army reached the city of Stalingrad, on the banks of the Volga River. With the river at their backs, Soviet soldiers finally stood their ground. In the ferocious street fighting, the German forces were ground down and eventually trapped in the city, when in November 1942, a surprise Soviet counteroffensive surrounded Sixth Army. Attempts to relieve the now-besieged German forces failed, and by early February 1943, the 90,000 men left from the once-proud army of 295,000 surrendered. Overall, the Germans and their allies lost about 800,000 men, while Soviet casualties numbered 1.1 million soldiers and over 40,000 civilian deaths.

The Soviet victory at Stalingrad was a major psychological turning point, signaling to Germans and Soviets alike that the *Wehrmacht*'s campaign in the USSR was doomed. A last major German effort in July 1943 against the heavily defended Kursk salient failed with heavy losses, and the Soviets responded with their own devastating counteroffensive, which, by November 1943, led to the liberation of Kiev. Throughout 1944 and 1945 the Red Army battered German defenses in a series of offensives up and down the front. By May 1945, the Red Army had captured Berlin and the Hammer and Sickle flew over the *Reichstag*.

The victorious Red Army of 1943–5 differed significantly from that of 1941 and 1942. First, its leadership had improved significantly. The war had been a cruel but effective teacher, and the Soviet command learned much from the terrible first two years. Stalin also eventually realized his own limitations as a commander and relied increasingly on his better generals for advice (in sharp contrast to Hitler who only became more convinced of his own infallibility), who after two years of the war were becoming more skilled in operations and tactics.

Second, by 1943, the Red Army had also been transformed, according to John Erickson, into a highly mobile and powerful tank and mechanized "army of quality," supported by the larger "army of quantity" made up of mostly infantry units.[20] It now enjoyed firepower superiority over the *Wehrmacht*. Soviet arms production, especially in tanks and artillery, far outstripped Germany's; for example, in 1942 and 1943, the Soviet Union (fighting on a single front) produced over 48,500 tanks, while Germany, fighting on multiple fronts, built only 26,500. Moreover, while by 1943, some German tanks, such as the Panther and Tiger, had superior armor and firepower compared to the Soviet mainstay, the T-34, there were far too few of the former to make up for latter's numerical advantage. American Lend-Lease trucks and jeeps provided Red Army infantry with the mobility necessary to sustain armored breakthrough, and relieved Soviet factories of the need to manufacture these nonlethal but nonetheless critical vehicles.

The combination of improved Red Army experience and weaponry significantly changed the dynamics of the battlefield in the final years of the war. From the second half of 1943 through the spring of 1945, the Red Army launched a series of offensives that devastated the German forces. To cite just one example, in Operation Bagration in June 1944, the Red Army engineered a "reverse blitzkrieg" and in just one month advanced several hundred miles from eastern Belorussia to the gates of Warsaw and in the process destroyed Germany's vaunted Army Group Center, which lost over 400,000 men and twenty-five divisions.

Yet even as the Red Army transformed institutionally, for the *frontoviki* many of the characteristics of daily life remained fairly constant throughout the war years. Recruitment, training, living conditions, the quantity and quality of food, the brutalities of combat, and negotiating the boundaries of military discipline and political control all marked the experiences of Red Army soldiers.

The war was a voracious consumer of human lives. The USSR's military mobilization was so extensive that many villages lost all their young men to conscription, and even vital skilled war workers, desperately needed for production, were sometimes swept up. Later in the war, facing depleted manpower reserves, the advancing Soviet armies drafted able-bodied men from age 17 to age 45 who had been living in the formerly occupied territories. Often these new recruits were given a rifle and basic uniform, and sent directly into the ranks as replacements without any formal training.[21] Approximately 8 million non-Slavs were drafted into the military, although the inclusion of these forces sometimes raised social tensions in an institution dominated by Russian language and cultural customs. For example, Jewish and Muslim soldiers were forced to eat pork as there were no other alternatives.

Training, particularly in the first years of the war, was often quite rudimentary. Recruits wore ill-fitting uniforms and footwear, lived in substandard barracks (often without proper sanitation or hygienic facilities), and ate inadequate, often spoiled, food. Battlefield tactics were taught with wooden "weapons," especially in periods when scarce equipment was more urgently needed at the front. One soldier, trained to be a mortarman, recalled that in his four months at a mortar specialist training school he did not fire a single mortar round, while a tank crewman related that much of his training consisted of "tank walking" (i.e., walking but pretending to be in a tank).[22] Recruits also contended with harsh discipline and brutal hazing, and beatings for mild disciplinary infractions were common punishments. Many viewed going into combat as an escape from the horrors of the training regiments.

While all frontline combatants endured harsh daily conditions, daily life in the wartime Red Army was particularly severe. At first, uniforms were poorly made and equipment kits were lacking necessities. The dislocation of Soviet textile factories and the overemphasis on producing weapons and ammunition exacerbated these problems. Corpses were often stripped of any valuable clothing. The clothing and equipment situation gradually improved in 1942, as Soviet production recovered and was readjusted to include nonlethal but nonetheless essential equipment. Winter gear, such as the *valenki* (felt boots), padded jackets, and fur hats, was especially critical and far superior to what German soldiers had.[23]

The extraordinarily cold weather added to the misery of soldiers' lives. Contrary to the racialized beliefs of German soldiers, Russians and other Soviet citizens were just as vulnerable to the cold as they were. The British war correspondent Alexander Werth described this cold in the aftermath of the fighting at Stalingrad:

One has to experience 44 degrees of frost [−47 degrees Fahrenheit] to know what it means ... If you breathe on a glove, a thin film of ice immediately forms on it. We couldn't eat anything, because all our food— bread, sausage, and eggs—had turned to stone. Even wearing valenki and two pairs of woolen socks, you had to move your toes all the time to keep the circulation going ... Once I took out a pencil to write down a few words: the first word was all right, the second was written by a drunk, and the last two were the scrawl of a paralytic; quickly I blew on my purple fingers and put them back in the fur-lined glove.[24]

Food, or rather the lack of it, obsessed the always-hungry Red Army soldiers. Even before the war, for many Soviets, obtaining sufficient food was problematic at best. The occupation of Ukraine, the USSR's "breadbasket," and the shortage of tractors, livestock, and able-bodied workers in non-occupied areas drastically reduced food production. Although military rations were given the highest priority, there was rarely enough food for the soldiers. The calories allotted were inadequate for the rigors of combat and even for the work performed in the rear areas. In theory, frontline soldiers were to receive approximately 3,500 calories per day (rear-area troops received significantly less), consisting primarily of bread, potatoes, kasha (buckwheat), and cabbage, supplemented by small amounts of meat and fish. However, even these norms were often not met, particularly when units were on the move. Soldiers were then expected to forage for themselves. It is therefore not surprising that one of the most valued items of American Lend-Lease aid was Spam (canned processed meat), which provided essential fats and protein.[25]

Veteran Yevgeny Nosov summarized the daily travails experienced by Red Army soldiers. War, he said, consisted of

marching for hours on end, carrying heavy loads, pushing and pulling with all your might, digging with a substandard spade you have found in an empty farmyard, feeling cold, your teeth chattering, stamping your feet in your frozen felt boots, damp, rain, overcoming heat and thirst, sometimes waiting days for a stray field kitchen, gnawing on that miserable, stale, hard bread because you have nothing else, smoking dry grass and moss, lighting a fire with flint, sleeping with your boots on, often on damp ground and sometimes simply in a hollow in the snow, enduring being shot at with bullets and under heavy mortar fire, not to mention the fighting itself when you have to face the machine guns in the open or defend yourself from a tank with grenades.[26]

The difficulties experienced by the men were magnified for the over 1 million women who served in the Soviet military. Women served in all military branches, predominantly as nurses (Soviet nurses often accompanied soldiers into combat and sometimes carried weapons) but also as anti-aircraft gunners, pilots (the Red Air Force had three all-women squadrons), snipers, tank crew, and partisans. They had to make do with field uniforms and boots designed for male bodies, and no provision was made for feminine hygienic needs. Moreover, while the Soviet Union proclaimed the full emancipation of women, there nevertheless remained official and popular ambivalence about the idea of women as fighters and killers. As women were customarily viewed as the givers and nurturers of life, many men, and even some women, believed that women killing, even if the target was the hated enemy, perverted their "true" nature. As one male Red Army veteran told a Soviet journalist,

> Perhaps I would take a women like that along on a scouting mission but not for a wife ... , No .... I can't imagine myself having a sniper for a wife. We are used to thinking of a woman as a mother or a bride.[27]

The Germans, too, believed that women soldiers were "unnatural" and often executed captured Soviet female fighters.

Although men may have been reluctant to marry women veterans, they nevertheless sought their companionship at the front. Many female soldiers certainly entered into relationships with their male comrades voluntarily, but others were pressured to do so, especially by superior officers. Regardless of how bravely women performed in combat or how conscientiously they fulfilled their duties, their fellow soldiers and civilians frequently sniggered that their hard-earned awards and medals were given for sexual prowess rather than for defending their country.[28]

Despite these popular misgivings, female combatants, whether in the regular armed services or in the partisans, were celebrated in Soviet wartime media as heroes. Figures such as Zoia Kosmodemianskaia, a young partisan tortured and executed by the Germans in 1941, and Liudmila Pavlichenko, a sniper credited with over 300 "kills," became the personification of Soviet bravery and heroism, willing to sacrifice their lives for their families, homes, and nation. Even though, as Roger Reese points out, women were often subjected to official and social pressure to serve; Soviet public rhetoric since the days of the Revolution proclaiming women as full and equal citizens had made a tremendous impact on many young women. As one woman partisan recalled after the war, "My only dream was to avenge, to die, and to have a book written about me ... I was ready to do anything for my homeland," while another stated, "I was a Komsomol member and could not remain passive."[29]

For both male and female combatants, the intensity of destruction meant that the threat of death was ever present. In 1943, soldiers could expect, on average, to serve at the front three months before being wounded or killed, and during offensive operations the life expectancy of an infantryman was fewer than eight days.[30] Units engaged in offensive operations from early 1943 onward often lost a quarter of their men, and infantry units involved in breakthrough operations endured casualty rates of over 50 percent. Material losses were also extraordinary: on average, the Red Army needed to replace one-tenth of its tank forces every week.[31]

Given this scale of destruction, death was a constant companion. As one veteran reported,

> We were afraid of death. Death was around us every day, every hour, and on all sides. You could sit quietly, drink tea, and a stray shell would fall on you. It was impossible to get used to that. It doesn't mean that we were all constantly jittery and that everyone sat and walked expecting death at any moment. Death simply came or it didn't ... Those who returned from the war either became fatalists or found faith in God. Nowhere could the hand of fate be found so clearly, so rigidly and unavoidably, like there. I experienced this myself, and not just once.[32]

Not only was death often random and sudden, but it frequently consigned its victims to oblivion. Soviet soldiers often lacked personal identity markers like the US Army's "dog tags," and they were usually buried in mass, unmarked graves without their families being informed of their deaths. Even now, decades after the war, volunteers still scour the woods and fields of former battlefields searching for the remains of unburied soldiers to give them a proper resting place.

What enabled Soviet men and women to endure such grievous loss of life and immense personal suffering, especially when fighting in the name of a regime that had displayed both in its recent past and wartime present such a profound disregard for its own citizens' lives and well-being?

There is no single answer to this question; each soldier would probably have his or her own complex set of reasons. In general, however, soldiers were motivated by a mix of factors, including personal relationships, patriotism, coercion, and hatred for the enemy.

Scholars have argued that personal relationships among soldiers are one of the most powerful reasons why people fight, and Red Army soldiers were no different in this regard. Despite—or perhaps because of—the omnipresent danger, relationships were very intense and quickly formed. "It's enough for a person to be with you two to seven days for you to know his qualities, all his feelings, the things it takes a year to know in civilian life," declared one soldier."[33] As in many other armies in the Second World War, small groups of soldiers, usually within a squad or a tank crew formed "primary groups," often described in familial terms. The love for and fear of letting down members of one's primary group, similar to those in other armies, became one of the essential reasons why Red Army soldiers braved the extraordinary dangers they faced on the battlefield.[34]

Patriotism, in particular the call to defend the *Rodina* (motherland), was inspiring for many, especially since the Russian word "motherland" without a defining adjective could mean anything soldiers wanted it to mean. Thus, *frontoviki* who were indifferent or even hostile to the communist Soviet Union, could interpret *Rodina* to mean their republic, province, or even their local town or district.

Hatred for the enemy was another powerful factor. For once, Soviet propaganda did not exaggerate when it portrayed the enemy as an existential threat to both the country's and the population's existence. The Soviet media cleverly connected defending the country with protecting one's family, especially as soldiers saw with their own eyes the consequences of German occupation as they moved through destroyed cities and villages. As one soldier-turned exile recalled after the war, "Now ... we fought like heroes, in contrast to the earlier years ... [when we] had seen the results of Hitler's policy and we knew that he was no better than Stalin," adding, "The Soviet government was terrible, but at least we felt it was better than an alien government."[35] The desire to avenge these atrocities proved to be a powerful motivator for soldiers. When the Red Army crossed into Germany and German-allied countries, Red Army soldiers transformed the abstract concept of hatred and revenge into the very real atrocities of mass rape, plunder, and arbitrary killings of civilians.[36]

As with all other armies, fear and discipline also kept soldiers fighting, although in the Red Army's case, these measures were extreme compared to the other Allied armies. Like their German counterparts, Soviet soldiers were subjected to a harsh disciplinary regime that gave little consideration to human frailty in the face of battle. About 158,000 Soviets were shot for cowardice, desertion, and draft evasion.[37] Soldiers also faced surveillance from political officers and the security services distributed among the troops.

One notorious aspect of discipline in the Red Army were the so-called blocking detachments made up of either Red Army or NKVD troops, with orders to prevent unauthorized retreats. Blocking detachments had been first used in the Russian Civil War and were deployed sporadically in 1941. They were formally instituted as part of the earlier mentioned Order 227, or "Not One Step Back," issued during the dark days of July 1942. Although video games and films have popularized the image of blocking detachments massacring retreating soldiers, most units simply rounded up soldiers found behind the lines, or prevented retreats using nonlethal methods. While shootings did take place, the admittedly scanty evidence available indicates that such instances were relatively rare.[38] Indeed, many Soviet veterans believed that such units were an unfortunate necessity in the context of an extraordinarily brutal war. As one former soldier argued, the blocking detachments actually paradoxically *saved* lives, especially when frontline troops panicked and retreated en masse:

[A] chain reaction of massive flight began and only the direct threat of death could stop it. Very often the flight provoked by the cowardice of one or several men resulted in the death of many more soldiers. That is why it would be inappropriate today ... to judge wartime incidents, which, on the surface, seem to contradict common moral standards.[39]

Soldiers deemed guilty of crimes or "cowardice" were often assigned to " 'punishment' battalions," where they would "expiate their sins before the motherland."[40] Punishment battalions were given the most dangerous missions, such as spearheading offensives and clearing minefields. Historian David Glantz estimates that, during the 1944 offensives, punishment battalions suffered monthly casualty rates of over 50 percent, three to six times higher than that of regular Red Army units. A survivor of a penal unit recalled,

I went on an attack many times after I arrived in the penal battalion. I was lucky since I was never even wounded. In the first company, out of the 198 soldiers who were assigned, only six survived. I then served in the second company, but once again I escaped injury. They threw us into the most dangerous sectors, sending us to almost certain death, at first even without artillery cover.[41]

The strict discipline, the constant presence of political and state security officers, and the draconian punishments meant that soldiers had little respite from Stalinist repression even as they were fighting the *Wehrmacht*. Although the fighting in Europe ended in May 1945, many Red Army soldiers did not return to their homes for several years as they remained on occupation duty in Central and Eastern Europe. From the soldiers' point of view, this delay was not all bad, as it gave them the opportunity to send looted goods such as furniture, bicycles, or radios to their families. However, when they returned, they and their families scarcely recognized each other. Many were dismayed that their own families lived in similar or in even more impoverished circumstances than what they had seen in occupied Europe. Furthermore, within a few years the Soviet government ceased all but the most perfunctory recognition of the soldiers' achievements, instead conferring upon Stalin the glory of the Soviet people's victory. Just as critically, material benefits and aid to veterans, especially the wounded and invalid, were wholly inadequate to meet the high demand for services. Not until the 1960s did the Soviet state begin to recognize the contributions of and provide some material support to the tens of millions of surviving veterans, but even then, the resources allocated were insufficient.

The political impact of the war on Soviet service members was ambiguous, even contradictory. As in the past, the Red Army was a school for citizenship, though the results of the wartime lessons it taught were not always clear. The war experience shaped veterans in a variety of ways, which could either reinforce or undermine the existing Soviet system. Millions of soldiers joined the Communist Party during the war, though they may have been motivated as much by material benefits as by patriotic and ideological reasons. These same veterans provided essential political support for the Soviet system. Wartime military service practically became a prerequisite for a postwar administrative career as veterans filled the ranks of the state and party at all levels. Although some observers credited the *frontoviki* for applying the same determination to fulfill their bureaucratic tasks as they did to win the war, other claimed that they were obsessed with power, careerism and advancing up the social ladder, and cared little for the higher ideals the Party supposedly espoused.[42]

Other veterans learned different behaviors from the war. Many veterans, particularly from among the intelligentsia, reported that they never felt as free or as responsible as *citizens* as during the war. The veteran and literary critic Lazar Lazarev related that for him and his friends, just out of high school, "those first two years of the war coincided with a spontaneous de-Stalinization, a true emancipation [and we] felt that everything depended on us personally, and that gave us an extraordinary feeling of freedom."[43] Historian Elena Seniavskaia argues that the war made possible an inner liberation for soldiers who could relate to the world around them with sincerity, honesty, and authenticity.[44] She notes that the "front generation" was also the "generation of the Twentieth [Party] Congress" and contends that the crucible of the war forged a new citizen who was "inclined to take risks, capable of making independent decisions in extreme situations, courageous and decisive."[45] These veterans believed that postwar Soviet society should reflect the same values of honesty, authenticity, and responsibility that had marked their war experience. While these former servicemen remained fully supportive of the Soviet Union and its sociopolitical system, nevertheless, their service in the Red Army had indeed transformed them, though perhaps not in the way Stalin and his generals had intended. In this sense, they helped the lay groundwork for the de-Stalinization campaigns in the postwar decades and subsequent efforts for political and social reform.

Notes

1   Cited in *Slovo tovarishchu staliniu*, Moscow: Eksmo "Algoritm," 2003, 212–13.
2   Catherine Merridale, *Ivan's War: Life and Death in the Red Army, 1939–1945*, New York: Picador, 2005, 4. By comparison, the United Kingdom and the United States lost a little over 380,000 and 400,000 killed, respectively. Red Army was the name (a synecdoche) given to all of the Soviet armed forces combined; the land army was officially called the *Raboche-Krest'ianskaia Krasnaia Armiia*, or Workers' and Peasants' Red Army; the color red was an important revolutionary symbol). The words Red Fleet (for the navy) and Red Air Force were also in use.

3 Elena Seniavskaia, *Frontovoe pokolenie, 1941–1945*, Moscow: Institut Rossiiskoi Istorii-RAN, 1995, 91.

4 Michael Geyer and Mark Edele, "States of Exception: The Nazi-Soviet War as a System of Violence, 1939–1945," in Michael Geyer and Sheila Fitzpatrick, eds., *Beyond Totalitarianism: Stalinism and Nazism Compared*, Cambridge: Cambridge University Press, 2009, 394.

5 Merridale, *e*, 3.

6 For a more extended discussion and analysis, see Mark von Hagen, *Soldiers in the Proletarian Dictatorship: The Red Army and the Soviet Socialist State, 1917–1930*, Ithaca, NY: Cornell University Press, 1990.

7 See Roger Reese, *Stalin's Reluctant Soldiers: A Social History of the Red Army, 1925–1941*, Lawrence: University Press of Kansas, 1996, 59, 84–92.

8 Many of the officers purged were not shot but instead were sent to the *Gulag* camps, see Reese, *Stalin's Reluctant Soldiers*, 134.

9 Mark von Hagen, "Soviet Soldiers and Officers on the Eve of the German Invasion: Towards a Description of Social Psychology and Political Attitudes," *Soviet Union/Union Sovietique* 1–3, 1991, 92.

10 Harvard Project on the Soviet System [hereafter referred to as HPSSS], Schedule A., Vol. 9, Case 118 (interviewer A.D.), 32, available at: http://nrs. harvard.edu/urn-3:FHCL:946680, accessed January 18, 2018.

11 Finnish casualties numbered 66,000; see Roger Reese, *Why Stalin's Soldiers Fought: The Red Army's Military Effectiveness in World War II*, Lawrence: University of Kansas Press, 2011, 32.

12 Von Hagen, "Soviet Soldiers and Officers," 99.

13 David Glantz, *Colossus Reborn: The Red Army at War, 1941–1945 (Modern War Studies)*, Lawrence: University Press of Kansas, 2005, 624.

14 Richard Overy, *Russia's War: A History of the Soviet War Effort, 1941–1945*, New York: Penguin Books, 117.

15 Jörg Echternkamp et al., eds., *Germany and the Second World War, vol. IX/II: German Wartime Society, 1939–1945: Exploitation, Interpretations, Exclusion*, trans. Derry Cook-Radmore et al., Oxford: Clarendon Press, 2014, 824–5; Glantz, *Colossus Reborn*, 624.

16 See George Fischer, *Soviet Opposition to Stalin: A Case Study in World War II*, Cambridge, MA: Harvard University Press, 1952; Reese, *Why Stalin's Soldiers Fought*, esp. 82–100.

17 Cited in Rudiger Overmans, "German Policy on Prisoners of War, 1939–1945," in Echternkamp et al., eds., *Germany and the Second World War*, vol. IX/II, 812–13.

18 Mark Mazower, *Hitler's Empire: How the Nazis Ruled Europe*, New York: Penguin Books, 2008, 163.

19 Boris Gorbachevsky, *Through the Maelstrom: A Red Army Soldier's War on the Eastern Front, 1942–1945*, Lawrence: University Press of Kansas, 2008, 111–13.

20 John Erickson, *The Road to Berlin: Stalin's War with Germany*, New Haven, CT: Yale University Press, 1999, 84.

21 Glantz, *Red Colossus*, 541–4.

22 Gorbachevsky, *Through the Maelstrom*, 38; Interview with Vasily Pavlovich Bryukhov, March 29, 2015, available at: https://iremember.ru/en/memoirs/ tankers/bryukhov-vasily-pavlovich/, accessed January 18, 2018.

23 German military planners assumed that the USSR would be defeated before winter 1941 and therefore did not supply *Wehrmacht* soldiers with winter uniforms. Desperate soldiers in subzero conditions grabbed any warm clothing they could find or plunder. Soviet comedy troupes made fun of the so-called Winter Fritz, dressing him up odd assortments of women's clothing.

24 Alexander Werth, *Russia at War, 1941–1945*, New York: Dover Books, 1964, 511.

25 Glantz, *Red Colossus*, 555–60. Spam even appeared in Soviet war films, such as Grigory Chukrai's *Ballad of a Soldier* (1959), which shows soldier eating from a can marked in English "U.S. Meat."

26 Cited in Marius Broekmeyer, *Stalin, the Russians, and Their War, 1941–1945*, trans. Rosalind Buck, Madison: University of Wisconsin Press, 2004, 191.

27 Cited in Svetlana Alexiyevich, *War's Unwomanly Face*, Moscow: Progress Publishers, 1988, 64.

28 Alexiyevich, *War's Unwomanly Face*, 8, 71; Merridale, *Ivan's War*, 240–1.

29 Cited in Alexeyevich, *War's Unwomanly Face*, 38, 40.

30 Merridale, *Ivan's War*, 199; Broekmeyer, *Stalin and the Russians*, 193.

31 David Glantz and Jonathan House, *When Titans Clashed: How the Red Army Stopped Hitler*, Lawrence: University Press of Kansas, 1995, 180; Glantz, *Colossus Reborn*, 621; John Barber and Mark Harrison, *The Soviet Home Front: A Social and Economic History of World War II*, London: Longman, 1991, 181.

32 Cited in Glantz, *Colossus Reborn*, 584–5.

33 Cited in Merridale, *Ivan's War*, 200.

34 Reese, *Why Stalin's Soldiers Fought*, 216–27.

35 HPSSS, Case 27 (interviewer H.D., type A2). Male, 26, Great Russian, Kolkhoznik. [67] p. Case 27 (interviewer H.D., type A2), 15, 17.

36 It is estimated that Soviet soldiers raped approximately 2 million German women; see Jeffrey Burds, "Sexual Violence in Europe in World War II, 1939–1945," *Politics and Society* 1, 2009, 35–73: 53–5.

37 Reese, *Why Stalin's Soldiers Fought*, 175. This figure does not include soldiers who were shot summarily on the battlefield. By comparison, the German army on the Eastern Front executed between 13,000 and 15,000 of its soldiers for cowardice and desertion.

38 A report from the NKVD authorities in the autumn of 1942 indicated that for the Stalingrad and Don fronts, about 1 percent of fleeing soldiers detained by blocking detachments were shot, while over 90 percent were returned to their units (cited in Alexander Hill, *The Great Patriotic War of the Soviet Union, 1941–1945: A Documentary Reader*, Routledge: London, 2010, 103).

39 Cited by Alexander Statiev, "Blocking Units in the Red Army," *The Journal of Military History* 2, 2012, 475–95: 494; see also Reese, *Why Stalin's Soldiers Fought*, 163–5.

40 See K. Slepyan, "People's Avengers or Enemies of the People," available at: http://www.ku.de/forschung/forschen-an-der-ku/forschungseinr/ forschungseinrzimos/publikationen/forum/zeitgeschichte/slepyan-peoples-avengers/, accessed January 18, 2018.

41 Cited in Glantz, *Colossus Reborn*, 578.

42 See, for example, Ludmilla Alexeyeva and Paul Goldberg, *The Thaw Generation: Coming of Age in the Post-Stalin Era*, Pittsburgh, PA: University of Pittsburgh Press, 1993, 30–1.

43 Cited in Nina Tumarkin, *The Living and the Dead: The Rise and Fall of the Cult of World War II in Russia*, New York: Basic Books 1994, 66.

44 Seniavskaia, *Frontovoe pokolenie*, 32–4.

45 Seniavskaia, *Frontovoe pokolenie*, 158, 161–2.

7

The History of Disability during Stalinism

Frances Bernstein

Comrade Deputy! We, Soviet soldiers and invalids, have always fought and will continue to fight for our Soviet motherland. If it becomes necessary, invalids will always be first in line to go wherever Comrade Stalin sends us.
—LETTER FROM A. D. SUVOROV TO V. M. MOLOTOV, 1950

Introduction

Several months after Nikita Khrushchev (1894–1971) delivered his "Secret Speech" unmasking the crimes of Stalin on February 25, 1956, a demonstration took place outside the headquarters of the Communist Party's Central Committee in Moscow. The event was unusual in several respects. An unsanctioned protest—in front of the Central Committee building, no less—was a bold, even reckless move, given that other such actions following Khrushchev's address, whether domestic or in Eastern Europe, had been (or would be) harshly suppressed.

Second, the thirty participants were not marching, but rolling. All disabled and using motorized wheelchairs (a notoriously scarce commodity in the Soviet Union), the mostly male group, composed primarily of war veterans, had gathered to oppose shutting down the system of sheltered workshops founded specifically to provide them with jobs, as most workplaces refused to do so, though required by law. Now these same positions were to be open to anyone; in fact, a sizable percentage of those already working in the shops was not disabled. This meant that people with disabilities were losing one of the very limited advantages they possessed.

In a city that was inaccessible to people with mobility disablements, the fact that so many wheelchair users could leave their apartments and make it to the center of town is also remarkable. Finally, and most significantly, it was perhaps an assessment of the group's demands as strictly economic—in contrast to the overtly political protests following the Secret Speech (e.g., as in Soviet Georgia, or the Soviet satellite state of Hungary)—that explains the state's surprisingly different response. The demonstrators were invited into the building to discuss their complaints—and then allowed to leave.

The 1956 group demonstration signaled a fundamental shift in the relationship of disabled people to the state and was the kernel of what would eventually become an organized disability rights movement. The event also serves as a fitting conclusion to the history of disability during the Stalin era. If leniency toward the protesters was due to their disability, it was a novel response on the part of the state; Stalin had been unmoved by such considerations. In this respect, if no other, people with disabilities were truly equal to everyone else.

Moreover, aside from the range of regularly occurring impairments found across cultures and nations (congenital, infection- or age-related, etc.), Stalinism itself was the Soviet Union's chief disabling condition. The two signature elements most closely associated with his regime, industrialization (and the collectivization that funded it) and the *Gulag*, plus the events of the Second World War, produced the vast majority of people with disabilities during these years.

This chapter presents a general overview of disability history from the beginning of the First Five-Year Plan (1928) to Khrushchev's speech. What does "invalidism" mean in the context of the Workers' State?[1] How closely does the understanding of disability as presented in state policy align with lived experience? What impairments (disabling condition) were "cured," prevented, or neutralized, and who was to blame for these conditions in the first place? Were any groups harder to integrate into the Soviet project or more dangerous than others? And finally, what of the experts charged with treating them?

Defective Children

In the nineteenth-century Russian Empire, the word "invalid" came into use primarily in reference to soldiers and other military personnel who had been physically disabled in service. After the Revolution, a very different understanding of invalidism emerged, describing those so labelled as incapable of working. Whereas the prerevolutionary usage of invalid was neutral, after 1917 those unable to work were in-valid and by definition suspect. Governing the regime's approach to disability was a belief in the transformative power of labor, as both method for rehabilitation and evidence of a cure. With health and normalcy defined in relation to work capability and loss thereof, those who could not work were not recognized by the state as disabled and therefore not provided for in terms of benefits and protections. More surprising, perhaps, was that this work calculus was applied equally to children as well as adults, and most especially to children with cognitive disabilities. Incapable (in the future) of working, the most severely impaired children were in principle denied unmerited benefits.

As understood in Russia, and building upon prerevolutionary and international developments, the discipline responsible for the education, care, and upbringing of children with disabilities was defectology. Similar in certain respects to contemporary special education in the United States, the term applied to children with a wide range of impairments, including speech and language, sensory, physical, neurological, psychiatric, and intellectual. Also under this umbrella were the behaviorally or "morally defective," a category including the abandoned, orphaned, and homeless children who were a pervasive fixture of the 1920s.

As with people with disabilities more generally, there are few statistics available for the number of disabled children in the early Soviet era, and what figures do exist we can assume to be substantially underreported. In 1930, 6,700 students attended schools for the deaf, with 5,400 in Russia, 800 in Ukraine, 150 in Belorussia, and 300 in the other republics combined. Two thousand blind and visually impaired children were educated in 37 schools, with 1,500 of these students in Russia. All told, 3,530 teachers trained in defectology educated 40,000 children with special needs in 1930. Significant progress was made by a decade later, as 1,095 special schools educated 274,000 children with disabilities. This growth, however, was spread unevenly. Between 1932 and the 1937–8 school year, 116,000 children, or 25 percent of the total, were cut from enrollment in special schools, the vast majority from rural areas. Unsurprisingly, far fewer schools survived the Second World War: in 1945–6, a total of 85,000 children attended 706 special schools.

In the 1920s, a number of newly established institutions, including the Commissariats of Education, Health, Social Welfare, and Justice, divided responsibility over these children. Schools for the deaf and blind were administered by the Commissariat of Enlightenment (known by its Newspeakish contraction as *Narkompros*), and for those children with health problems, chronic diseases, psychiatric disorders, or physical impairments, by the Commissariat of Public Health (*Narkomzdrav*). Children with intellectual deficits were under the jurisdiction of the Commissariat of Social Welfare (*Narodnyi komissariat sotsial'nogo obospecheniia*).

By the time of introduction of the First Five-Year Plan (officially spanning the years from 1928 to 1932), the vast majority of disabled children were separated into different establishments and programs catering to their specific learning needs. These were primarily residential; parents were deemed unqualified to care for and educate such children and were strongly pressured to send them away. There were schools for the hard of hearing and the deaf, for the visually impaired and the blind, for those with mobility or motor impairments, and for others with such health ailments as scoliosis and heart conditions. The developmentally delayed represented a special category, with the educable (defined as able to complete a seven-year factory worker school) capable of entering the workforce, separated from the uneducable, who would instead be placed in custodial institutions. In 1931, education for the former population was made compulsory.

For a brief period, there had been the possibility of an alternative and much more optimistic approach toward children with disabilities, one articulated by Lev Vygotsky (1896–1934), the developmental psychologist and founder of the Experimental Institute of Defectology (1929). Vygotsky believed that every child had special gifts and was capable of learning; it was the teaching methods that had to change, not the children. An advocate of "positive differentiation," he supported inclusive classrooms and the opportunities for socialization they provided to both those children with disabilities and those without.

Vygotsky's understanding of disability comes remarkably close to the social model of disability, a theory articulated several decades later in the United Kingdom. He distinguished between two levels of "defects": primary (organic) and secondary (social-environmental). Disability, he argued, was determined not by any sort of biological imperfection in itself but rather by the social and cultural context in which the person with that impairment lived. It was society, not defect, that disabled. Whereas in the social model, removing barriers to full participation by people with disabilities is the key, for Vygotsky it was education, or "correction." According to him, defectiveness was not "irreparable," and even those with severe deficits could find a place in Soviet society.

However, what began so optimistically ended with a crude separation between those considered capable of learning and those who were not, a reorientation made possible in part by Vygotsky's early death at the age of 37 from tuberculosis in 1934. During the Great Turn's cultural revolution, defectology was tainted by its association with pedology (the study of the nature and development of children), which shared the same fate as many other academic and scientific disciplines with roots in the West, such as social hygiene, venereology, and eugenics. In 1931, the main journal of the field, *Questions of Defectology*, ceased publication. Vygotsky's writings were banned in 1936 and only republished in the late 1950s, after Stalin's death. In 1930, Vygotsky's school was renamed the Scientific-Practical Institute of Special Schools and Children's Homes. In 1943 the name again changed, to the Defectological Scientific Research Institute, a title it bears to the present. Vygotsky was rehabilitated in 1956, and schools and programs following his methods gradually reemerged starting in 1958, with Krushchev's educational reforms.

In 1936, the Party accused defectologists of classifying *too many* children as defective, when their deficits, it claimed, were really the result of neglect or lack of discipline. They argued that what was needed instead were remedial schools and a far less gentle approach to recalcitrant students. Gradually, facilities which had earlier (before the revolution privately and afterward by the state) cared for the intellectually disabled now housed typical children, with the previous inhabitants moved to poorer facilities. Essentially, the severely delayed were not considered highly functional enough to be considered defective and thus worth the effort at correction. From this point, their care became and would remain custodial. Once they turned eighteen, most of these children were moved to facilities for adults and likely passed the rest of their lives there. Children with multiple or severe disabilities such as cerebral palsy, multiple sclerosis, and childhood schizophrenia (autism) would share the same fate; often they too would be diagnosed with mental retardation.

Pension and Social Insurance

During the first years of Bolshevik power and into the 1920s, a number of disability-related measures were introduced, though inconsistently and unequally. Social insurance included support for the following: permanent disability, old age, and death benefits; temporary conditions such as sickness, accidents, and maternity; access to rest homes, resorts, and sanitaria; and grants for births, burials, and rehabilitation. Health care and allowances for children were universal. In late 1918, and in keeping with Bolshevik ideology, it was announced that insurance would be extended to any individual engaged in wage labor, including "freelancers" (such as artisans) and landless peasants, to be paid for by their employers. When industry was nationalized in 1921, this obligation fell to the state. Needless to say, given the chaos and wrecked economy, the country was in no position to provide such support. For instance, in March 1921 the entire health insurance budget earmarked for disabled military veterans was exhausted after purchasing 775,000 artificial limbs.

With the transition to the New Economic Policy in 1921, eligibility for state social insurance was based upon how and where one worked, not financial or physical hardship. Entitled were wage laborers, meaning the proletariat, first and foremost. Excluded were peasants, who, along with other "independent" workers (such as artisans and members of producer cooperatives, including those for the disabled), instead, could enroll in mutual aid societies. An official estimate at the time found 2.7 million people with disabilities, most of them peasants, of whom 75 percent had been injured in the First World War or the Russian Civil War, and who received no regular financial support from the government.

Even after collectivization, peasants were disqualified from state insurance because they were "self-employed," and the aid societies established in the 1920s migrated with them into the collective farms from 1929 onward. While not required to establish these funds, once in the *kolkhoz*, peasants were strongly urged to do so. Collectives were supposed to support those unable to work, including widows, orphans, pregnant women, the elderly, and the disabled. The money could be used for loans to members and other services as well. How the funds were distributed, the amount and duration of the aid, and whether there were strings attached to the grants was up to each individual *kolkhoz*; such a system was rife with opportunities for graft and retaliation. These payments were typically much lower than the amount state insurance paid to white- and blue-collar workers. It took the state until the 1950s to establish some oversight, and only in January 1965(!) did farmers become entitled to state social insurance.

In 1930, unemployment insurance was abolished and never reinstated, in part because it was deemed unnecessary, thanks to universal employment. A second justification had to do with concern about supposed malingerers and freeloaders who, it was believed, had been able to exploit the system. Beginning in 1933, insurance agents were given the right to deny benefits to those so labeled. As with the *kolkhoz* aid societies, there was a great deal of abuse: personnel elicited bribes, ran protection rackets, and sexually manipulated women; for their part, many workers did indeed engage in simulation and self-mutilation. When efforts by the state to end corruption failed, blame was placed on class enemies old and new: former factory owners and nobles, tsarist officers and priests, as well as the "Menshevizing, right opportunists" unmasked in the Commissariat of Labor and All-Union Central Council of Trade Unions throughout the 1930s.

With industrialization, the country's highest priority was to get as many people working as possible, and the chief purpose of social insurance for people with disabilities the pursuit of that goal. Thus efforts were made to restrict entitlements and provide those still eligible with the bare minimum of assistance. State support was to be an option of last resort, reserved for only the most severely disabled, who had no remaining capacity to work. According to a July 19, 1930 law, the Commissariat of Social Welfare was required to provide vocational training and job placement, rather than merely pensions, to those with disabilities. Notably, instruction for rural invalids was virtually nonexistent before the war.

The higher one's salary before the disablement or the higher one's rank, the greater the benefits to which one was entitled: the severity or location of the injury was largely irrelevant. As before, pensions for peasants, students, and rural workers were lower than those for urban workers or administrators, although by the end of the decade, entitlements also were raised for those who had served in the Red Army or Navy. Workers who quit or were terminated from their jobs had their benefits reduced or lost them altogether.

Industrial Trauma

Industrialization was one long gash on the social body. There were the traumas to the land itself, the deep cuts to the earth made in the building of Magnitogorsk, the Belomor (White-Sea) Canal, and the Moscow subway system, to name but a few projects. Because these were constructed with convict labor, the enormous loss of life and scores of mangled bodies were of limited concern.

The state's relationship with the (nonprisoner) proletariat was more complicated; after all, the 1917 Revolution had been made in its name. The government sought to right the wrongs perpetuated by Capital and the tsar by passing a series of measures devoted to safeguarding workers' bodies and health in the decade following 1917. Supervisors and shop managers were required to record and inform local labor inspectorates of cases of work-place trauma; notice of on-site deaths and work absences longer than one day were to be reported within forty-eight hours. For their part, sanitary and technical inspectors were charged with monitoring workplace safety. A 1927 law called for the establishment of on-site health and safety bureaus, and in 1929, the Commissariat of Labor took to task the numerous enterprises not using money earmarked by the state for safety and first aid measures. In 1932, the chair of the Central Council of Trade Unions made a similar complaint, excoriating management for continued violations.

Over the same period, a number of scientific institutes, some building upon their prerevolutionary counterparts, developed to study occupational health, safety, and job performance. The first group was established in the 1920s, and in the 1930s a second wave followed, established as a companion to industrialization. Sometimes their agendas worked at cross purposes. For instance, the Central Institute of Labor sought to rationalize assembly-line work, controlling for extraneous movement in the goal of greater productivity, whereas the State Institute for the Protection of Labor worked to guard against fatigue and repetitive motion injuries caused by assembly lines. Whatever the institutes' different emphases, all their efforts were in one way or another devoted to the relationship between human beings and machines, and to the circumstances in which those interactions took place.

With industrialization, worker health, safety, and interests were definitively subordinated to production. Piece rates were introduced and salary linked to output. Now individual records were championed, replacing the earlier emphasis on collective labor, and enormous wage differentials developed between top and bottom producers. The culmination of this reward system was the Stakhanov movement, named for the Donbass miner Alexei Stakhanov (1906–1977), who in 1935 allegedly surpassed his production goal by fourteen times, mining 102 tons of coal in six hours. Competition was likewise encouraged through industry-wide contests (this was called "socialist emulation," or "socialist competition"), pitting different enterprises against one another to win prizes and honors, as well as within individual factories, with top workers feted and underperformers shamed. Similarly, in 1930, previously universal health care was replaced by a gradated system favoring those sectors of the economy that were the most productive, with peasants and the nonworking (including people with disabilities) in last place. Financial assistance and benefits, likewise, were determined according to this hierarchical structure, based upon such factors as one's job history and behavior as well as the kind of work being performed. Such a calculus was also applied to determine access to children's camp, resorts, and rest homes. The imbalance in pensions continued after the war, with an enormous gap between what the favored groups of the population received versus everyone else.

As late as 1929, top industry journals published statistics on workplace injuries and articles pointing out the correlation between increased productivity and accident rates; the physical strains and dangers of assembly-line production; and the impact of a three-shift system on worker fatigue and the ensuing injuries, illnesses, and absences. Poor ventilation, insufficient training, neglect or absence of safety protocols and equipment (goggles, for instance), shoddy materials, inadequate medical care, impossible production quotas, and stress on machines from overuse and round-the-clock shifts resulted in serious work-place injuries and fatalities, and the production of industrial goods was matched by the production of disabilities. In addition to mangled limbs, workers lost their vision and hearing, suffered from lung cancer and other respiratory diseases, or were poisoned by toxins. Another factor contributing to the high rate of accidents was the changed composition of the labor force: the vast majority of new workers were recent peasants, many uneducated or only newly literate, unaccustomed to industrial conditions and the pace of urban life and work. Women entering the industrial workforce for the first time faced similar obstacles and injuries.

From this point onward, there were few opportunities available to discuss openly "work invalidism," and the magnitude of the phenomenon remained unacknowledged until after Stalin's death. One forum where public admission was still possible was in reference to the experts on whom these traumas were blamed, a process initiated in 1928 with the Shakhty Trial. In that year, a group of engineers and other technical personnel in the mining industry in Shakhty (in the Donbas region) was arrested and charged with sabotage and colluding with the bourgeoisie abroad to destroy the country's economy. In this inaugural case of "wrecking," as spelled out in Article 58 of the Russian Republic's Penal Code, five of those convicted were executed and the remaining forty-four sent to prison.

On the other end of the spectrum were those in danger of being "wrecked." Significant efforts were made to educate industrial workers and get them to take responsibility for their own well-being. To this end, the Commissariat of Health's Division of "Sanitary Enlightenment" and a cohort of regional Institutes for Sanitary Culture oversaw the production of pamphlets, posters, poems, and even plays depicting a healthy lifestyle (*byt*) for the proletariat. The more benign advice had to do with workers' lives beyond the factory: this meant clean dorm rooms and clothing; personal hygiene; untainted food and water; sanitized dishes, cups, and utensils; exercise; fresh air; and, of course, sobriety.

Within the factory, the main focus of sanitary enlightenment, chiefly in the form of posters, was workplace trauma and accidents. Unlike the amorphous, unidentified victims of wreckage invoked in the Shakhty affair, as depicted in industrial safety education, workers had only themselves to blame. The war against alcohol played an important role in propaganda aimed at workers in both spheres. Outside of the factory, it was held responsible for absences, sick days, tardiness, vision loss from alcohol poisoning, and the dissolution of the family, with the violence that often went with it. Inside the factory walls, alcohol was depicted as even more pernicious and damaging. One poster produced during the First Five-Year Plan showed a man with a sling and bloody bandage where his hand used to be, captioned, "I came to work drunk." Despite the soaked bandage, this poster was downright restrained in the amount of blood it displayed, as compared to many others debuting at the same time, where blood spurted and pooled. Posters showed limbs caught in gears, tools left on scaffolds piercing the skull of the person below, bodies ablaze from matches and cigarettes dropped into flammable liquids, careless workers electrocuted, decapitated, crushed, or impaled.

As with other areas of sanitary enlightenment, health educators conducted research with test audiences to determine which posters were most effective. They discovered that workers were more attentive to the message of posters showing a little blood rather than a lot and responded better to positive images (depicting the moment before an accident occurred) than to negative ones, featuring the violently disabling act itself or the moment immediately following it. Writing in 1932, one education specialist confirmed that these graphic posters were scaring new workers, and contrasted (negatively) the gore of the Soviet versions to the light and humorous tone of safety posters found in the West. Even after the disappearance of statistics and opportunities for professional discussion of workplace injuries and fatalities in the early 1930s, or contacts with the West, for that matter, the Great Medical Encyclopedia nonetheless felt it necessary in 1935 to accuse the West of lying about a purportedly high incidence of industrial accidents in the USSR. Instead, the encyclopedia explained, the vast majority of such occurrences were related to transportation and *non*-mechanized—rather than mechanized—labor.

Nonetheless, these are the images that predominated. There are a number of possible explanations for their gruesome content. First, there could be no ambiguity in who or what was responsible for these accidents: human error, and never the hazardous work itself, or the grueling pace and quotas, and certainly not the ones who put the Plan into place. Absent from visual depictions were the frequent accidents involving storming, socialist competitions, and Stakhanovism. Finally, the new workers' squeamishness aside (which suggests that the posters worked!), bodily violence was an essential and explicit component of Stalinism. In their vividness and ubiquity, these illustrations present a sharp contrast to the handling of injury and disability in the Second World War. During and for a long time afterward, visual depictions of severely injured and disabled soldiers were virtually nonexistent: not even the remotest suggestion of self-mutilation on the part of soldiers could be entertained, although that, along with desertion and draft evasion, certainly occurred.

In addition to posters, a range of different art forms were mobilized to educate the newly disabled masses (and everyone else) about what it meant to be a good versus a bad invalid. This particular genre swelled during and especially after the war, principally in relation to war invalids. *One Million, Two Hundred Thousand*, a silent film made in 1931 by the Central Institute of Disabled Labor, contrasted the heroic invalid-shock worker, celebrated by the worker state, with his (almost always his) prerevolutionary counterpart, whose pain and need were ignored by the callous government, compelling him to beg or rely on charity. One also had to have the right *kind* of disabling event and injury: it had to be someone else's fault, not caused by one's own negligence. Thus a 1939 poster, depicting a male, above-the-knee amputee on crutches, was captioned: "I ignored traffic regulations." *One Million* featured other "bad invalid" types as well. Also implicated were malingerers, as well as workers who took sick days instead of soldiering on through their pain or illness. The same was implied even about those "legitimately" disabled who took a pension, although they still had the capacity to engage in some form of labor.

Industrial safety propaganda occasionally, though infrequently, featured women. One such poster showed a woman whose kerchief was so loose that her hair got caught in a power drill. This is a rare image where we don't see the gore to follow. More often, women in safety propaganda appeared in rural settings, as they did in visual collectivization propaganda, to indicate that this once "backward" population enthusiastically supported the campaign. Except that here, the same strong and happy female collectivizers who had mastered the tractors and other farm equipment were being sucked into fan belts or pierced by agricultural tools. Thus the poster "Be careful with your spade!," in which one of two women working in a field has her head turned away and cuts off the toes of the other. Images of non-Russians—also deemed culturally backward—served a similar function. Captioned "Be careful with pitchforks!," another poster depicted two Central Asian men, one of whom has pierced the leg of the other with the implement. There is blood on the fork and leg, and dripping onto the ground.

Cooperatives

In 1921, the All Russian Cooperative Association of Disabled People (VIKO) was established out of economic necessity, as the state was in no position financially after the civil war to offer much help or job opportunities to this population. Over the next several years, the growth of this mutual aid society was limited, in part due to governmental neglect. The situation changed dramatically by the end of the decade, when the system of closed workshops (*arteli*) and cooperatives expanded rapidly, producing items such as clothing, toys, and shoes, and providing services such as repair work and hairdressing. There were also facilities (*internaty*) that combined functions, providing the disabled with vocational training, an occupation and salary, and room and board. In 1927, invalid cooperatives were extended the same benefits as other cooperatives with the nondisabled enjoyed, such as access to credit. Administered by their own elected officials, VIKO also had its own vacation and rest homes, sports clubs, and cultural programs. About 36,000 people with disabilities worked in the enterprises during the decade, and the All-Russian Organization of the Blind (VOS, 1925) and the All-Russian Organization of the Deaf (VOG, 1926) had their own, similar bodies. VIKO was liquidated in 1956, its workshops appropriated by other enterprises; this move was behind the wheelchair protest described at the beginning of the chapter.

In the context of industrialization, the goal was to get invalids working as soon as medically possible, whether in the cooperative system or in industry.

The Council of People's Commissars (*Sovnarkom*) instructed the localities to make use of whatever potential they could find, including within the ranks of the disabled. Those desiring to work had first to undergo a medical examination (to be discussed below) to determine how much work potential they had retained, and the sort of labor they were capable of performing, be it skilled or unskilled. Once they completed rehabilitation therapy, they received work recommendations and training. For invalids seeking positions in the general workforce and no longer capable of returning to their former profession or of taking up another skilled occupation, at the very least they would free up some of the nondisabled for more physically demanding work. The Commissariat of Labor came up with a list of recommendations for the disabled in these circumstances, including employment as service personnel (courier, cleaner, porter); salespeople (receptionist, clerk, vendor); medical/sanitary workers; railway workers (station masters, guards, conductors); food workers (packer, riveter, packer, etc.); instructors; or foremen. Unsurprisingly, measures put into place to ensure that people with disabilities be hired were largely unsuccessful. A 1931 law required all enterprises to reserve a minimum 2 percent of its total workforce for people with disabilities. Another issued in 1934 obligated former employers to find appropriate jobs for invalids who had lost some but not all of their former work capability. With most possibilities for integrating into the general workforce closed off, people with disabilities turned instead to the closed cooperative and workshop system.

By 1929, inspections of these facilities were conducted by social welfare personnel to confirm that all those working there were severely disabled. Those deemed insufficiently impaired were responsible for finding work through labor bureaus, where they would be competing for jobs with the general population. Those who were not officially disabled but had managed to get a work referral from a physician or medical clinic were barred from the sheltered system beginning in 1933. In turn, by 1935, with the entire population mobilized for industrialization, invalids who wanted to participate in the general workforce were prevented from doing so and restricted to the disability *artels* and cooperatives, leaving all other positions to the nondisabled.

In the determination of whom to recognize as a proper invalid (and hence deserving of state benefits), purges served a second, no less crucial function in the context of early Stalinism: guarding against the infiltration of the workshops by class aliens. There were concerns about non-proletarians penetrating the cooperatives, intent upon destroying them from the inside. In fact, some maintained, *kulaks* and former merchants were *the* most active members of the *artels*; moreover, they were not *really* disabled. What conclusions might be drawn from this formulation? First, as with the intellectually delayed children who were deemed too defective for defectology, class enemies automatically become non-invalids, their social position canceling out their impairment. And second, what did it mean that class enemies, even if faking their disability, outperformed the proletariat?

In order to be permitted to work, those with the most severe disabilities consented to be classified into the higher "functioning" category, to whom employment was permitted. And yet few turned down this opportunity, with the exception of some military invalids, whose pensions were higher. They were motivated by the incentives and privileges to which they would now be entitled, such as free public utilities and access to hard-to-find goods, including prostheses. The reservation system was also quite successful, with the vast majority of positions in industry going to labor invalids and the remainder to other reserved posts. Regardless of where they worked, salaries were low and most likely insufficient to support them fully, given that the vast majority were engaged in unskilled labor.

Purges

Politically, the experience of living with a disability under Stalin was little different from that of anyone else; in its totalizing impulses, this was an equal-opportunity regime. Nor were those with disabilities spared later in the decade from the Great Terror. Perhaps the best-known example was the 1937 Trial of the Leningrad Society of the Deaf-Blind, in which fifty-four members were arrested for belonging to a fascist and terrorist organization. Thirty-four were executed, and the remainder sent to the *Gulag*. The evidence of their treason was a collection of postcards featuring Hitler found in the apartment of a deaf German immigrant who was a member of the Society, and which were included in the packages of the German cigarette brand he smoked.

Another mass persecution action involving people with disabilities during the 1930s took place in Ukraine, which targeted the blind itinerant minstrels known collectively as *kobzary*. Playing the *bandura* (similar to a lute) or *lira* (a kind of hurdy gurdy), they sang traditional folk songs and epics. If the justification for the repression of the deaf Leningraders was a fear of external enemies, this purge was part of the state's repression of what it deemed to be internal ones. As with the broader crackdown on Ukrainian culture, in keeping alive a rich native art form and history, the *kobzars* threatened the Union's "Russia first" nationality policy that gathered momentum after 1932.

Numerous sources claim that there was an organized, large-scale execution of the musicians following a congress of *kobzars* convened on Stalin's orders and held in Khar'kiv, although this has not been confirmed by official documents, and most details of the incident (including the year, place, and method of execution) are disputed. What is certain is that by the late 1930s, traditional blind minstrels had almost completely disappeared, and execution orders for individual *kobzar*s during the decade have been located in the archives.

People with disabilities also were well represented in the *Gulag*, where they died in droves in an unforgiving and inaccessible environment. While there is indirect mention of the existence of scattered prison camps for the infirm and disabled dating back to the first years of the regime, by the 1930s, as the number of camps and prisoners climbed, so, too, among the latter did the disabled. Over the next two decades, a variety of actions were taken to accommodate this growing population. In 1931, camps introduced weak prisoner recovery teams, which gave to those so designated a one- to two-month break from hard labor and increased rations so they could recuperate enough to be returned to the general work force. Understandably, caps were established on how many inmates could be assigned to this detail at any given time. Prisoners whose conditions were deemed permanent enough to disqualify them from ever returning to heavy work were excluded altogether as a pointless drain on resources. Additionally, personnel were always on the lookout for simulators as well as those who mutilated themselves in the hope of hospitalization or even release. Among the most frequent methods, prisoners cut off or intentionally frozen fingers, toes, and limbs, reopened old wounds, or burned themselves. Such efforts were considered sabotage, for which one could be executed or receive an additional camp sentence.

Administrators attempted to identify and weed out the permanently disabled before they could be transported to the camps. A second pool consisted of prisoners made ill or disabled during the lengthy and arduous journey to the camps from European Russia. Whereas, initially, special sections for prisoners with disabilities were established within larger camps, by the end of the war and into the postwar years, a number of camps devoted entirely to disabled prisoners had opened. Simultaneously, medical labor commissions were established across the *Gulag* system to assess prisoners' fitness for work. The biannual inspections were held outside, in view of other inmates and camp staff, and required prisoners to expose their buttocks for commission members to pinch to determine if there was enough fat on them to warrant their return to hard labor.

Medicine and Expertise

Another factor shaping the response to, and experience of, people with disabilities was the role of experts, in particular physicians. The reorientation of Soviet society following Stalin's consolidation of power and the initiation of the industrialization drive entailed a radical transformation of the profession. Medicine underwent a sea change, starting with the purges of the discipline in the Cultural Revolution. Beginning in 1929, specializations originating in the West were eliminated and contact with foreign colleagues cut off; non-proletarian practitioners and those trained and working before the 1917 revolution were suspected; institutes, universities, and journals were closed or had their staffs replaced; and diseases and conditions were retheorized, with any understanding or explanation of illness as emanating from social conditions removed. All these factors shaped the delivery of care and played a role in the profession's unpreparedness for military conflict, evidenced by its poor performance at the skirmishes with the Japanese at Lake Khasan (1938) and Khalkhin Gol (1939), in the war with Finland (1939–40), and, most significantly, during the early stages of the Second World War.

Beyond the hospitals and treatment facilities, where their illnesses and injuries were first treated, the institution with perhaps the greatest and lengthiest influence over the lives of the newly disabled was the Medical Labor Expert Commission (VTEK), established in 1918 as the Bureau of Medical Expertise and renamed as the Medical Expert Commission in 1927, before adopting its current name in 1931. Evaluation by this body would initiate one's formal interaction with the state as a disabled person and the first of many hurdles to acquiring all the things that had been promised. Frequently changing jurisdictional homes (moving between the Commissariats of Labor, Social Work, Health, and the All-Union Central Council of Professional Unions), by 1937 the peripatetic institution was permanently placed in the Commissariat (later Ministry) of Social Welfare.

Before the Revolution, compensation for workplace disability was calculated according to a piece rate system, with certain losses (right arm) valued more highly than others (a foot). With the introduction of welfare payments for disabled people for the first time in Soviet Russia in 1918, invalidism and its compensation were linked explicitly to work performance, rather than to a percentage system of loss weighed against a normative body. In 1921, a six-part disability classification system was introduced, ranging from Group I, for those incapable of performing any work and requiring full-time care, to VI, for those able to continue in their former profession but with lowered productivity. With the reduction of one group from the original six, the system remained in place until 1932.

In response to the sharp increase in workplace injuries associated with industrialization, on February 9, 1932, a three-category, less complicated system replaced the five, a change, which, with minor modifications, would remain in effect until the collapse of the Soviet Union. In the first two iterations of the Soviet classification scale, disability had been determined by how much work capability had been *lost*. According to the new formula, now disability would be calculated according to how much work potential *remained*. Those who had completely lost their ability to work and required full-time care were assigned to Group I; Group II was for those who couldn't work but did not need outside care; and Group III was designated for those unable to resume their former occupation under the same conditions as before, but whose condition would allow for some work that was either irregular, with a shortened workday, or significantly lower qualifications.

Comprised of three physicians (therapist, neuropathologist, and surgeon) and one representative each from the All-Union Central Council of Trade Unions and the Commissariat of Social Welfare, VTEK boards determined the nature and cause of the subject's impairment and the likelihood of restoring work-readiness. Ideally, the invalid would resume his *former* occupation; by the beginning of the Second World War, returning to one's prewar position meant effectively that one was no longer disabled, and hence ineligible for the (meager) benefits to which war invalids were entitled.

The Great Patriotic War

Hundreds upon hundreds of thousands of soldiers returned home disabled from the Second World War. Beyond its proclamations of indebtedness for their sacrifices, as a matter of policy, the state sought to rid itself of them as soon as possible. One method, as mentioned above, occurred at the level of representation. Other than a few iconographic examples, visual depictions of the Invalids of the Patriotic War (IOV), as they were known, went missing from popular culture and commemorative practices. Several other strategies also served to make their damaged bodies disappear.

One involved the physical removal of the most severely disabled to boarding facilities where they could get care or learn a trade (*internat bol'nichnogo tipa*, or *dom invalidov*), far from public view. A number of factors motivated this response, among which offending public sensibilities was certainly one. Both during and after the war, the spectacle of amputee veterans in uniform, begging on street corners and in crowded railway stations was common, a constant reminder of the brutality of war *and* of the state's neglect. Others were rounded up as part of the postwar crackdown on "antisocial and parasitical elements." Those who had nowhere else to go (meaning no one who would accept financial responsibility for their care) also ended up here. Often they went voluntarily, to avoid being a burden to their families.

Conditions in these places varied, but many were without some or all of the following: running water, access to a banya, soap, coats, blankets, linens, shoes, wool tights, winter clothing, boots, fuel, dishes, and cutlery (at the

Andoga Internat in Vologda *oblast'*, the 132 inhabitants shared 14 glasses and 30 spoons). Often there was little to eat above subsistence-level rations, in part because it was expected that the patients would grow their own food and raise livestock. (Facilities for disabled children were similarly unprovisioned, usually with even less food.) Given the poor pay and remote locations, it was difficult to retain workers, not to mention qualified medical personnel. A number of staff engaged in criminal behavior, appropriating or reselling items meant for the inhabitants; only a few of these were ever prosecuted.

Prostheses represented another solution for those whose disabilities could be masked. Yet, for all the celebration of artificial limbs and their role in getting invalids back to work and to the collective, the Soviet prosthetics industry was not up to the task. Deficiencies in planning, communication, training, transport, materials, and the manufacturing process itself led to whole-scale technological failure and for many invalids, the experience of acquiring an artificial limb could be prolonged, humiliating, and often painful. First, there was the colossal demand alone: the small number of prosthetic research institutes and manufacturers operating at the start of the war were utterly unprepared and overwhelmed. The Ministries of Social Welfare and Health, each responsible for different types of devices, were embroiled in a prolonged turf battle over control of the industry. Labor shortages meant that factories were often understaffed and undertrained, resulting in shoddy construction and requiring the wearers to return the limbs for repairs several times a year (according to one report, it was unusual if a device did *not* break during the first three months). Sometimes repairs stretched for many months or even years. Primitive conditions made standardization next to impossible. At the farthest possible remove from the assembly-line model of production, an individual prosthesis might be entirely fabricated and assembled manually, by a single worker.

The disabled were required to make repeated trips, some traveling great distances, for fittings and receipt of the devices and subjected to long delays waiting for their appointments, typically in unheated corridors with no place to sit (including for those missing legs). There were no accommodations provided for those forced to wait overnight or longer and, once in receipt of their limbs, they were given little instruction in how to properly use and care for them. Not surprisingly, many chose to forego wearing their prosthetics entirely, or used them purely cosmetically. The inadequacies of the industry continued into the late 1950s.

Finally, there was the state's ongoing practice of revising disability classifications to reduce its substantial support obligations to invalided veterans, effectively defining this population out of existence. First developed in response to the massive number of injuries resulting from the brutal conditions of industrialization, this calculus was then applied to the massive number of injuries resulting from the brutal conditions of war. Less than two months after Barbarossa commenced on June 22, 1941, the Commissariat of Social Welfare issued its first wartime revision to the 1932 protocols. Emphasizing the urgency of mobilizing as large a labor force as possible, the directive called for VTEK boards to be more exacting in their assessments. Furthermore, if VTEK found no medical contra-indications, invalids would be subject to the common wartime work schedules, including night work and overtime, from which they had earlier been exempted. That so many previously nonworking invalids were now classified as fit to work greatly boosted the state's triumphant claims about its success and devotion in treating and rehabilitating the war disabled.

Because so many VTEK physicians were reluctant to award invalid classifications more strictly, in June of 1942, the People's Commissariat of Social Welfare changed them. Of chief importance in the modified directive was the revision to Category II. Whereas earlier the classification signified that the designee was incapable of performing any kind of work, in the new version it was redefined as meaning work-ready, even if at a greatly reduced skill level and salary. Further, regardless of the severity of one's disability/ies, any invalid returning to his previous or a similar occupation and making the same salary as before the injury, was not disabled (for purposes of pensions). Thus a right-handed bookkeeper who had lost both legs and his left arm but could resume his former profession was entitled to no compensation for his physical sacrifices.

Initially, patients were required to have follow-up exams every six months for Categories II and III, and twelve months for Category I to reassess any changes in the invalid's work capacity, whether owing to a general improvement in their health or to their adaptation to prosthetics or other assistive devices. Not only would this free up less demanding jobs for more challenging or skilled ones but also would allow benefits to be adjusted accordingly. Beginning in November 1942, all Category II designees, with their six-month window, were subject to reevaluation within the following *two* months, regardless of when their next appearance was scheduled to take place. In addition, it was expected that going forward fewer war-wounded would be given an initial classification of Category II to begin with. The effort was successful: whereas 52.7 percent received this designation in 1942, the number declined to 35.4 percent in 1944 and 21.1 percent in 1948. Given the strains under which VTEK already routinely operated, this call for the reexamination of all Category II disabled within two months doubtless placed an enormous additional burden on these bodies. It also demonstrates an urgency bordering on desperation on the part of the state.

In January 1943, A. N. Sukhov replaced A. P. Grishakova, the previous Commissar of Social Welfare, after she was fired for her "unclear" approach toward the IOV, meaning, presumably, that her efforts to get more of them working were deemed inadequate. Shortly thereafter, an order was issued mandating that all Group III men under the age of 52 and women under the age of 45 work, or they would lose their pension. The measure had the desired effect: their numbers increased dramatically. In fact, so many Category III were removed from the pension rolls that Sukhov himself intervened, issuing a special order against the "groundless, mechanistic" application of the law.

In May 1943, the interval between exams was halved, obliging Group I designees to appear every six months and Groups II and III every three months. Notably, the reexamination schedule for labor invalids remained as it had been: once a year for Group I and every six months for Groups II and III. They justified the shorter deadline for war invalids, who were younger and (initially) healthier than industrial workers, by noting that substantial improvement in the health of IOV's, and hence fitness for work, often occurred long before the next scheduled appearance. By the fall of 1943, VTEK actively worked to reduce the number of those originally assigned to Group II. According to social welfare statistics, although 52.7 percent received this designation in 1942, this number declined to 35.4 percent in 1944 and 21.1 in 1948.

War invalids with irreversible conditions such as complete blindness bitterly objected to having to recertify their impairments. Motivated perhaps by recognition of the senselessness of this requirement, in December 1943, Politburo member V. M. Molotov (1890–1986), Deputy Premier as well as People's Commissar of Foreign Affairs, decreed that war and labor invalids in this category be required to appear only once per year. Yet Molotov's intervention didn't go far enough for the Red Army, which petitioned to have these war veterans exempted altogether from reevaluations, a request that was denied. Only in 1956 did VTEK publish a list of permanent conditions for which it was no longer necessary to recertify.

Those dissatisfied with their VTEK designation could appeal to the regional VTEK office. Officially, recourse stopped with that decision, though many continued to seek redress above and around that administrative body. Most frequently protesting a Group III classification, veterans wrote to the Commissariat of Social Welfare, the Army, the trade unions, the Council of People's Commissars (or Council of Ministers after March 1946), the Supreme Soviet, the Central Executive Committee, newspapers, journals, and important individuals; few decisions were successfully overturned. One dissatisfied veteran, himself an employee of the Ministry (People's Commissariat) of Social Welfare (the organization administrating VTEK), who was missing a leg and using an artificial limb was assigned to Category III, while someone else with the identical amputation who appeared on crutches was awarded Category II.

IOV registered other injustices as well. However hard the state tried to advance a definition of disability as the inability to work, many were not buying it. In 1946, blind and handless Captain I. P. Tsvetaev, an engineer from Odessa before the war, wrote to Stalin, complaining about the unfairness of a system that equated him by classification (and thus pension) with someone only missing his legs, as the latter was physically capable of performing a desk job.

At the time, the most acceptable way to air grievances was via appeal to an agency, a newspaper, or, failing that, an Important Person. The state monitored expressions of dissent that went much beyond that for evidence of more serious and potentially seditious speech; it was particularly concerned about discontent on the part of war veterans, whether disabled or not, who already had a separate, collective identity. Many war invalids ended up in the *Gulag* at one of the camps established for people with disabilities, such as the Spasskaia Labor Colony in Central Asia.

Nervous Disorders and Mental Illness

In the late 1920s and 1930s, Soviet psychiatrists were applying many of the same methods as their foreign counterparts to people with mental disturbances, both mild and severe. Conditions warranting more attention and of greater potential danger to themselves and others, such as schizophrenia, dementia, clinical depression, and neurosyphilis, ideally would be cared for on an in-patient basis. Of the various treatments attempted, it was the introduction of shock therapies and especially insulin shock therapy in 1936 that was hailed by practitioners as a wonder drug, potentially capable of radically transforming the practice of psychiatry and the care of the mentally ill.

At the outset of the First Five-Year Plan, psychiatric hospitals were in dire shape: shabby and dilapidated buildings with too many patients and too few staff. In Saratov, one facility had 360 beds for 550 patients, and of the 2 million residents in the region, 6,000 were in need of psychiatric treatment, with half of those requiring hospitalization. Often, there were no resources or personnel to conduct labor therapy, deemed the core of rehabilitative care throughout the Stalinist era. Worker turnover was frequent due to low pay, violent patients, and, when the war came, the exodus of many to the front.

While there were certainly some model institutions, offering a range of therapies in clean, fully staffed, and modern wards, many were closer to what Molotov's letter writer described above. Some hospitals lacked a separate section for those deemed dangerous, or had men and women sharing bathing facilities and wards, while others lacked electricity and other basic necessities; a building in Voronezh was missing a roof. Ambulances refused to transport the mentally ill to psychiatric hospitals, dropping them instead at general hospitals or the nearest psychiatric outpatient clinic. Facility directors petitioned to keep for their own patients' use some of the items produced in their workshops, one saying, "We sit here naked, undressed, unshod, but give away our wool."

By far, the biggest problem faced by psychiatrists working in hospitals was the surplus of the chronically ill, leaving almost no room for new patients who needed immediate attention. These long-term patients had not responded to treatment and were too dangerous to discharge; others were forced to remain because their families could not afford to care for them. Whereas previously, in rural locations some mentally ill were looked after by their families or by other households paid to take them in, collectivization had put an end to the practice. *Kolkhoz* leadership and village councils were afraid of them; moreover, as one hospital chief complained, collective farm leadership did nothing to protect returning patients from ridicule and abuse.

Shown to be effective with this category of long-term patients, insulin shock therapy was expensive, required quiet, separate spaces, and oversight for ten to twelve hours per session by staff who were sorely needed elsewhere. Its use, therefore, was restricted to just a few institutions located in places like Moscow, Kiev, and Leningrad. Whatever enthusiasm greeted insulin and other shock therapies as a curative before the war, after the invasion by Germany, the goal in most Soviet psychiatric hospitals was basic survival, for the buildings and the patients. Despite heroic efforts by many hospital workers to save them, most mentally and intellectually disabled patients (including children) in the country's western territories, such as Litvinov Psychiatric Hospital in Kalinin Region and Mogilev Republic Psychiatric Hospital in Belarus, suffered the same fate as did the disabled and Jewish staff shot or gassed in other German-occupied countries. With so many treatment facilities destroyed or severely damaged during the war, the same problems of poverty, an excess of patients, and shortages of space and staff continued to be major obstacles to effective treatment for many years afterward. After the war, electroshock therapy was widely utilized because it required only electricity. Crowding became such an issue that in some hospitals two patients shared one bed.

Outside of hospitals, in the 1920s, the Soviet Union was plagued by an entirely different species of mental upset: an "epidemic" of weak and exhausted nerves. Psychiatrists attributed this phenomenon to the heady and stimulating tempo of life after the 1917 Revolution, and counseled rest, healthy food and lifestyle, and the avoidance of overwork: essentially a dampening of revolutionary enthusiasm. Such asceticism was incompatible with the goals and pace of industrialization, with its overfulfilled plans, staged competitions, and the completion of the First Five-Year Plan a year early. Most of those psychiatrists who subscribed to the theory of nervous exhaustion were purged during the Cultural Revolution of the early 1930s.

In the 1930s, leading (surviving) psychiatrists argued instead that most activists, including members of the Party, avoided these dangers through the power of their will. In those lacking, severe disruptions to the environment and body could result in *physical* injury to the nervous system, and for those with the predisposition, a full-blown case of the disorder. With the war, psychiatrists were greatly concerned about the nerves of soldiers. Like their colleagues elsewhere, Soviet psychiatrists debated whether war neurosis (known in other contexts as hysteria or shell-shock) was caused by somatic or psychic disruptions. By this time Western practitioners had largely settled this question for themselves in favor of a mental rather than a physical cause.

For soldiers presenting with symptoms including paralysis; tremors; confusion; impaired speech, hearing, or vision; nightmares or insomnia; heart palpitations; and disorientation at the start of the war, the recommended treatment was a short rest, ample food, and then back to one's unit. It was stressed that under no conditions should soldiers be moved from the front, nor ever entertain the possibility as a way to avoid military service. In fact, the number of soldiers with mental fatigue was proportionally higher in the Soviet Union than elsewhere, as the country did not follow the standard practice of providing regular rest leaves for mental health reasons.

Protocol and circumstances gradually changed. By 1942, those presenting with psychological trauma went to newly established transition hospitals nearer but not on the front, and after a twenty-day rest, either returned to their units or were transported further east for more intensive treatment. Psychiatrists noted that half the soldiers in these hospitals diagnosed as "concussed," which meant, in this case, a head injury with no discernible physical symptoms, were not responding to the standard treatments. As with "shell-shocked" soldiers of the First World War, the only successful remedy for war neurosis was the talking cure of psychotherapy, and the competition between psyche and soma in the USSR was resolved in favor of the former.

Conclusion

After the war, becoming injured in defense of one's country was no longer sufficient evidence of dedication to the state; additional sacrifices were called for in the name of postwar reconstruction. To rebuild the country's devastated economy and infrastructure, those with disabilities, like everyone else, were expected to work. Beyond the general ideological value of labor, the ability to work was deemed to be central to a wounded soldier's recovery, and labor therapy was used in all treatment and rehabilitation centers. Moreover, disability benefits were too low to live on without supplemental income from working.

Regardless of the country's grave labor shortage once the war began, veterans with disabilities nonetheless encountered numerous impediments to working. State laws requiring factories to take people whose impairments would not interfere with work performance were ignored, despite the (unenforced) penalties attached. The situation became even worse after the war ended, with administrators and managers often outright refusing to hire disabled veterans to make room for demobilizing, nondisabled servicemen, or offering them low-status and low-paying jobs, such as that of security guard. Ironically, few invalids (25 percent!) worked in the system of invalid artels and cooperatives established specifically for them before the war. Options for vocational training were limited, and not necessarily popular, available, or nearby. Commenting on the frequent practice of sending blind veterans to accordion (*baian*) school, social welfare personnel complained on more than one occasion that the country was saturated already with blind accordionists and that a more useful occupation had to be found for them.

Note

1 While the word *disabil'nost'* is becoming more common, *invalidnost'* and "invalid" remain the accepted terms in professional and popular lexicon.

8

Gender and Sexuality

Amy Randall

Let us imagine a few social types in Imperial Russia—a married Russian peasant woman, a gay soldier, and a Muslim urban Uzbek woman—and how their lives might have been transformed by the Russian Revolution. If in 1912 the young peasant wife Masha had to endure a loveless marriage with a philandering husband because divorce was virtually unattainable, in the new Soviet Union of the 1920s she could leave her marriage by request. If Masha became pregnant in Imperial Russia, she had to become a mother unless she procured an illegal abortion, whereas in the 1920s she could choose to keep or terminate a pregnancy. Meanwhile, if in prerevolutionary times, the soldier Pyotr had reason to fear a potential blackmailer, or arrest and imprisonment, as he strolled on Nevskii Prospekt in St. Petersburg in search of a same-sex liaison, in the 1920s Pyotr could cruise gay men in Leningrad without fear of criminal sodomy charges because of its decriminalization in the new Soviet Russia. If in Imperial Russia Mirza had been compelled to wear some kind of veil in public, a tradition among urban and wealthier women in some parts of Central Asia, in the second half of the 1920s the Communist Party launched a campaign to end this practice, which she may or may not have supported. Moreover, if Mirza had been unable to procure higher education before the Revolution because of traditional gender norms, in the 1920s she could pursue it as the new Communist regime developed educational opportunities for women as well as men throughout the new Soviet Union.

At first glance, these social types, and the transformations they experienced, might suggest a narrative of oppression in Imperial Russia and liberation in the Soviet Union. This narrative of progress, however, does not do justice to the complexity of the Soviet approach to gender and sexuality in the first decade after the Revolution. Nor does it contextualize how certain "Soviet" ideas and policies were not *sui generis* but rather linked to prerevolutionary trends and changes. Thus, for example, some of the Jadidists (Muslim reformers) in Central Asia, who called for increased education of girls and women in Imperial Russia, became Communists who advanced this cause after the 1917 Revolution.

When it comes to changes in Soviet policies and discourses about gender and sexuality, the transition from the postrevolutionary years of the 1920s to the Stalin era is often framed by scholars in a similar way as the transition from Imperial Russia to the Soviet Union, but with the terms reversed: the changes under Stalin's rule are viewed as a turn to a more coercive and conservative order. If in 1936 the peasant Masha wanted to pursue divorce or an abortion, she faced new Soviet family laws restricting divorce and banning most abortions. Meanwhile, under Stalin's rule in 1934, the soldier Pyotr could no longer pursue same-sex relations without risk of punishment because of a new anti-sodomy law. And if Mirza's daughter was in school in Central Asia in the late 1930s, she might have been forced to learn Russian when the Communist leadership decreed it a compulsory second language in all non-Russian middle schools.

Scholarship that has argued that the Soviet approach to gender and sexuality was relatively more radical/progressive and emancipatory in the 1920s, and more reactionary/traditional and instrumental during the Stalin era, has yielded important insights into the history and politics of the "woman" question, the Soviet family, Bolshevik feminism, women and wage labor, gender and empire, sexual minorities, and other related topics. Nonetheless, as many scholars have noted, this analytic framework has obscured some of the complexities and contradictions, as well as continuities, in early Soviet and Stalinist discourses and policies.

This chapter explores gender and sexuality during Stalin's rule. It considers femininities and masculinities, gender identities and relations, sexual norms and practices, and sexual politics and identities. The Stalinist gender and sexual order was not unchanging, uniform, consistent, or entirely new; it was inextricably linked to Soviet discourses and policies about national minorities, religion, class, and broader historical events as well as gender and sexual norms and identities in Imperial Russia and early Soviet rule. It consisted of emancipatory and "radical" as well as repressive and conservative policies. At its core, the Stalinist gender and sexual order was designed to be in service to the Party-state, and was oriented toward mobilizing the populace to promote modernization, grow Soviet power, and advance a new industrial "Soviet" socialism.[1]

When the Bolsheviks established a new Communist government in 1917, they sought to create not only a new political and economic reality but also a new society in which the Russian people as well as national minorities in the newly constituted USSR would be radically transformed. To do this, the leadership introduced new laws, institutions, policies and practices. It also promoted the New Soviet Man and Soviet BecWoman, archetypes whom the populace was supposed to emulate. When Stalin established control in the late 1920s and launched his "Revolution from Above," he continued to pursue the early Bolshevik goal of widespread transformation, though he modified some polices, introduced new as well as more restrictive measures, and expanded the use of repression to achieve change.

Soviet propaganda, literature, and Party-state discourses characterized the New Soviet Man in the Stalin era, as in the 1920s, as a soldier defending the motherland from the threat of counterrevolution or war, an industrial worker laboring on the industrial "front," and a stalwart member of the Communist Party dedicated to the construction of a bright new future. In addition to these archetypes, the New Soviet Man in the Stalin era could also be a collective farm worker rather than a traditional *muzhik*, struggling to achieve a modern new agricultural order; a labor hero who outperformed others; and a master of technology and nature, such as a Soviet aviator, whose accomplishments signaled the educational, scientific, and industrial advances of socialism. In keeping with Stalinist nationality policy, the New Soviet Man was not necessarily Russian, but if he was from one of the Soviet Union's many national minorities, he was sometimes portrayed as having overcome cultural backwardness and benefiting from the tutelage of fellow Russians who were promoted in the 1930s as the "first among equals," as ostensibly the most revolutionary and "Soviet" ethnicity in the country. The New Soviet Man was supposed to be secular and reject what Communist leaders considered to be religious and unenlightened ways. Under Stalin, he was also represented as a model of culturedness (*kul'turnost'*), a man who displayed cultured behavior and taste. In general, the New Soviet Man demonstrated manly courage and strength, allegedly made possible by Stalin's leadership and by male camaraderie, a fraternal band of brothers under Father Stalin's direction. The New Soviet Man was supposed to be heterosexual, get married, and have children as well, but relegate his family to secondary priority as he performed a hegemonic robust masculinity on behalf of the Party-state.

In the Stalin years, as in the 1920s, the ideal New Soviet Woman was a working mother who produced children for the new socialist order; engaged in agricultural, industrial, or other wage labor; and took on public duties to help realize the new society. The New Soviet Woman was also modern and secular, hence not constrained by traditional peasant, ethnic, or religious practices. She did not wear *lapti* (bast sandals) or seek medical advice from *znakharki* (traditional wise women), nor did she wear a veil or remain secluded in the home. In contrast to the 1920s, the Stalinist government promoted several additional versions of the New Soviet Woman: the unemployed wife activist, who engaged in social mothering and civic housekeeping for the nation; the female collective farm worker who helped to create a new agricultural system; the female citizen-soldier who participated in direct combat to defend the Motherland; and the female luminary, whose achievements were celebrated publicly. In the late Stalin era, the party-state promoted yet another version of the New Soviet Woman: the *unmarried* working mother, whose virtue was officially defined by her reproductive and productive contributions to the state rather than some "bourgeois" notion of sexual morality and marital status.

The Family

If there had been some talk about the "withering away of the family" among Bolshevik radicals during the Revolution and early Soviet years—which Karl Marx and Friedrich Engels had earlier suggested would happen under communism—the new Communist government quickly clarified that this did not mean the eradication of the family altogether, but the eradication of the "bourgeois" model of family, in which women were exploited and treated as the property of men. In 1918, the government promoted the legitimacy of marriage and the family in the Soviet context by adopting a new Family Code that made marriage a civil rather than a religious matter, simplified divorce so that it was affordable and equally attainable by the male or female spouse, and granted the same legal rights to children produced in registered and unregistered unions. In 1926, it further undermined religious marriage and the bourgeois family by affirming the legitimacy of de facto marriages, and granting cohabitating couples the same rights and duties as those in "official" marriages. More generally, the Communist regime sought to eliminate not only bourgeois but also other patriarchal models of marriage and the family, including those of the "backwards" peasantry and national minorities. Targeting traditional cultural customs and religious practices, Soviet leaders established a minimum marriage age to end child marriages, banned bride price as well as polygyny, and promoted equal inheritance laws. In promoting these changes, the new Soviet regime claimed to "liberate" women and girls from traditional patriarchal marital and familial practices so that they could participate in the building of socialism. The ideal new Soviet family, comprised of a free and equal union between a man and woman who procreated, would advance the Party-state's goals. The reality of Soviet families was much more complex, however, and many women remained in difficult and abusive marriages because of social norms and the lack of economic opportunities to strike out on their own.

Under Stalin, a new Family Code of 1936 made divorce more difficult and expensive, strengthened men's responsibility for child support, and banned most abortions. Many scholars have interpreted these changes as proof of a Stalinist retreat from revolutionary values and a move toward a more conservative family model. Interestingly, many members of the Soviet populace—particularly women—expressed approval for the new restrictions on divorce. Divorce rates had skyrocketed in the 1920s and in the first half of the 1930s, usually at the behest of men, and women often suffered significant financial problems when their marriages ended. Although the new divorce procedures sought to strengthen family stability, after a temporary decline from 1936 to 1938, the percentage of divorces continued to increase.

If the changes in divorce law entailed a departure from the regime's earlier revolutionary ideas about free and equal unions by making it harder for people to leave unhappy marriages, some aspects of the Family Code did not. The code's focus on fathers' and husbands' financial duties amplified earlier Soviet family policies to combat male irresponsibility and was approved of by many women who wanted more stringent measures to ensure men's payment of child support. Another "radical" aspect of family policy remained unchanged: de facto marriages and divorces continued to be recognized, with attendant legal and financial duties for children born of such unions. Stalinist family policy was intended to bolster family stability and paternal responsibility so that women would have more children. It did not promote a return to a traditional prerevolutionary patriarchal model of the family, in which men had legal dominance and authority, and the family was a private entity separate from the state. Nor did the new family policy encourage women to return to the home and abandon wage labor. Stalinist family policy aimed to mobilize a modern and civic family that would advance Soviet objectives.

The 1936 abortion ban was a retreat from the regime's policy of allowing women to control their own bodies and lives. For Masha, discussed earlier, having an unwanted pregnancy or seeking an illegal abortion might have ended her studies, career advancement, or even her life. The Stalinist volte-face in abortion policy, however, was not a radical change in the Soviet leadership's perception of the procedure, which it had neither condoned nor considered a woman's right when legalizing it in 1920. Instead, the political elite had viewed it as a public health necessity—a necessary "evil" given the high rates of illegal abortions, their harmful effects on women's health, and the poverty that led many women to seek one. The excuse for recriminalizing abortion was also couched partly in health terms; the alleged deleterious effects of the procedure combined with the alleged improvement in people's material conditions made child rearing easier and abortion unnecessary. In actuality, recriminalization stemmed from official concern about the falling Soviet birth rate, particularly among Slavic populations. This is evident from a simultaneous secret government decision to limit access to contraception, even if this was already largely unavailable because of inadequate funding and supplies. Although the regime hoped to bolster procreation by banning most abortions, an initial surge in the Soviet birth rate was followed by a decrease in the late 1930s. Moreover, despite the procedure's new illegality, there was only a slight and temporary decrease in abortions after 1936. In the absence of contraception, illegal abortion served as a de facto method of birth control. As women turned to "back-alley" abortions, which posed greater risks than legal abortions, there was a sizable increase in abortion-related health complications, including death.

For many non-Slavic women, such as Kazakh and other Central Asian women, the abortion ban had little to no effect on their reproductive practices because the termination of unwanted pregnancies was culturally taboo, and abortion rates were quite low. The abortion ban was accompanied by pronatalist measures, however, that did affect the daily lives of at least some Central Asian and other women who had large families. More specifically, the new Stalinist policy of awarding birth bonuses in the form of annual state allowances for mothers with seven or more children provided social prestige and important monetary assistance (albeit limited). Trumpeting the government's role in easing the burdens of motherhood to legitimize Communist rule, the Stalinist regime pointed in particular to how the plight of female national minorities had improved; birth bonuses, in conjunction with other new pronatalist measures, such as increased funding for the expansion of maternity homes, children's nurseries, and kindergartens, underscored the Soviet break from the "backward" past. Purportedly, rural and urban as well as Slavic and non-Slavic mothers were the happy beneficiaries of the Soviet commitment to improving the lives of mothers and children.

Soviet pronatalism was not new under Stalin; since the early days of the Revolution, Communist leaders, including even radical Bolshevik feminists such as Aleksandra Kollontai (1872–1952), had praised motherhood as woman's natural and civic obligation, and adopted various measures to protect and encourage it.[2] Stalinist birth bonuses for mothers of large families, however, were novel. During the Second World War, the government sought to further incentivize motherhood by reducing the number of children necessary to receive birth bonuses. It established a tax on bachelors, childless adults, and couples with fewer than three children, underscoring to men *and* women the patriotic duty to procreate. Communist authorities also introduced new maternity awards to further glorify motherhood. Such pronatalist policies were not uniquely Soviet. In the interwar era, many European governments viewed reproduction as a state matter and adopted similar measures to increase populations, while also restricting access to birth control and abortion.

male role

In the ideal Stalinist family, gender roles were fixed. Women assumed primary responsibility for the household and child rearing, even when working full time. Meanwhile, Soviet leaders expected men to marry, procreate, and provide financial assistance to their families, but not to engage actively in domestic chores and children's upbringing, expectations mirrored in daily life. By affording women equal legal rights and greater economic autonomy as well as establishing a "state-mother-child-triad," early Soviet policies undermined the institution of fatherhood, diminished men's family authority, and fostered gender asymmetry in parenting. During the Stalin era, in actuality, some fathers were actively involved in family affairs, and many men retained a dominant family position. Still, Stalinist policies in the 1930s reinforced fathers' discursive and legal marginality by removing them from their families via forced collectivization and dekulakization, the drive for rapid industrialization, and the purges. The Second World War ruptured men's connection to their families even more, as many fathers marched off to war from which most never returned.

Work

In the early Soviet years, Communist leaders promoted a social contract with women that encouraged them to pursue full-time employment and motherhood, supported by maternity leave, state-sponsored childcare, and other resources and benefits, but it was only in the Stalin era that the Party-state ideal of the Soviet working mother became a significant reality. The mass influx of women into the wage economy began in 1929. As families struggled in the face of declining real wages and living conditions, many households that had previously functioned with one wage-earner needed two to make ends meet, and more women turned to paid labor. This organic process was harnessed by the Stalinist regime. Faced with the ambitious goals of the First Five-Year Plan and enormous male labor shortages, it launched a campaign to recruit women, and between 1929 and 1941, over 10 million women joined the industrial labor force and service sector. Although female employment varied by region and nationality, by 1939, women made up 39 percent of the paid workforce. A 1942 labor conscription decree and wartime propaganda contributed to a significant wartime increase of women workers. By 1950, women constituted half of the workers in the national economy (excluding agriculture).

Instead of integrating women from the outset as equals alongside men in all sectors of the economy, Soviet authorities pursued a policy of labor inclusion through segregation. They encouraged new women workers to pursue jobs in traditionally "female" sectors of the economy. In addition, the regime regendered the economy and labor force by reassigning positions that had previously been designated as male as primarily or exclusively female. Soviet policies opened up employment opportunities for women, affording them new skills and training as well as greater entry into rapidly expanding sectors of heavy industry, such as mining and metallurgy. Nonetheless, because of hostility against women workers, central directives to promote female skilled labor were often undermined at the local level. As Zueva, a railroad worker during the 1930s, explained: "Men see the woman worker as an enemy, a wrecker of production, not a comrade."[3] When women filled jobs formerly held by men, they mostly worked as unskilled and semiskilled laborers, and rarely held managerial and other leadership positions. Ultimately, the regime's policies reinforced a gendered division of labor, which meant that "women's work"—even in previously "male" sectors—tended to be less prestigious and lower-paying than "men's work." Meanwhile, labor laws to protect working women's reproductive capacity, such as exempting nursing mothers from night shifts and providing them with breastfeeding breaks, were often not enforced. The gap between Party-state policies about women workers and actual workplace practices persisted in the postwar period. Nonetheless, despite discrimination, harassment, and limitations on professional advancement, Soviet women took pride in their work. As Tania, a construction engineer, noted, "Work was my life. At first I worked in order to live, later it was more, it went deeper inside and as a result it turns out that I cannot imagine myself without work."[4]

Just as wage labor was gendered, so too was unpaid labor in the home. In the early Soviet years, Bolshevik leader Vladimir Lenin denounced the drudgery of housework, Party-state leaders called for the increased socialization of housework and childcare, and propaganda heralded women's liberation from "kitchen slavery." Innovations such as maternity leave, communal childcare, public kitchens, and laundries were intended to allow women to enter and remain in the paid workforce with fewer biological or domestic constraints. During the New Economic Policy (NEP) era of the 1920s, however, state expenditures for such resources dropped significantly, and many factories and other workplaces allowed existing services and facilities to atrophy. It was only during the Stalinist drive for rapid industrialization and modernization that a substantial network of nurseries, kindergartens, public canteens, and laundries began to develop. From 1928 to 1936 the number of children in childcare centers increased tenfold. The number of communal dining halls also multiplied significantly, serving approximately 25.5 million citizens by 1933. Given the overall number of women entering wage labor, and an overall population of approximately 165 million in the mid-1930s, even such significant increases in resources were entirely insufficient to meet demand. Meanwhile, in the new socialist society, an assumption of "natural" sexual differences

women had to fill two roles

between men and women remained. As domestic work and childrearing continued to be associated with women, working mothers struggled to fulfill their dual roles as mother/homemaker and laborer.

In its initial years, Stalin's policy of forced agricultural collectivization devastated peasant men and women alike, and millions lost their lives in the resulting famine of 1932 and 1933. Collectivization was intended to be an efficient and modern agricultural system for fueling rapid industrialization and extending Soviet power into rural communities. In Central Asian regions with nomadic national minorities, such as Kazakhstan, Kyrgystan, and Turkmenistan, it was also an instrument to compel people to settle down and become "Soviet." Dekulakization, the forced removal of "*kulaks*" (wealthy peasants) supposedly opposed to collectivization, led to the summary execution of tens of thousands and the exile and deportation of millions from their villages.[5] Stalinist propaganda, nonetheless, touted the importance and successes of collective farming. Frequently, it featured a young woman as the public face of the new agricultural landscape, who represented the transformation of the "backwards" *baba* into a *kolkhoznitsa* (female collective farmer), capable of mastering new ideas, processes, and technologies. Visual culture frequently depicted this new *kolkhoznitsa* as a tractor driver, underscoring women's new opportunities and the benefits of agricultural mechanization. To some extent the discursive centrality of the image of the *kolkhoznitsa* reflected reality; as millions of men departed the countryside because of dekulakization or the search for industrial jobs, women played an increasingly important role in agriculture. But even so, men occupied the vast majority of leadership posts because of discrimination and a gendered division of rural labor, despite repeated instructions from the central government to promote women. Moreover, many men ignored or undermined the few women in higher positions, sometimes violently.

The official celebration of the *kolkhoznitsa* stood in stark contrast to the reality of hundreds if not thousands of *bab'i bunty* (women's riots) against collectivization in its early years.[6] Frequently at the forefront of peasant resistance, women in Slavic and Central Asian regions blocked efforts at grain requisitioning and dekulakization, repossessed "socialized" seed and livestock, and verbally and physically abused Soviet officials and activists promoting the new agricultural policies. Interestingly, peasant men often stood back from the angry women, and joined in protests only when they could justify their actions as masculine rather than anti-Soviet—for example, that they were safeguarding female relatives. Because Party-state authorities did not usually utilize force against these unruly peasant women, and rarely punished them compared to their male counterparts, women's riots allowed for the relatively safe expression of peasant resistance to Soviet policies. Communist and rural leaders tended to characterize women's opposition as a product of irrational female behavior and *kulak* manipulation as a way to diminish its significance. The rebellious women, however, often articulated specific goals and rational socioeconomic interests as they obstructed Soviet collectivization.

If the *kolkhoznitsa* served as the public face of collectivization, the male industrial labor hero served as the public face of Stalin's drive for rapid industrialization.[7] Although the male worker had been central to Soviet imagery in the 1920s, the Stalinist regime promoted the labor hero as another version of the New Soviet Man in the 1930s. Whether a "shock worker" engaged in socialist competition, or a "Stakhanovite," this was a brawny heroic worker who went above and beyond to achieve greater productivity. The term Stakhanovite came from Alexei Stakhanov, a Donbas miner who allegedly hewed 102 tons of coals instead of the 6.5 norm in one shift in 1935. Industrial leaders applauded and rewarded Stakhanov for his "individual" feat, even though he had auxiliary assistance, and encouraged others to emulate his purported strength, will power, and novel work techniques to surpass production quotas. As Stakhanovism spread beyond heavy industry to other sectors, various markers of success demarcated Stakhanovites from ordinary workers. Many female salesclerks, for example, achieved Stakhanovite status by promoting cultured trade and excellent customer service. The message behind the labor hero movement was that, despite limitations, such as inhospitable work and living conditions, an ordinary individual worker—male or female—could become an exemplary one, even a Soviet celebrity. Indeed, part of the appeal of becoming a Stakhanovite was that it conferred a variety of rewards, including some that marked recipients as members of an emergent new Soviet elite.

Tens of thousands of wife-activists provided free labor during the Stalinist drive for industrialization and modernization. The wife-activist (*obshchestvennitsa*) movement first emerged among elite housewives of industrial managers and engineers in the mid-1930s, and then encompassed wives of more rank-and-file workers, including those in the countryside. While some scholars have argued that this movement cast unemployed wives as the helpmates of husbands, reaffirming traditional gender roles, the movement also afforded wives more complex social roles as they moved beyond their husbands to assist society as a whole by promoting education, mannered behavior, and cultured taste among workers and their families, improving work and living conditions, and engaging in voluntary labor at workplaces. By encouraging wife activists to use their allegedly feminine traits, maternal nature, and domestic experience to contribute to the Soviet project, the Stalinist regime valorized them and the domestic, in sharp contrast to the Party-state's denigration of homemakers as ignorant and counterrevolutionary and the domestic sphere as feminine and unproductive in the 1920s. The wife-activist became another version of the New Soviet Woman, a new model of Soviet womanhood.

Politics and the Public Sphere

Women's involvement in paid labor as well as in politics and social and community initiatives demonstrates how the public sphere was regendered under Stalin. Soviet visual culture reflected this change. In the 1920s, women had been marginalized in political iconography of the new socialist order and rarely depicted unless the target audience was female. Moreover, when represented, women were usually cast in supporting roles to men, as happy recipients of the new regime's revolutionary policies, or as unenlightened, or petty bourgeois, and, therefore, potentially counterrevolutionary. Under Stalin's rule, there was a significant expansion of, and far more, positive female images. In a wide variety of print and artistic representations as well as social and political events, women were characterized as active citizens and positive symbols of the new Soviet order. This was no small matter. During the 1920s, for example, over 300 Soviet postage stamps—official items of the new state—had featured people, but they have been without exception men; in contrast, after 1929 under Stalin, women began to appear, signaling their inclusion in the body politic. Stalinist narratives of women as exemplary figures underscored their modern transformation as well as the successes of the Revolution and the new Stalinist order; women had gone from being poor and benighted peasants and workers to successful laborers, and even unemployed housewives had become contributors to the Soviet project. Depictions of newly visible women notables, along with images of women as scientists, masters of technology, and physically fit and strong athletes, coexisted with more conventional displays of mothers, underscoring women's ability to be working mothers, including heroic ones. In narratives about female luminaries from national minorities, becoming a public heroine also involved breaking with traditional and "backward" religious and ethnic practices.

Despite women's public recognition under Stalin as invaluable participants in the construction of a new order, and Communist ideology that posited women's active involvement in politics as integral to their overall emancipation and the building of socialism, the political elite did not treat women as political equals. In the 1920s, women's political marginalization had been explained in part as a result of women's alleged ignorance and lack of economic independence, both of which supposedly hindered their ability to act as autonomous political agents. Wage labor was supposed to allow women to become more economically and thus politically independent from men, and education was supposed to transform women into politically aware and active citizens. But despite women's increased education and mass entry into paid labor in the 1930s, they remained largely outside of high politics under Stalin's rule (and indeed beyond). Few women occupied top positions in the

All-Union Council of Ministers (before 1946 called the *Sovnarkom*), the All-Union Supreme Soviet, and the Communist Party Central Committee, and not a single woman served on the Politburo, the highest policy-making body of the CP between 1919 and Stalin's death. Women constituted between 12 and 21 percent of total Communist Party members in Stalin's time, although they fared a bit better numerically in the All-Union Leninist Communist Youth League (*Komsomol*), constituting 34 percent of its members in the mid-1930s. Female involvement in both the CP and the *Komsomol* was constrained by anti-women prejudice as well as most women's daily double burden of having to labor in the home and workplace.

Women's leadership in lower-level party and government bodies was also limited, though it did increase during the Stalin era. Female leaders largely served in political sectors directly related to women's everyday responsibilities as mothers, wives, and caretakers, such as education and public health. Interestingly, some female national minorities might have been better represented in government and party institutions than their Slavic counterparts, for as the regime sought to extend Soviet power in predominantly Muslim regions, it established quotas mandating one-third of posts for women in such bodies.

In 1930, one of the main vehicles for women's political activism and advocacy, the women's section of the Communist Party (*Zhenotdel*), was abolished. In the 1920s, the *Zhenotdel* organized literacy campaigns, consciousness-raising activities among women, and a delegate system that offered women political training and experience. It also sought to emancipate female national minorities from "oppressive" religious and indigenous customs. Although acting on behalf of the party, the *Zhenotdel* offered women some political autonomy, and frequently advocated on behalf of "women's" issues. In 1930, Communist leaders framed the liquidation of the women's section positively—ostensibly because the woman's question had been "solved" and women had gained equality. In actuality, women lacked political parity or equality, and the *Zhenotdel*'s dissolution eliminated a major vehicle for advancing women's voices and concerns.

The regime's failure to treat women as political equals to men is underscored in its structures of repression. To be sure, millions of women and men suffered immensely during Stalin's purges in the mid-to-late 1930s, but women constituted only about 6–9 percent of the prison-camp population of the *Gulag*. The secret police targeted the wives and family members of political prisoners, however, and established a special camp for them in Karaganda. Female criminals and prostitutes also ended up in camps when police forces targeted them as "socially harmful elements" during the mass operations stage of the purges in 1937 and 1938. Even though Stalin and the Soviet leadership did not deem women politically threatening enough to incarcerate them en masse, the Great Terror inflicted deep violence on the psyches and lives of women who remained outside the camps, particularly those directly connected to male "enemies of the people." Guilty by association, these women often lost their jobs and friends, and struggled to survive in conditions of economic deprivation and social isolation.

Soviet Power, Islam, and Gender

Despite some changes in Soviet nationalities policy during the Stalin era, the regime continued to link the Sovietization of national minorities to the eradication of traditional religious and ethnic practices viewed as anti-Soviet and oppressive to women. As a result, Communist authorities promoted women's "emancipation" in the predominantly Muslim regions of Soviet Azerbaijan and Central Asia, believing that this would win over local women, undermine indigenous power and patriarchal family structures, and lead to widespread social transformation. The Communist liberation narrative about freeing Muslim women from male oppression contained problematic Eurocentric and colonial assumptions, however.

Under Stalin, Party and local activists abandoned the *Hujum*, the very public assault on religious and indigenous customs in Central Asia of 1926 and 1927, which had included mass unveiling campaigns in Uzbekistan and Tadzhikistan, which had resulted in a violent backlash against women who unveiled. Still, in the late 1920s and throughout the 1930s, unveiling and ending female seclusion remained priorities. In regions where veiling was not common among indigenous women, Soviet officials focused instead on promoting women's education and medical care as well as enforcing recent laws against bride-wealth, polygamy, and underage marriage. In the first seven months of 1929, for example, Soviet courts tried over a thousand Turkmeni men for engaging in these illegal marital practices. The police and judiciary also went after local men who harmed women for unveiling or engaging in public life. In addition to using criminal prosecutions to advance change, the Stalinist government linked Communist Party loyalty to compliance with new Soviet laws and initiatives, and punished or expelled men for gender transgressions in the mass *proverka* (verification campaign) of members that began in 1929. In the purges of the 1930s, Party men who failed to unveil their wives or abandon other traditional gender and family customs were often deemed "enemies of the people." Despite Soviet print and visual culture in the 1930s that trumpeted the successful modernization of female national minorities (such as newsreels featuring Russian *and* Kazakh women doctors treating Kazakh male patients), significant opposition to gender reforms led many national minorities to ignore or subvert new Soviet laws and prescriptions.

Some Muslims, including Jadidists who advocated Islamic modernization before the 1917 Revolution, and local women activists who supported changes in gender norms and, in some cases, had initiated personal reforms in their own lives in advance of Communist initiatives, supported the regime's liberation policies for women. Other Muslims saw the campaign against Islamic and ethnic practices as an imperialist assault on their way of life and an attempt to impose Russian and foreign ways. From this perspective, the practice of religious and indigenous customs became an act of political and cultural resistance. Ironically, by politicizing everyday familial, marital, and gender customs, the Soviet regime advanced Muslim women's political agency, a Communist goal, which they didn't always exercise in support of Soviet power. Whereas some Muslim women chose to eschew old practices and adopt new "Soviet" behavior, others did not, either because of male pressure and domination or in defense of their own religious and ethnic identities. Women's actions, however, were not necessarily political or anti-colonial. Stalinist policies of collectivization and modernization, as well as the Second World War, wrought not only massive economic but also social changes, which undermined traditional gender norms. As girls began to attend Soviet schools, and women began to work as full-time collective farm laborers or urban wage earners, female seclusion lessened. Because Soviet schools did not allow students to wear veils, and veils were impractical in many workplaces, veiling also became less common. Nonetheless, even as Muslim women became better educated, adopted new jobs and public roles, discarded their veils, exercised personal freedoms such as divorce that Communist power had introduced, and gained access to basic Soviet healthcare, many acted as guardians of religious faith, indigenous customs, and ethnic identity in their private lives, both during the Stalin era and in later years.

The Military and the Great Patriotic War

As toward 1939 the Stalinist regime readied for possible war with the capitalist West, particularly Nazi Germany, it promoted another version of the New Soviet Woman, the female soldier, who both disrupted and reaffirmed existing gendered landscapes. Although some women had fought during the First World War, the Russian Revolution, and the Civil War (1918–21), gender roles in the early Soviet years marked men as the "defenders" of the country and women as the "victims" of war and aggression in need of men's protection. Stalinist authorities, however, encouraged female teenagers and young women to enroll in an expanding network of paramilitary classes, and by the mid-1930s, their participation was reportedly around 50 percent in many regions. The *Komsomol*, and, to a lesser extent, the Society for the Promotion of Defense, Aviation, and Chemical Industries (*Osoaviakhim*), likewise promoted girls' and women's military training. In the last few years before the Nazi invasion, the Soviet press and popular culture also began to feature the accomplishments of female snipers, parachutists, and sharpshooters, suggesting that womanhood and military service were not incompatible. The regime's celebration of three female aviators who set a new world flying record in 1938 underscored women's technical and potential military prowess.

As approximately 800,000–1,000,000 women joined the Red Army and partisan forces during the Second World War, women soldiers became increasingly recognized as a distinct group in society. If, at first, female volunteers signed up only as individuals, in early 1942, the Stalinist regime shifted course and began to mobilize women officially because of the need for new military recruits, given the decimation of fighting forces in 1941. Soviet women served in many military capacities, in contrast to female service in the armed forces elsewhere, in which women were cast as "noncombatants." In the Soviet context, the previously male space of combat was regendered as a mixed space as hundreds of thousands of women served at the front. Significantly, many women did not feel the need to erase their "female" differences to become soldiers and asserted their womanliness instead of cultivating a masculine soldierly self.

The gender transformation of the frontlines challenged the soldierly identity of male troops. As a result, most male soldiers and commanders initially viewed the identity of soldier and woman as antithetical, and reacted to women soldiers in combat units with incomprehension and hostility. As the war wore on, the experience of fighting alongside women, and sometimes being commanded by them, appears to have changed some men's minds about women's capacity to be military comrades. Many men, nonetheless, sought to reaffirm their differences from women, and did so by asserting a military masculinity that sexualized female forces, and contributed to women's sexual harassment and assault. Focusing on female soldiers' sexual rather than military roles allowed men to disassociate combat from women and construct them as sex partners rather than military comrades. Communist leaders, meanwhile, celebrated men's hyperviolent masculinity and focused on their outstanding individual feats of killing and courageous support for their male comrades. Despite women's presence at the front, official discourse and male soldiers touted the importance of this camaraderie to military successes, linking frontline brotherhood to soldierly masculinity.

The Soviet press did not report the many difficulties female soldiers faced, from sexual abuse to the lack of women's-size boots or of supplies for menstruating women. Yet it also did not treat these women as an oddity. Instead, the press extolled women soldiers' exploits as daughters fighting on behalf of the Motherland. Many narratives also emphasized female soldiers' femininity, which may have reflected individual woman's self-presentation but additionally served to reassure readers that a distinct binary gender order was still intact. Significantly, reportage focused on exemplary women combatants but not on female troops as a whole or the state's mobilization of women into the armed forces, which effectively obscured the scale and nature of women's involvement. As the silencing of this broader military context suggests, the Stalinist regime did not intend for the female soldier to be a permanent identity.

Although many women were recognized during the war as heroes and lauded for their military valor, in the immediate postwar and late-Stalin years the central press and official war narratives largely marginalized female combatants' contributions, focusing instead on women's war efforts as workers and mothers. Soviet authorities rejected the female soldier as a permanent model of womanhood by accelerating women's demobilization at the end of the war and encouraging female troops to pursue nonmilitary careers. The great Moscow Victory Parade reasserted the masculinity of combat by *not* featuring women veterans. This suppression of female soldiers' sacrifices was deeply painful for them; as one explained,

> Men were victors, heroes, wooers, the war was theirs, but we were looked at with quite different eyes ...
> I'll tell you, they robbed us of the victory.[8]

In some postwar regional narratives, however, women veterans received greater attention. In recently occupied Latvia, for example, they were honored as symbols of the "liberation" of the new Soviet republic from past oppressors, bourgeois, and Germans.

After the war, silence also surrounded the brutal sexual violence male Soviet troops inflicted on perhaps 2 million German, Austrian, and other women as they liberated Nazi-occupied regions and claimed victory over Germany. Even if not official policy, soldiers perpetrated mass rape to express their Soviet *and* masculine dominance over women, and the Third Reich and Axis enemies more generally. By acting in groups, they reinforced their collective brotherhood and transformed rape into a social act of male soldierly bonding, while pressuring reluctant comrades to participate. Although this sexual violence might have reinforced many soldiers' sense of virility, damaged from the war, it might also have undermined their masculine identity by transgressing gender norms that positioned men as male protectors of women and children. How did men's sexual violence inform their postwar masculine selves and their reintegration into civilian life? How did it affect their relationships with women?

As the Stalinist regime applauded returning male soldiers, it encouraged them to return to the workforce and "renew their military glory every day in their work."[9] This transition proved difficult for many men who suffered emotional and physical damages from the war, especially the 2.75 million physically disabled veterans who often lacked medical support, including prosthetic devices, for their impairments. For many veterans, moreover, the workplace was hardly a vehicle for heroic glory or even self-realization. Alienated from work, politics, and their families, many veterans met in taverns, bathhouses, and other homosocial venues where they reasserted their frontline brotherhood. Meanwhile, many younger Soviet men who did not serve during the Great Patriotic War and could not claim a military masculinity sought to emulate soldiers, while others began to distinguish themselves by developing an alternative and nonmilitary model of manhood rooted in jazz, Western-style fashions, and dancing. Although these stylish young men (*stiliagi*) faced significant public disapproval, they were not repressed because many were sons of the Stalinist elite and their "rebellion" was not explicitly political. Joined by other young men and women from different social strata in the late-Stalin and post-Stalin years, they contributed to a new Soviet youth culture.

Enormous wartime losses, particularly of male lives, resulted in a terrible population imbalance in the male-to-female ratio. Men constituted approximately four-fifths of war deaths. Cognizant of this demographic crisis, and a decline in the birth rate, the Stalinist government adopted a new Family Law in 1944 to spur reproduction. By making divorce much more difficult and redefining legal marriage to encompass only registered unions, the law was supposed to promote family stability, and therefore greater procreation. The law was hardly conservative, however. By stripping unregistered marriages and any children of such unions of any legal standing, including paternal child support, promising financial and other forms of government assistance to newly defined "unwed" mothers and "out-of-wedlock" children, and relieving men of responsibility for offspring of sexual liasions, the law unintentionally encouraged men to pursue extramarital affairs and impregnate unmarried and widowed women. Finally, by offering increased financial assistance and new awards to mothers of large families, and lowering the number of children required to receive such aid, the law was supposed to incentivize motherhood.

The new law legitimized "single" motherhood, as did Soviet propaganda, which heralded unmarried mothers' successes in raising happy and healthy children. This does not mean, however, that unmarried mothers and their children faced no social opprobrium. Meanwhile, the state's monetary aid proved inadequate, and many "single"-mother families received less help than they would have from child support payments. Moreover, religious and cultural opposition to the new policy, for example, in the new Lithuanian Soviet Socialist Republic, as well as bureaucratic incompetence, meant that some "single" mothers never received state aid.

The war and the 1944 Family Law changed the structure of Soviet families. The huge number of widows, the greater difficulty in heterosexual pair bonding given the unbalanced sex ratio, and the legitimization of unmarried motherhood meant that "fatherless" families became an increasing reality. By uncoupling marriage from reproduction, and adopting new pronatalist policies, the Party-state made motherhood even more of an imperative for normative womanhood. Meanwhile, Soviet public discourse, including literature, directed women to be healers of men's physically and psychologically damaged bodies. This had the effect of gendering wartime trauma male, erasing the very real trauma that female soldiers and women on the home front had experienced.

During the war and in the postwar period, Stalinist propaganda and visual culture asserted Soviet men's roles as fathers and protectors of their families. Homecoming narratives continued this trend, emphasizing demobilized soldiers' happy reunions with their families, and some postwar popular magazines and paintings depicted returning fathers' bonds with their children. These representations marked a shift from Soviet men's earlier marginalization as fathers, and suggested a new familial masculinity for men to embrace. At the same time, however, the 1944 Family Law—and the realities of the war—undermined fathers' familial roles. Moreover, postwar visual culture and media trumpeted Stalin's role as not only the paternal leader of the great Soviet family but also the surrogate father in individual families.

Sexual Politics

The sexual politics of the Stalinist regime—like its gender politics—were oriented toward transforming and regulating sexual norms, practices, and identities to promote a new Soviet order and Party-state objectives. Soviet discourses and policies regarding gender, the family, ethnic and national minorities, religion, and class, as well as the regime's economic and political agendas, informed Stalinist sexual politics.

During the early Soviet and Stalin years, Communist authorities promoted heterosexuality as the natural and "normal" sexuality for Soviet citizens. Although they promulgated this construction of heterosexuality in new family laws, court cases, visual culture, and printed media, as already discussed, they also rejected various forms of heterosexual relations and practices, such as underage marriages, which were associated with women's oppression and "backward" religious and national customs. Under Stalin, female prostitution, which had been decriminalized in 1922, came under increased attack. If during the early Soviet years public health and medical officials sought to rehabilitate female prostitutes and integrate them into society, in the early 1930s Communist authorities adopted more punitive tactics and increasingly sent them to corrective labor colonies in the *Gulag* system. This change was a result of new police efforts to regulate urban areas and cleanse them of "social anomalies," given the massive social dislocation caused by Stalin's economic policies. In addition, in the context of the drive for rapid industrialization and women's mass entry into paid labor, the alleged causes of women's prostitution—unemployment and dismal material conditions—were purportedly resolved. According to Communist authorities, women were no longer compelled to sell their bodies, and, thus, if they did, deserved to be punished.

The previously discussed Stalinist Family Law of 1936 affirmed the regime's sexual conservatism, including its rejection of the more liberated heterosexuality of the postrevolutionary years and 1920s, which was marked by an increase in premarital and nonmarital sexual relations as well as divorces. Indeed, as the new policy explained, making divorce more difficult was intended to combat "light-minded attitudes toward the family and family obligations."[10] Nonetheless, although the new law indicated a shift, most Communist leaders had in fact long promoted sexual conservatism. In the early 1920s, they rejected Kollontai's radical sexual ideas and viewed sexual liberation as distracting to the socialist cause. The *Komsomol* sought to channel young people's sexual energy into the collective building of socialism. Many Soviet officials, social commentators, and medical professionals decried sexual libertinism, linking "excessive" sexual activity to moral degradation and poor health. Sanitary enlightenment propaganda of the 1920s talked about non-procreative and casual sex only in negative terms, associating it with venereal disease, men's infidelity to their wives, and the sexually deviant prostitute.

The regime's sexual conservatism, nonetheless, intensified under Stalin's rule. Public discussions about sexuality disappeared in the 1930s. By 1932, the nascent field of Soviet sexology was dead, and plans to host the Fifth Congress of the World League of Sexual Reform in the Soviet Union were abandoned. Studies of sexual behavior, venereal diseases, or related publications were either destroyed or removed to special divisions in the libraries that were closed to the general public. As Soviet authorities terminated the public health sexual enlightenment efforts of the 1920s, citizens were schooled, instead, via "moral education" and the punishment of "deviant" behavior. Freudian ideas about sexuality and psychoanalysis were discredited as perverse. In 1934, the government (re-) criminalized sodomy (meaning male homosexuality), and in 1935, it passed an anti-pornography law.

The Stalinist regime's criminalization of male homosexuality in 1933 and 1934 marked a significant policy change. In 1917, Bolshevik leaders repealed tsarist criminal statutes, including the criminalization of male sodomy, and the new Russian Criminal Code of 1922 reaffirmed this change. So, too, did the penal codes in Soviet Ukraine and Belorussia. The legalization of consensual male same-sex relations, partly a product of the new regime's decision to secularize criminal law, did not indicate widespread acceptance. Instead of viewing homosexuality as a crime, Communist leaders, Soviet officials, and experts adopted a biomedical perspective and characterized it as an abnormality, illness, and psychological "perversion." Significantly, homosexuality was decriminalized in the more "modern" and "European" parts of the Soviet Union, but not in Azerbaijan, Georgia, and the Soviet Central Asian republics. In these, more "primitive," regions with a majority of non-Slavic peoples, Communist authorities viewed homosexuality differently, claiming that it was particularly common and "an endemic form of depravity" that warranted punishment.[11] In Central Asia, they also outlawed the "keeping of *bachi*," that is, the practice of hiring cross-dressed feminine dancing boys as entertainers and prostitutes for men, which they associated with the persistence of local "primitive" and capitalist customs. Communist authorities also rejected a biomedical approach to same-sex relations among Russian Orthodox clergy, or between clergy and laymen (particularly boys), claiming, instead, that homosexuality and pederasty were the result of the perverted conditions of a monastic and religious life. The regime's approach to male same-sex relations in the early Soviet years, therefore, was multifaceted and inconsistent. Even in regions where homosexuality was legalized, Soviet censorship limited public discussion about same-sex sexuality or its artistic and literary representation, while homophobia led many gay men in the 1920s to get married to advance their careers, as Communist and medical authorities deemed marriage a cure for same-sex desire.

A new domestic and international context in the late 1920s and early 1930s contributed to the (re-) criminalization of male sodomy. During the First Five-Year Plan (1928–32), Communist Party leaders directed the Commissariat of Health and related professionals to adopt new medical priorities and strategies to boost industrial and agricultural workers' productivity. This coincided with the imposition of new orthodoxies in a variety of scientific and cultural fields and delegitimization of "bourgeois" and non-Party specialists (professionals associated with the Old Regime) as part of the so-called Cultural Revolution. Together, these changes contributed to attacks against "biologizing" doctors and scientists who supported a biomedical understanding of homosexuality, psychiatrists who promoted a biosocial and therapeutic approach to same-sex desire, and sexologists who sought to better understand human sexuality. In this environment, research about and "treatment" of Soviet homosexuals— male and female—appears to have ceased. Meanwhile, as the police stepped up efforts to control urban areas and remove social problems, gay men were targeted in visible male homosexual subcultures. After raids against gay and bisexual men in Russian and Ukrainian urban communities in 1933, Genrikh

Iagoda (1891–1938), the deputy chief of the secret police, contacted Stalin with a new draft anti-sodomy law, arguing that "pederasts" threatened state security by engaging in espionage and debauching "healthy young people." In these new domestic circumstances, Soviet leaders rejected the earlier medical and psychiatric approach to homosexuality in favor of a new penal approach involving compulsory labor treatment.

The politicization of male homosexuality in the context of the growing Nazi threat also played a role in recriminalization. Speaking in 1934 on behalf of the anti-sodomy law, the world-famous writer Maxim Gorky (Gor'kii; 1868–1936) justified it as a blow against the forces of fascism by asserting that homosexuality was a product of fascist degeneracy and foreign perversion. Arguing that homosexuality had no place in the Soviet Union, he proclaimed "Destroy the homosexuals—Fascism will disappear."[12] Other Communist leaders also envisioned homosexuals as political enemies involved in anti-Soviet activities. Official discourse that associated homosexuality with the corruption of male youth and bourgeois depravity further delegitimized it. Purportedly "normal," politically loyal, non-fascist, and non-bourgeois Soviet people did not engage in same-sex relations.

The number of male victims of the new anti-sodomy law is difficult to determine, given the lack of access to relevant archives and the bureaucratic complexity of surveillance and prosecution. Existing evidence, however, suggests mass arrests occurring in several major Soviet cities in 1934 and thousands of prosecutions (if not more) during the Stalin era. In this context, Pyotr, the gay soldier mentioned earlier in this chapter, would have become a target. Still, despite repression, male urban homosexual subcultures continued to exist, as men rejected the heteronormative sexual order by meeting for love and sex. Meanwhile, male same-sex relations that were more "private" appear to have garnered less police attention, and some gay and bisexual men, including well-known figures, lived their lives without persecution, especially if they married women and kept their same-sex desires from the public. For gay men living more openly, punishment was a real possibility during the purges of the 1930s, including not only imprisonment but also execution. The poet Nikolai Kliuev (1884–1937), for example, who wrote about homosexual love and refused to compose "normal verses," met this fate. While undoubtedly the all-Union anti-sodomy law and official homophobia adversely affected the lives of men-loving-men during the Stalin era, details of the lived experience of such men are not well known, particularly in rural areas and regions with national and religious minorities.

Significantly, female homosexuality was not criminalized under Stalin or any other Soviet leader. Unlike their male counterparts, women-loving-women were not characterized as a potential political threat since women generally lacked political power. Authorities didn't view female same-sex sexuality as a social threat either; women's lesser economic power to establish urban subcultures as well as their more private forms of social organization meant their same-sex relations were not as publicly visible as that of queer men. Soviet discourses that promoted motherhood as essential to womanhood and as women's civic duty also compelled many queer women to enter into heterosexual marriages so they could become mothers, which masked their identities and desires. Meanwhile, medical professionals argued that "genuine" female homosexuals were uncommon, and associated female homosexuality with "masculine" women who demonstrated gender nonconformity in their dress, behavior, and adoption of "male" jobs. Interestingly, although most experts condemned these women for their sexual transgressions, some viewed their gender transgressions more equivocally, for they associated these women's masculinity with political consciousness, skills, and public competency. Doctors and psychiatrists argued that "feminine" and gender-conforming women who pursued same-sex relations did so because of bad heterosexual relations, or because of temporary corruption by the "mannish" female homosexual. Although female same-sex relations were not criminalized, it appears that at least some lesbians faced punishment in the early Soviet and Stalin eras for their sexually transgressive behavior, charged with crimes such as engaging in "depraved acts" with a minor, "crimes of nature," and "hooliganism."[13]

Despite the Stalinist regime's condemnation and criminalization of male homosexuality, policies regarding it were not consistent. In the *Gulag*, the forced-labor penal camp system initiated under Stalin's rule was apparently pervasive, and largely ignored (or tolerated) by camp officials who viewed it as a product of incarceration and a homosocial environment. They also viewed it as a product of carceral power relations, in which prisoners established a hierarchy, enacting sexual violence against other inmates and reducing "passive" homosexuals to the lowest status. Authorities permitted this system of sexual dominance, which they could and did manipulate, particularly since it often involved "criminal" inmates (supposedly friendly to the Soviet regime) abusing "political" inmates (those deemed hostile to Communist rule). Many camp officials also indulged queer relations because of the perception that they helped to preserve order and enhance labor output. If some men engaged in homosexual sex to experience pleasure and enact violence against others, others pursued consenting queer relationships for intimacy and love. Some men also engaged in sexual barter to receive benefits, such as additional food.

Female same-sex sexuality in the camps also appears to have been largely ignored or tolerated by officials. Like male same-sex sexuality, many interpreted it as acquired and temporary homosexuality due to incarceration; ostensibly when released, the majority of women would abandon same-sex relations in favor of heterosexual ones. Although female prisoners of all social classes engaged in same-sex relations—for the sake of pleasure, love, or in exchange for improved living and work conditions—women of the intelligentsia often sought to conceal their lesbian affairs in an effort to maintain their class distinction. According to them, it was "criminal" inmates who engaged in such relations, allegedly seducing innocent prisoners and shamelessly parading their desires. Educated women also constructed "criminal" queer women as different, even disgusting, because many violated gender norms. In the lesbian subculture of the camps, some women assumed a "masculine" and assertive role (the *kobly*, butches), while others assumed a "feminine" and "passive" role (the *kovyrialki*, femmes). Although such "butch-femme" couples existed in the 1920s and earlier, and were not merely a product of the *Gulag*, some scholars allege that camp life helped to mainstream this relationship model and subculture, eclipsing most other models and an earlier "salon" lesbian subculture. This argument is moot: It underscores the need for more research to better understand the nuances and complexity of female queer relations under Stalin's rule and in subsequent years.

Whereas Communist Party meetings and procurators' reports from camps appear to have evinced no concern about homosexual relations, the same cannot be said of heterosexual sex. Communist authorities and camp administrators frequently discussed it as a problem and sought to limit sexual contact between male and female prisoners by officially banning cohabitation, punishing inmates for heterosexual relations, and imposing sex-segregation in the camps. This might have been because of the potential economic problems resulting from heterosexual sex: any pregnancies and births hindered women's labor productivity and required the allocation of scarce camp resources to support pregnant and nursing mothers as well as babies and children. In the broader context of the regime's pronatalism, however, this procreation was still useful to the state, and many camps established maternity wards and nurseries. Despite the efforts to curb heterosexual sex, it flourished in the camps. Although some female prisoners sought heterosexual intimacy, many others experienced sexual violence at the hands of male inmates and camp personnel. Some heterosexual female prisoners, like their queer counterparts, also used sexual barter to better their camp situations.

Under Stalin, Communist leaders adopted a relatively "radical" position on interethnic and interracial sexual relations. Unlike many governments around the world, which banned "miscegenation" and interracial unions, the Stalinist regime endorsed racial mixing and mixed marriages. Although in the early Soviet years some scholars and eugenicists objected to these unions because of their belief in a worldwide racial hierarchy and the idea that the mixing of the "races" would lead to physical and moral degeneracy, Stalinist authorities officially repressed these views in the late 1920s and early 1930s. Soviet laws already embraced the equality of all people, regardless of race or ethnicity. Moreover, according to Communist ideology, differences among people were a result of historical, cultural, and material differences rather than biological differences. As Nazi rule was established in 1933, the Stalinist regime explicitly rejected Nazi and eugenicist racist ideas. Rather than seeing mixed marriages as a negative, the Communist Party characterized mixed marriages as a positive means for bringing the Soviet Union's diverse groups together and generating a unified people. Mixed marriages also legitimized communism by exemplifying the Soviet commitment to racial equality and the "friendship of peoples," in contrast to the explicit racism of capitalist and fascist regimes.

Wartime and Postwar Sexualities

The mass upheaval of the Second World War contributed to the development of a new Soviet sexual landscape. As men and then women entered the armed forces, and families fell under German occupation, or were evacuated away from the front, many relationships collapsed. Wartime conditions led many husbands, wives, and non-married lovers to seek sexual and emotional intimacy outside of their existing unions. In the process, sexual norms and practices in Soviet society shifted, and extramarital as well as casual relationships became more common.

This kind of sexual behavior flourished in the Red Army. While some rank-and-file female and male soldiers fell in love with each other and established mutually affectionate unions, other military relationships were more hierarchical and tended to involve male officers with female subordinates. Women in these relationships—frequently called "field campaign wives"—provided sexual and other services to higher-ranking men in exchange for special privileges, such as supplementary rations. While some women actively pursued these relationships, others were essentially commanded to play this role by their superiors. Still other women felt compelled to enter into these relationships because of the constant male sexual harassment they faced. As one female soldier explained,

> It was very hard for us to exist in that zone. For that reason, many of the girls got off with one single guy, in order to protect themselves from advances from the rest of them. . . . It was very hard.[14]

Women soldiers were also raped by their male compatriots.

Although *both* men and women were sexually active in the Red Army, women were subjected to a sexual double standard. Many male soldiers apparently saw women's sexual activity either as a sign of weakness—a way to gain benefits or to get pregnant so they would be sent home—or a sign of immorality, whereas they saw their own similar sexual conduct as natural. Soviet society more broadly condemned women's sexual relations in the Red Army, holding them but not men accountable for what many perceived as a wartime breakdown in moral values. This double standard had serious consequences for military women at the end of the war, and effectively silenced the sexual violence that some had experienced. The perception that many female soldiers had been "loose" also stigmatized them and led many women to keep their bravery and military contributions at the front to themselves. "Try telling it," one woman veteran stated, "and who will give you a job then, who will marry you?"[15]

It is likely that the wartime conditions that led to a new morality and more temporary heterosexual relations on the home front also contributed to an increase in same-sex relations. As research about other countries has shown, the Second World War provided many opportunities for male troops to act on same-sex desires, which they may have been unable or unwilling to explore during peacetime. Moreover, despite Soviet women's military participation, the armed forces as a whole remained very male, and most men experienced the war in a homosocial context. Unlike elsewhere, Soviet authorities did not grant male troops regular leave or organize wartime brothels so that men could pursue heterosexual liaisons. As male troops experienced the challenges of war, they frequently took care of each other, performing "feminine" tasks such as tending to wounds and preparing food. Many men formed deep friendships and emotional bonds, and some even spoke of their great love for each other, which in some cases was presumably romantic love. As women soldiers also experienced the hardships of the war, and new opportunities for pursuing same-sex intimacy, undoubtedly some turned to each other for love and support, including sex. It is worth noting that although many of the same-sex relations during the war were consensual, inevitably some were also nonconsensual.

Freer sexual relations during the war were reinforced by the 1944 Family Law, which implicitly encouraged non-conjugal relationships and greater sexual promiscuity for reproductive purposes. This law too reaffirmed a sexual double standard; women were expected to be sexually active to become mothers, but not to pursue sexual activity for the sake of pleasure. Indeed, the Soviet regime regarded female sexuality with great ambivalence, particularly female youth sexuality. Anxiety among Communist and educational authorities in the late 1930s and early war years about "unhealthy relations" between boys and girls, and a perceived increase in youth sexual activity, fueled the Stalinist regime's decision in 1943 to abandon coeducation in urban schools. This policy to monitor and contain youth sexuality remained in place throughout Stalin's reign.

Although Stalin hardly promoted a politics of sexual freedom, there was a kind of sexual revolution after his first decade in power. The Great Patriotic War and the new Family Law of 1944 had a dramatic effect on sexual norms and behaviors. The *Gulag* also appears to have fostered new sexual practices, and its revolving door—a yearly release of perhaps 20 percent of inmates during the Stalin era as well as an amnesty in 1945—meant that Soviet society was flooded with released prisoners, some of whom likely pursued similar sexual conduct at home. Finally, the demographic imbalance at the end of the war contributed to a crisis of heterosexuality in the postwar period, as reproductive-aged women vastly outnumbered their male counterparts. For millions of Soviet women, marriage was simply unattainable, and since motherhood was tied to normative womanhood, millions of widows and single women became unmarried mothers in the late 1940s and 1950s. Indeed, from 1945 to 1955, 8.7 million children were officially born out of wedlock. As "looser" sexual relationships between men and women prevailed in the postwar and late Stalin era, the divorce rate also continued to climb, despite the greater difficulty in procuring one.[16] Sexual norms and practices, of course, varied in different Soviet communities, so overall trends do not do justice to regional and local variations.

If the regime effectively sanctioned new heterosexual norms and behaviors, it did not approve of new expressions of same-sex desires or liaisons. Authorities' condemnation of "pair friendships" among cadets at the Suvorov military academies in the late 1940s, which they deemed "the worst, most unhealthy form of individualism," suggests official anxiety about postwar military same-sex relationships.[17] Concern by *Gulag* doctors and administrators about the spread of homosexual identities and queer sex in Soviet society as millions of prisoners were released after Stalin's death suggests that they might have had similar fears upon the release of at least 600,000 inmates in Stalin's 1945 amnesty. Notwithstanding official homophobia during the Stalin era, however, there doesn't appear to be evidence of an active homophobic campaign and punitive policies against the Gulag queer until after Stalin's death. Moreover, despite criminal prosecutions of men having sex with men in the postwar period, evidence from court cases suggests that many Soviet citizens knew about but did not report them to authorities. This "quiet accomodationism" may have existed as well in the earlier Stalin era, but it is also possible that this limited tolerance was a result of new "popular notions of domestic privacy and accepted official intrusion" after the Second World War.[18]

Conclusion

When Stalin died in 1953, the Stalinist gender and sexual order was not replaced by a more liberal one, despite destalinization and various liberalizing reforms under Nikita Khrushchev's leadership. Instead, the new regime increased the persecution and prosecution of male same-sex desire—both in the *Gulag* and in wider society. As lesbians, too, received renewed attention, medical professionals often subjected them to psychiatric "treatment" and hospitalization for their "perversions." Seeking to replace Stalin's overt coercion and repression as a method of control, Khrushchev instead promoted moral renewal as official policy as a way to discipline citizens. The campaign to promote "communist morality," combined with Khrushchev's efforts to reinvigorate socialist democracy (popular participation in the administration of society), resulted in the more overt regulation of gender and sexual norms and practices in the everyday lives of Soviet people, as new and revived mechanisms for peer surveillance were established.

Notes

Special thanks to Elizabeth Wood and Naomi Andrews for their feedback on this chapter.

1 Because the Communist Party was so much entangled with the Soviet government, many scholars call it a "Party-state."

2 Kollontai was briefly people's commissar (government minister) of social welfare after the 1917 October Revolution, and was a member of the highest Party committee (the Central Committee) from 1917 to 1921.

3 Wendy Goldman, *Women at the Gates: Gender and Industry in Stalin's Russia*, Cambridge: Cambridge University Press, 2002, 219.

4 Greta Bucher, *Women, the Bureaucracy and Daily Life in Postwar Moscow, 1945–1953*, Boulder, CO: East European Monographs, 2006, 65.

5 See more on this in the chapter of the peasantry.

6 See, for example, Lynne Viola, "Bab'i Bunty and Peasant Women's Protest during Collectivization," *The Russian Review* 1, 1986, 23–42.

7 The reader can see this clearly on this book's front-cover.

8 Svetlana Alexievich, *The Unwomanly Face of War: An Oral History of Women in World War II*, New York: Random House, 2017, 109.

9 Robert Dale, "Being a Real Man: Masculinities during and after the Great Patriotic War," in Corinna Peniston-Bird and Emma Vickers, eds., *Gender and the Second World War: The Lessons of War*, Basingstoke: Palgrave, 2017, 116–34, 124.

10 Rudolf Schlesinger, ed., *The Family in the U.S.S.R.: Documents and Readings*, London: Routledge, 1949, 278.

11 Dan Healey, *Homosexual Desire in Revolutionary Russia: The Regulation of Sexual and Gender Dissent*, Chicago, IL: University of Chicago Press, 2001, 162.

12 Ibid., 189.

13 Ibid., 68, 225.

14 Kerstin Bischl, "Telling Stories: Gender Relationships and Masculinity in the Red Army 1941–45," in Maren Roger and Ruth Leiserowitz, eds., *Women and Men at War: A Gender Perspective on World War II and its Aftermath in Central and Eastern Europe*, Osnabrück: Fibre, 2012, 117–34, 129.

15 Alexievich, *Unwomanly Face*, 109.

16 Mie Nakachi, "N. S. Khrushchev and the 1944 Soviet Family Law: Politics, Reproduction, and Language," *East European Politics and Societies* 1, 2006, 40–68.

17 Erica Fraser, *Rearming Masculinity: Martial Brotherhoods and Postwar Recovery in the Soviet Union*, Toronto: University of Toronto Press, forthcoming, 81.

18 Dan Healey, *Russian Homophobia from Stalin to Sochi*, London: Bloomsbury, 2018, 70.

9

The Educational Experience in Stalin's Russia, 1931–45

Larry E. Holmes

In Stalin's Russia, the state alone determined the structure and curricula of the nation's schools. Soviet youths responded to its initiatives with both enthusiasm and defiance. They embraced Moscow's effort to provide them with multiple opportunities for an education. But they also made schooling an experience that deviated from the center's plans and expectations in several ways. First, their behavior undermined the state's designs for a perfectly disciplined environment. Second, despite proud pronouncements above of a uniform school system for all, many youths departed from it by enrolling in trade schools or by not attending any educational institution. Third, even when confronted with officially prescribed and, presumably, mind-numbing drill, many children nevertheless enjoyed their time at school. Fourth, pupils learned and teachers taught their lessons in ways unintended in the grand halls of the capital.[1]

A Popular Embrace of State Schools

By 1934, the Soviet state demanded that every child receive at least seven, and preferably ten, years of education. Correspondingly, from 1932 to 1937, funding for schools increased fourfold and the number of schools, teachers, and pupils increased dramatically. By the end of the 1930s, enrollment, which had been a mere 12 million in 1928, reached 31 million and remained so thereafter until a significant expansion in the 1960s. Almost half of the pupils were girls.[2]

Children, male and female alike, later recalled their warm embrace of an opportunity to attend school. They gave two chief reasons. First, they believed that schooling provided the means to get ahead. A mother, an illiterate, whose husband was also illiterate, convinced her children, as one of them later recalled, to get at least an elementary education because

> one who cannot read and write is like a blind man[, while a former pupil remembered thinking that] in order to get along in life, it is necessary to read and write.... It meant getting a job [still another asserted, while many youngsters hoped that an education would help them avoid a life of manual labor, recalling how] I wanted to learn more in order not to dig the earth [, or that] individuals without an education are not considered people ... They are just like horse-power, human-power.[3]

Second, children hoped to make something of themselves by becoming a "cultured person," stating how [their parents] "did not want me to remain a fool," or that, "The desire to get an education was a pride in our family," while another mentioned, "My primary reason [for an education] was to become a cultured man."[4]

Adults fondly remembered their first day at school, a festive occasion, for which they wore their very best, perhaps something just purchased or sewn at home for the occasion. They remained in school despite hunger, poor shoes, and inadequate clothing. In rural areas, youngsters walked many kilometers to class, in the dark of winter carrying torches to scare off wolves. They might go not just for the education. The school was often a welcoming building, decorated inside with brightly colored posters and drawings. Youths also enjoyed the camaraderie there and the chance for teenage flirtation and romance. Repeatedly smitten, David Samuilovich Samoilov confided over and again in his diary his fondness for female schoolmates.[5]

During the Second World War, and not just in besieged Leningrad, schools became a primary, even exclusive, source of food, if only of a slice of bread and thin soup. A teacher in Leningrad, Aleksei Ivanovich Vinokurov, wrote on January 16, 1942, in his diary that pupils thought less of their studies and more of their lunch to come, albeit consisting only of "a lackluster badly smelling small ration of water called soup and a small piece of candy." Some children came to school only for the spare meal, skipping lessons before and after it. It was not always enough. In Leningrad, the instructor, Ol'ga Fedorovna Khuze laconically observed in her diary on January 20, 1942: "Teachers and pupils are dying."

And yet as we will see below, even in better times, not all youths could take advantage of expanding opportunities mandating seven or more years of education.

The Imperfect Perfect

In the early 1930s, the Soviet state imposed a single school system with a traditional curriculum of subjects, homework, grading marks, and promotion examinations. It determined when the school year began, the length of a lesson, and the type of pencils, pens, paper, ink, and chalk suitable for classroom use. Such an obsession with uniformity led in 1936 to the closure everywhere of separate classes and schools for physically and mentally challenged children. In the city of Kirov, located about 500 miles northeast of Moscow, a special commission headed by the head of the Regional Department of Education transferred all but 16 of 272 pupils at the city's school for mentally and physically challenged children to normal schools with disastrous consequences for everyone concerned.[6] In 1943, however, the state introduced a measure of structural disharmony with segregated education by gender in the largest cities of the Soviet Union. It hoped thereby to improve discipline among schoolboys. From then, until the return of coeducation in 1954, about 13 percent of Soviet youths attended separate schools for boys and girls.

Pupils' everyday experience defied the state's best-laid plans. Rules for the quality of notebook paper and type of pencils required their systematic violation if students were to write anything at all. With Moscow's encouragement, local governing organs disrupted a school's schedule and its academic mission when requiring teachers and pupils to bring in the fall's harvest, sell state bonds, and get out the vote on election day. In rural areas, children skipped school in the spring to plant and then in the fall to harvest their parents' privately held kitchen gardens. During the Second World War, in cities threatened by German bombardment, most notably Leningrad during its 900-day siege by enemy forces, pupils (and teachers) masked schools and other buildings, brought flammable items down from the attic, and hauled sand back up to extinguish fires ignited by incendiary bombs, rather than taking lessons.

A rapid expansion of schools and enrollment outstripped increased funding. Teachers and students everywhere, even in Moscow, experienced shortages of everything imaginable from pens, pencils, and desks to items most essential to a highly centralized system—syllabi, textbooks, and teaching manuals. A notebook might consist of old newspapers glued together on which pupils wrote in small print in the margins or in large letters on the printed page itself. During the late 1930s, almost half of all schools with more than a quarter of the total enrollment of the Russian Republic operated in two or more shifts. "Everybody hated the second shift," a pupil recalled.[7] Despite campaigns to improve teachers' professional qualifications, 63 percent of elementary instructors in the Russian Republic had no more than five or six years of education, if that, beyond the elementary four grades.

Kids are kids wherever they are, of course. In class, pupils talked to each other, passed notes, some of them with sexual connotations, used crib notes during examinations, and prompted en masse a comrade called to the front of the class with the right (or incorrect) answer. They threw paper wads and launched rubber bands at classmates. More surreptitiously, when clearly out of sight of their adult supervisors, pupils mutilated portraits of Marx, Engels, and Soviet leaders, including that of Stalin, by tearing them or burning their eyes out with the ends of lit cigarettes. Before class, pupils placed dead flies in a teacher's inkwell, or loosened the legs of his or her chair. During class, they might ask silly questions or insist in unison over a teacher's initial objection that a pupil be allowed to go to the toilet. Boys enjoyed pulling the pigtails of girls seated in front of them.[8] One former pupil proudly recalled his role as his school's leading and most innovative prankster.[9] At Moscow's School No. 25, one of the worst offenders was none other than Stalin's younger son, Vasilii (1921–1962). He failed to complete his homework, "forgot" to bring pen and notebooks to school, wound up a mechanical mouse and let it go during class, showed more interest in soccer than in his studies, and supplied fellow smokers in the men's toilet with his father's favorite brand.[10]

Teachers, too, misbehaved. Driven by "percentage-mania" (the evaluation of their performance based on promotion of pupils from one grade to the next), they encouraged pupils to look at their notes during examinations, answered the very questions they posed, or surreptitiously corrected students' written errors. Pupils' testimonies and official, albeit understated, reports indicated more serious transgressions of proper comportment, such as predatory behavior on the part of some male teachers toward their female students.[11]

A Tripartite Arrangement

As just noted, many youths attended regular schools. Yet, so many others, in fact, enrolled in trade schools that the Soviet educational system consisted in practice of a vocational as well as an academic track. A third and large school-age cohort attended no school at all.

Soviet youth's choices made the state's goal of seven years of general education (and an implied commitment to ten years) more fancy than fact. During the 1930s, 6–8 percent of all pupils dropped out of grade school each year. Another 8–9 percent failed year-end promotion examinations and were then required to repeat the grade. A further 8–9 percent failed, but could retake the examination. Many students forced to repeat a grade quit school altogether, however. Half of those permitted to retake the tests failed to show up in the fall and an unknown percentage left of those who returned and failed the examination again. Many dropouts enrolled in trade schools that provided brief specialized instruction. An extensive network of factory apprenticeship schools offered a course of less than one year with training in skills associated with an industrial enterprise and a full-time job there to follow.

Trade schools graduated 2 million Soviet youths during the 1930s. In 1940, they took on greater importance. That fall, the Soviet government imposed fees for enrollment in the senior division of schools (grades eight through ten), while it created a Labor Reserves System of tuition-free vocational schools for adolescents. To insure substantial enrollment numbers, the government assigned quotas to municipal soviets, collective farms, and orphanages. This combination of inducements and coercion produced immediate results. In the first year of its existence, the Labor Reserves System enrolled 602,000 students.

Then, as in the previous decade, vocational schools aggressively recruited students with less than seven years of general schooling. In the 1930s, only one-third of those attending factory apprenticeship schools had completed the seventh grade. As late as 1939, no more than 40 percent of the incoming class had done so. The Labor Reserves System aggressively recruited children from the ages of twelve to fourteen who had not yet completed and, in some cases, entered the junior division of the secondary school (grades five through seven). Some of these young recruits had not finished the elementary grades.

The vocational track included yet another institution for adolescents, the technical college (*tekhnikum*). It provided semiprofessional training of several or more years in such fields as transport, education, metallurgy, electronics, and meteorology. In the academic year of 1939–40, 4,000 *tekhnikums* enrolled a million students and graduated almost a quarter of a million. To be sure, these institutions rarely admitted anyone with anything less than seven years of schooling, and thus did not threaten to deprive the schools' junior division of its age-cohort clientele. However, throughout the Stalinist period, less than a third of youths admitted into *tekhnikums* had finished the tenth grade.

By the number of its pupils and graduates, this vocational track dwarfed its academic counterpart. From 1935 through 1939, 559,000 youths graduated from the senior division (the tenth grade) of regular schools. Many of them proceeded to enter a higher educational institution. During the same period, factory apprenticeship schools graduated twice that number and *tekhnikums* a third more, most of them then entering the workforce.

Some youngsters in trade schools might have preferred a regular school. In many cases, however, their academic shortcomings or an inability to pay for pens, paper, textbooks, and, after 1940, tuition gave them little choice than to opt for a free vocational education and a full-time job to follow.[12] A boy later recalled how after seven years of education his parents compelled him to attend a nearby trade school and then work in order to help feed and clothe the family. Yet he welcomed the opportunity and took pride in what he could accomplish at school and on the job. He regretted the removal in 1991 of the large statue of Feliks Dzerzhinskii, the first head of the Soviet state's secret police (*Cheka*), in Moscow's Lubianka Square, because he believed, in this case mistakenly, that Dzerzhinskii was responsible for the extensive network of vocational schools.[13]

Unlike this individual, many other youths who left school never proceeded to enroll in a trade school. Their numbers swelled in the early 1930s in many areas devastated by the collectivization of agriculture and especially by the famine of 1932 and 1933. By the tens of thousands, they begged for food at railroad stations and in the streets of major urban centers. One youngster who did manage to stay in school later recalled: "Your mind could not be on the lessons, it was always on food—food which we did not have."[14] Teachers, too, went hungry and fell gravely ill. Some of them managed to survive by selling everything in their possession, including their shoes. Others received something from a local collective farm in return for their manual labor.

Upon noting that many of his peers came up short of the state-mandated seven years of schooling, one pupil later off-handedly remarked, "You go to school in the Soviet Union if you have the means to do so, but many do not have the means."[15] When asked as an adult about the law mandating seven years of general education, a former pupil who had quit school after the sixth grade "simply shrugged his shoulders." Others recalled, "You didn't even have to go to school [and t]hey weren't so strict about that in the village." When the militia visited a family on a collective farm whose child dropped out after the second grade, the father responded: "There he is, sitting on top of the stove [, ... t]ake him, barefoot, as he is [, ... t]ake him." The militia departed without the child.

The number of school-age children beyond the reach of any educational institution increased dramatically during the Second World War and not just in areas overrun by the enemy. On the home front, school buildings became military hospitals, dormitories for workers, and army recruitment centers. Schools in turn crowded into offices, clubs, theaters, and other unsuitable structures, operating in three or, even, four shifts, the last one ending at 11:00 or 12:00 p.m. These conditions adversely affected the quality of instruction and led to the outbreak of infectious disease, all of which discouraged enrollment. Moreover, with the father and elder brothers away in the army in most families, younger children stayed out of school as never before to help raise younger siblings, tend a family's kitchen garden, or work in a collective farm's fields. In the Kirov region, enrollment in grades five through seven, attended primarily by children twelve to fourteen years of age, fell by 46 percent (from 116,370 to 63,323), The greatest decline occurred in rural areas where enrollment dropped by half (from 93,754 to 47,426).[16]

Drill, Politics, and Creativity

The Kremlin leadership demanded instruction of a prescribed body of information and discrete cognitive skills. As might be expected, teachers and pupils were to achieve those ends by extensive note-taking, homework, memorization, and drill. Pupils took turns reading their textbook aloud, and then retold in succession what they had just read. The teacher posed precise questions demanding from pupils equally precise responses based on what they had just heard.

Lessons in history condemned the pre-revolutionary old and praised the post-revolutionary new, and endeavored to instill a love of the Communist Party, Soviet state, and Stalin, and glorified the transformation of Russia by national planning and machine technology that had begun in earnest in 1929. During the terror that began to engulf the country in the mid-1930s, teachers and pupils revised their textbooks on the fly to correspond to the latest disappearance of former revolutionary heroes who had turned out to be "enemies of the people." A pupil later recalled that

> every now and then there would come an order that a page would have to be pasted over or certain sentences would have to be crossed out. By the end of the year [he mentioned by way of exaggeration], only a few pages of the original books were left.[17]

Older Russian literature was now harnessed to demonstrate how from ancient times writers had defended the Russian land against outside invaders. A pupil later remembered that "after 1936 the nineteenth century Russian writers, Alexander Pushkin and Leo Tolstoy, were made to seem the forerunners of Communism [; ... w]hat those Communists could do!"[18] By 1944, syllabi spoke favorably of the biologist Ivan Vladimirovich Michurin (1855–1935) and agronomist Trofim Denisovich Lysenko (1898–1976), who denied classical genetics by insisting that characteristics induced in plants by human manipulation of the environment could be transmitted to offspring.[19]

During the late 1930s, Moscow responded to diplomatic tension in the west and military clashes with Japan in the east with the introduction of formal military training in grades five through ten. Students practiced hand-to-hand combat, studied poison gases, practiced first aid, learned how to extinguish flames ignited by incendiary bombs, and fired small caliber arms. In the Second World War, curricula for history and geography added patriotic and martial themes and those for the sciences expanded sections on military technology. Students spent more time in basic training at school and at summer camps.

In such a highly charged political environment, teachers felt vulnerable. Later, they recalled a constant monitoring of their work by inspectors, school directors, fellow teachers, and senior pupils prepared to report any political slip to the secret police.[20] In 1937 and 1938, when tension with Nazi Germany was already high and an innocent remark about anything German might be taken as subversive in the heated atmosphere of the Great Terror, authorities in the city of Kirov fired in succession three teachers of German at a single school.[21]

And yet the image of the tough, regimented, and thoroughly politicized Stalinist school, praised by friends and scorned by foes, concealed much. Moscow's own emphasis on teaching the three Rs and the development of cognitive skills meant, in practice, limits on the politicization of the curriculum. In the mid-1930s, the Party's leadership quashed several initiatives by the Russian Republic's People's Commissariat of Education (*Narkompros*, the Russian Republic's ministry of education) to add courses on Marxist-Leninist theory and Communist Party history. Politicized instruction on the new Soviet constitution adopted in 1936 played only a bit part in the overall curriculum, limited to a two-hour segment each week in the seventh grade. Syllabi only occasionally attacked religion on the assumption that knowledge itself, especially of the natural sciences, would spell the end of it. A recertification campaign of teachers from 1936 to 1939 that, to be sure, took on political overtones in the end removed only 3 percent of the 603,000 instructors questioned. Many of them soon returned to the classroom. "Teachers appear to have been *less* victimized than other social groups," concludes the leading historian for the Stalinist period on this period, Tom Ewing.[22]

A school's faculty may have felt threatened, but on a day-to-day basis it remained remarkably free from political interference. Communist Party cells in schools were rare because relatively few instructors joined the Party, or the Young Communist League (*Komsomol*). One teacher later recalled that "the Party did not mix directly into our work," adding how, "I liked my work very much [and] I enjoyed teaching."[23] After mentioning that his director and inspectors could check his work at any time, another teacher nevertheless observed that he was "the master of the class, a real teacher."[24] The state's educational program, as Ewing has noted, corresponded to teachers' professional ethos.[25] Like the state, teachers supported an expansion of the school system, accepted the need for order and discipline, and equated education with the learning of a prescribed body of knowledge. In pursuing their own as well as the state's agenda, Ewing suggests how "teachers contributed as much to the formation of Stalinist education 'from below' as did the political leaders who set policies 'from above.' "[26]

Those teachers with the most confidence and know-how, usually the veterans, made instruction interesting for their pupils by a creative use of prescribed syllabi. One pupil later recalled: "We liked those teachers who spoke least about politics," while another recalled how, "A teacher's personality meant a lot," and one former pupil put it well: "If there is a good teacher, the subject is good; a bad teacher, and the subject is no good."[27]

Teachers of politicized subjects could make the classroom a fascinating place. George Counts (1899–1974), a prominent American educator, visited Moscow's School No. 25 for almost two weeks at the end of 1936. While there, he observed that after a lesson on Stalin and the First Five-Year Plan, ninth graders "gathered around their teacher in considerable numbers obviously interested in this subject."[28] At the same school, pupils later recalled lessons in geography that were like a "picture book" as their imagination roamed from one point on the globe to another.[29]

The son of a Russian mother and Western correspondent, George Fischer, recalled fondly his life as a Soviet schoolboy from 1929 to 1939. He liked the emphasis on social awareness that gave him and his peers a sense of importance and purpose. "I had few if any doubts about the Soviet system," he later remembered, "when I left Russia after ten years of schooling there."[30] Wolfgang Leonhard (1921–2014), son of a German Communist who emigrated to the Soviet Union, attended school in Moscow from 1935 to 1939; he recalled that he and fellow pupils were passionate about politics and read enthusiastically political literature, including works by Lenin and Stalin. That passion remained even when he discovered whole paragraphs inked out in books at the Library of Foreign Literature.[31] "I was loyal," another pupil recalled, "I did not know anything else[;] I thought that all this was right[;] our State, and our Stalin and so on."[32] The pupil, Samoilov, who, as we will see below, could think for himself, nevertheless accepted much of what he was told. On October 12, 1935, when he was fifteen years of age, he wrote in his diary, "My favorite dream is of my death for our country." The following year, on June 15, 1936, he thought that with the new constitution "at last the dictatorship has ended and the epoch of the ideal socialist republic with a truly peoples democracy begins." Two months later, on August 24, he declared that those Old Bolsheviks, "terrorists," as he called them, condemned in show trials to death had been "doomed by history." "In such moments," he added, "one feels the strength and genius of Stalin, who understands history." On December 21, he wrote, "For me there is no life without Soviet power."

When interviewed as adults, former students at School No. 25 fondly remembered their schooldays:

> Propaganda gave meaning to our lives. For us, the tsarist sky was gray, the socialist, blue. We believed in communism. We wanted to become warriors for the world revolution. We were all convinced communists.[33]

They realized problems faced the country and its government, but they were quick to blame authorities lesser than those in the Kremlin and to trust in the future. "I was a believing orthodox," one acknowledged, "who believed in the state, country, and revolution as things sacred," while others declared that, "Our generation believed itself to be chosen ... [; w]e were pure, unspoiled ... [; n]o wonder we won the war."[34]

Other Lessons Learned

In December 1934, Iuliia Borisovna Kapusto, a student at School No. 25, wrote a poem dedicated to Sergei Mironovich Kirov (1886–1934), the Party leader in Leningrad who had just been assassinated. The state's chief newspaper, *Izvestiia*, published it. Not to be outdone, the Party's Central Committee's newspaper, *Pravda*, summoned the youngster to its offices. When asked what she wanted to be when she grew up, Kapusto answered, "In no way whatsoever a poet or prose writer, but a propagandist (*publitsist*), only a propagandist."[35] And Kapusto made good on her promise. As an adult, she wrote fictional memoir accounts of young girls who had participated in the 1917 Revolution and in the Second World War. The Young Communist League (*Komsomol*) printed her works in large runs, with one book appearing in 165,000 copies.

And yet thanks to the irrepressible exuberance of youth and to teachers who encouraged a degree of spontaneity, students were not robots. They surreptitiously slipped notes to visiting inspectors with complaints about the class schedule, poor instruction, or "some kind of broth" served by the school's cafeteria.[36] Upon recalling the study of different poison gases, a female student added, "That was pretty stupid." Another girl who remembered that at school "we did shoot a lot," added, "I never really learned to shoot." She also recalled that "we had to learn the constitution practically by heart. It was very silly." A boy disliked the introduction of gender-segregated education: "Nobody liked it. It was impossible to have so much fun any more."[37]

His readiness to die for his country and veneration of Stalin notwithstanding, David Samoilov frequently expressed in his diary heretical opinions. When chastised in early January 1935 for coming to school without the red scarf that he and fellow Young Pioneers—members of the Party's youth arm at school—were required to tie around their necks, Samoilov responded sarcastically: "The scarf is a rite," he wrote on January 5, "the same formality as icons in a church." Communism, he thought a month later, on February 9, could not last even if achieved, because people with greater abilities would always want more. On April 22, he responded negatively to the celebration in society and at school of Pushkin's work: "I adore Pushkin the poet but hate Pushkin the fetish." Probably in part because he had read at home and in public libraries Voltaire, Shakespeare, Sergei Esenin (1895–1925), and Boris Pasternak (1890–1960), the latter two of whom were authors not in especially good odor in the Soviet Union at the time, Samoilov denounced the state of literature in his country. On December 15, 1934, he confided in his diary: "Unfortunately now there are no good poets, and generally the arts are not able to develop under a dictatorship."

Like Samoilov, other children mixed belief with doubts. The eighth grader Nina Nikolaevna Kosterina questioned the guilt of her close relatives and then of her father upon their arrest. And yet she voted for the expulsion from her school's *Komsomol* unit of a schoolmate whose parents had been imprisoned.[38] At School No. 25, the pupil Svetlana, Stalin's daughter, could not believe that all those arrested in the terror were guilty. She thought instead that it was all the result of a tragic misunderstanding that not even her father could grasp. Another pupil at the school, Dina Kaminskaia, admitted that the school and its instruction "sheltered me from real life," but, she added, it also "favored my development into an intelligent, well-educated person."[39] During Leonid Brezhnev's rule, Kaminskaia vigorously defended Soviet dissidents arrested and placed on trial for their political protests.

Conclusion

Education in Soviet Russia from the early 1930s to the end of the Second World War defied official declarations of a single and unitary system. Many Soviet youths embraced the opportunity to study in regular schools, many others enrolled in trade schools. Still others attended no school, regular or vocational, their numbers increasing dramatically during the Second World War. Proud manifestoes to the contrary, schools never came close to fulfilling the state's schemes for them. Pupils pulled pranks (for which they remained intensely proud as adults). Teachers in their instruction and pupils in their learning proceeded in ways well beyond the prescribed curriculum.

And yet schools served the ruling Party-state well in ways largely unacknowledged by it then and by its historians later. They imbued many pupils—Vasilii, Stalin's son a notable exception—with the norms and values of modernization, such as reliability, punctuality, perseverance, and an acknowledgment of a hierarchy of power and privilege. They legitimized the Stalinist system by providing so many (albeit not all) youths an opportunity for an education, a job, and a sense of self-worth. For many students, schooling was part of a process for the creation of a better, just, and prosperous Soviet Union and world. As one of them recalled, they took pride in being part of an effort to replace the "*samovar* of the old" with a "revolution of movement and progress."[40] For many of the children enrolled in a regular or vocational school, no disjuncture existed between their own private identity and what the school trained them to be in public. This convergence of attitudes about self, school, and state resulted, to be sure, from politicized instruction at school and, more broadly, in society. It also emanated, above all in schools that followed the general (academic) curriculum, from creative modifications of the officially approved content and methods of instruction made by both teachers and pupils.

Soviet citizens who emigrated to the West following the Second World War praised the educational system they had left behind. Although they complained of politicized instruction, "no aspect of Soviet society received more warm and spontaneous support than did the system of Soviet education."[41] One adult who had received seven years of education recalled: "The schools are really not bad in Soviet Russia [... ; i]f everything else were like that, nobody would be against the regime."[42] At the close of her memoirs, Elena Bonner (1923–2011), wife of the famous dissident physicist, Andrei Sakharov (1921–89), mused that critics "would really let me have it for that happy childhood ... [and t]hey'd bring up everything including the poster in the school lobby: 'Thank you Comrade Stalin for our happy childhood.'"[43]

Students attending the nation's schools experienced a host of contradictions: an academic and vocational track, compliance and defiance, drill and spontaneity, manipulation and initiative, and uniformity and variation. Precisely, those contradictions made schooling a great success, often in unexpected ways. A divergence of pupils' experience from officially prescribed norms meant for them an education that was productive and enjoyable. Despite some of the Kremlin's schemes that might have had the opposite effect, schools offered something of considerable benefit to the individual, society, and state.

Notes

1 For the experimentalist Soviet school curriculum of the 1920s, see Larry E. Holmes, *The Kremlin and the Schoolhouse: Reforming Education in Soviet Russia,* 1917–1931, Bloomington: Indiana University Press, 1991. In this article, I rely extensively on pupils' and teachers' telling of their own experience during the 1930s and 1940s in their diaries and, later, in memoirs and interviews. Four sources are of particular importance: The first is the

online "Prozhito," which consists of unpaginated diaries of pupils (and a few teachers) and available at http://prozhito.org/. Of particular importance are the diaries of the pupils David Samuilovich Samoilov, future poet, a student in Moscow in grades seven through ten from 1934 to 1938; Nina Nikolaevna Kosterina, a pupil in Moscow in grades eight through ten from 1936 to 1939; Georgii Sergeevich Efron, son of the poet, Marina Tsvetaeva, senior pupil in Moscow in 1940 (who died from wounds suffered at the front in 1944); and Elena Vladimirovna Mukhina and Mikhail Vasil'evich Tikhomirov, pupils in Leningrad in 1941. Also especially valuable are diaries from 1941 and 1942 of two schoolteachers in Leningrad: Ol'ga Fedorovna Khuze and Aleksei Ivanovich Vinokurov. Material from these diaries is henceforth cited in the text by name of the diarist and date of the entry. The second source consists of interviews from the Harvard Project on the Soviet Social System. In the early 1950s, it interviewed over 700 refugees who had left the Soviet Union from 1943 to 1946. The interviews and materials from questionnaires are available at http://hcl.harvard.edu/collections/hpsss/about.html. I use the testimony only of people who can be clearly identified as attending or teaching school during the 1930s and early 1940s. This source is henceforth cited as HIP. Third are the interviews I conducted from 1990 to 1996 of thirty-six former pupils for another book, see Larry Holmes, *Stalin's School: Moscow's Model School No. 25, 1931–1937*, Pittsburgh, PA: University of Pittsburgh Press, 1999. It should be noted that this school catered to the children of the elite, including, among others, Joseph Stalin's daughter, Svetlana, and his youngest son, Vasilii. Fourth is the testimony in interviews from an impressive cross-section of former teachers and pupils that are part of the Oxford Archive of Russian Life History. These interviews were conducted for a project sponsored by the Leverhulme Trust under grant no. F/08736/A "Childhood in Russia, 1890–1991: A Social and Cultural History" (2003–6) and are copyrighted by the University of Oxford. This source is henceforth cited as "Oxf/Lev" with a coding system that usually consists of a project identifier, place code (St. Petersburg [SPb], Moscow [M], and villages in Leningrad [2004] and Novgorod [2005] provinces [V]), a date code, a cassette number (PF), and a transcript page. For further information about the project, see www.mod-langs.ox.ac.uk/russian/childhood. My thanks go to the interviewers, Aleksandra Piir (St. Petersburg), Yuliya Rybina and Ekaterina Shumilova (Moscow), Oksana Filicheva, Veronika Makarova, and Ekaterina Mel'nikova (village interviews); to the project coordinators, Professor Al'bert Baiburin and Professor Vitaly Bezrogov; and to the project leader, Professor Catriona Kelly, for making this material available. On the validity of interviews for an understanding of Soviet school education under Stalin, see Alex Inkeles and Raymond A. Bauer, *The Soviet Citizen: Daily Life in a Totalitarian Society*, Cambridge, MA: Harvard University Press, 1961, 3–64; and Larry E. Holmes, "Part of History: The Oral Record and Moscow's Model School No. 25, 1931–1937," *Slavic Review* 56, 1997, 280–305.

2 For these and other state decrees mentioned below, see *Narodnoe obrazovanie v SSSSR: Obshcheobrazovatel'naia shkola. Sbornik dokumentov, 1917–1973 g.g.*, Moscow: Pedagogika, 1974, 108–20, 156–82. Statistical information cited here and below may be found in *Kul'turnoe stroitel'stvo*

SSSR: Statisticheskii sbornik, Moscow-Leningrad: Soiuzorguchet, 1940; *Narodnoe obrazovanie, nauka i kul'tura v SSSR: Statisticheskii sbornik*, Moscow: Statistika, 1977; and Nicholas DeWitt, *Education and Professional Employment in the USSR*, Washington, D.C.: US Government Printing Office, 1961. For trade schools, see A. N. Veselov, *Professional'no-tekhnicheskoe obrazovanie v SSSR: Ocherki po istorii srednego i nizshego proftekhobrazovaniia*, Moscow: Vsesoiuznoe uchebno-pedagogicheskoe izdatel'stvo Proftekhizdat, 1961.

3 This testimony in the order of its presentation in the text is in HIP, Schedule A, vol. 34, case 109, 24; Schedule A, vol. 28, case 537, 2; Schedule A, vol. 29, case 631, 5; Schedule A, vol. 16, case 319, 13; and Schedule A, vol. 17, case 336, 61.

4 This testimony in HIP, Schedule A, vol. 9, case 111, 53; Schedule A, vol. 14, case 240, 51; Schedule A, vol. 36, case 333, 29. Editor's note: Note here again the use of *kultur'nyi*, the word that signified intellectual sophistication and good manners and was writ large in the "cultural revolution" that was part of the Great Turn.

5 See entries, for example, of September 18 and October 10, 1935 and September 7 and November 30, 1936.

6 Larry E. Holmes, *Grand Theater: Regional Governance in Stalin's Russia, 1931–1941*, Lanham, MD: Lexington Books, 2009, 158–9. See for more in Francis Bernstein's chapter in this book.

7 HIP, Schedule A, vol. 36, case 127, 3a.

8 For these and similar cases of misbehavior, see Oxf/Lev V-04 PF7B 8, 14, 19; Oxf/Lev M-03 PF26, 12; Oxf/Lev V-04 PF7B 8, 14; Oxf/Lev V-04 PF19, 21; and Oxf/Lev SPb-05 PF13 [A,B], 26.

9 Oxf/Lev V-05 PF17B, 18A, 18B, 33.

10 Holmes, *Stalin's School*, 58, 165–6 (and on bad behavior by Vasilii as an adult, 168). For more on "bending the rules" at School No. 25, see 56–61. On childhood mischief as part of an official celebration of a "sentimental idea of childhood as a space," see Catriona Kelly, *Children's World: Growing up in Russia, 1890–1991*, New Haven, CT: Yale University Press, 2007, 115.

11 The entry in Kosterina's diary of March 4, 1937 hints at one such case.

12 For an appreciation of vocational schools, see testimony in HIP, Schedule A, vol. 37, case 324, 36, vol. 19, case 378, 23, and vol. 7, case 93, 37.

13 Oxf/Lev V-04 PF12, 13,14, 18. Dzerzhinskii was responsible for the creation in the 1920s of several colonies for homeless children.

14 HIP, Schedule A, vol. 23, case 456, 33.

15 This paragraph's testimony can be found (in succession) in HIP, Schedule A, vol. 28, case 536, 37; Schedule A, vol. 9, case 619, 21; Schedule A, vol. 29, case 631, 6; Schedule A, vol. 10, case 133, 44a; and Schedule A, vol. 26, case 514, 8.

16 T. B. Khrabrikova, "Shkoly Kirovskoi oblasti v gody Velikoi Otechestvennoi voiny" (dissertation for a candidates degree in pedagogical sciences,

Moscow Regional Pedagogical Institute, Moscow, 1953), 385–7. Urban Schools for Working Youth and Schools for Rural Youth, founded in 1943 and 1944, respectively, accounted for only a small part of the decline of pupils attending secondary grades (i.e., grades five to seven).

17 HIP, Schedule A, vol. 16, case 314, 35.

18 HIP, Schedule A, vol. 34, case 420, 27.

19 See the syllabi in Eric Ashby, *Scientist in Russia*, New York: Penguin Books, 1947, 217–41.

20 HIP, Schedule A, vol. 9, case 11, pp. 1, 3, 19; vol. 13, case 166, p. 12; vol. 20, case 387, p. 21; vol. 25, case 493, 13, 21; vol. 33, case 1354 (NY), 10; vol. 34, case 1434 (NY), 3; vol. 35, case 1517 (NY), 12, 16, 18, 24–25. HIP, Schedule B, vol. 7, case 45, 7.

21 Holmes, *Grand Theater*, 156. The knowledgeable reader might ask why the absence, even in a brief essay about Soviet education under Stalin, of a discussion of Pavel (Pavlik) Morozov (1918–1932) or Anton Makarenko (1888–1939). For an explanation, see Larry E. Holmes, "School and Schooling under Stalin, 1931–1953," in Ben Eklof, Larry E. Holmes, and Vera Kaplan, eds., *Educational Reform in Post-Soviet Russia: Legacies and Prospects*, London: Frank Cass, 2005, 76–9. For Lev Vygotsky, see Francis Bernstein's essay in this book.

22 E. Thomas Ewing, *The Teachers of Stalinism: Policy, Practice, and Power in Soviet Schools of the 1930s*, New York: Peter Lang, 2002, 243.

23 HIP, Schedule A, vol. 24, case 476, 13–14.

24 HIP, Schedule A, vol. 20, case 387, 32.

25 Ewing, *Teachers of Stalinism*, 186.

26 Ibid.

27 In succession: HIP, Schedule A, vol. 25, case 501, 4; Schedule A, vol. 37, case 157, 3b; and Schedule A, vol. 12, case 153, 43. See similar testimony in Oxf/Lev M-03 PF26, 19.

28 Holmes, *Stalin's School*, 95–7.

29 Ibid.

30 George Fischer, "My Soviet School Days," *The Reporter*, August 16, 1949, 4, 6.

31 Wolfgang Leonhard, *Child of the Revolution*, Chicago, IL: Henry Regnery Company, 1958, 24–5.

32 HIP, Schedule A, vol. 10, case 125, 9.

33 Holmes, *Stalin's School*, 101–2.

34 Ibid.

35 Ibid., 48.

36 Larry E. Holmes, *Kirov's School No. 9: Power, Privilege, and Excellence in the Provinces, 1933–1945*, Kirov: Loban, 2008, 9–21.

37 In succession: HIP, Schedule A, vol. 32, case 642, 30; Schedule A, vol. 21, case 431, 17–18; and Schedule A, vol. 12, case 153, 43.

38 See references in her diary of March 25, April 16, September 10, September 13, and December 20, 1937.

39 Holmes, *Stalin's School*, 198 (Svetlana); and ibid., 104 (Kaminskaia).

40 Holmes, *Stalin's School*, 100.

41 Inkeles and Bauer, *Soviet Citizen*, 132.

42 HIP, Schedule A, vol. 10, case 133, 44a.

43 Elena Bonner, *Mothers and Daughters*, New York: Knopf, 1992, 320.

10

A Year of Celebrations in the Life of a Soviet Student

Karen Petrone

Imagine that you are an urban Soviet high school or university student in 1937. This year is perhaps the most infamous in the rule of Joseph Stalin, because it is the year most associated with the purges of the Communist Party (often called the Great Terror), complete with show trials, forced confessions under torture, and a public discourse of vigilance against enemies including mass demonstrations demanding "death to the traitors." Yet, if you were attending a Soviet school or university during that year, you would likely have participated in numerous Soviet holidays and public celebrations. While it might seem rather odd to emphasize celebrations and holidays during this time of intense political terror, it is important to understand that Soviet celebrations were not simply a diversion from terror, or an elaborate cover-up. The Soviet holiday calendar was one of the most significant and sustained ways in which the Communist Party and Soviet state sought to create and reinforce Soviet identities and to educate a new generation of Soviet men and women whom they hoped would be untainted by prerevolutionary culture, in the twentieth year after the Revolution of 1917. Given the political turmoil and chaos that the purges caused, the need to sustain and reinforce new Soviet identities became even more essential, at the same time that it became much more difficult. Celebrations were one of the prisms through which the Soviet young people at the time interpreted the very confusing and contradictory world that surrounded them.[1]

Using archival, memoir, literary, and secondary sources, this essay explores how urban, primarily, Slavic students and young people experienced Soviet celebration culture by describing the holiday calendar that such students might have experienced during the fateful year of 1937. In the 1930s, the Sovietization of culture in the massive multiethnic space of the Soviet Union was uneven at best. Russian-speaking cities and the capitals of the Slavic non-Russian republics were most likely to develop the array of celebration practices described here. Provincial and non-Slavic cities were less likely to participate in this celebration culture; the countryside, particularly in the non-Slavic republics, was the least likely to engage in such festivities. In short, the closer to Moscow or a major urban center you lived, the more likely you were to participate in the full range of celebrations. For the purposes of this essay, our hypothetical students live in a large, Russian-speaking city such as Moscow, Leningrad (now St. Petersburg), and Gorkii (now Nizhnyi Novgorod), or the capital of a largely Slavic republic such as Kiev (the capital of present-day Ukraine) or Minsk (the capital of present-day Belarus).

Students in 1937 experienced both constraints and choices as they participated in the year-long cycle of celebrations and commemorations. Every celebration that served the civic purpose of teaching students how to be Soviet was, to some degree, a negotiation between students and organizers. Although the Soviet state had a great deal of coercive power at its disposal, and during collectivization and the purges especially, used violence to ensure conformity, the state could only use coercive measures in as far as it would insure the presence of citizens at events. While coercion to attend could create a powerful display of unanimity that was quite useful for the state, no amount of coercion could make participants internalize the ideals espoused during holiday celebrations, unless they were inherently appealing and attractive to their audiences. Forced attendance could in fact be counterproductive if it made the students resentful of Soviet policies. For holiday demonstrations (in truth, ceremonial parades), particularly on International Workers' Day (May 1) and the October Revolution anniversary (November 7), students and workers typically had to gather at their institutions hours in advance; it could be "tedious and unpleasant" to wait one's turn to march past the tribune on which the local Party leaders stood.[2]

When participation in holiday events was mandatory, truancy was rare, as students' absence could have very serious disciplinary consequences. Yet, even when attendance was required, students then (like students now) always had some choice in the extent to which they became personally absorbed by the events. Outward compliance is not the same as internal engagement. Organizers understood that creating a popular event, which would effectively model how to be an ideal Soviet citizen, required that they provide appealing activities in which students desired to participate and that would give students a positive feeling about the Soviet ideals being celebrated. Such activities often included sporting events, concerts, dances, and the screening of feature films. Given that the Soviet Union had just barely recovered from the austerity and severe famine caused by collectivization between 1928 and 1933, another popular aspect of celebrations was the unusual availability of holiday foods. As one university student wrote in the mid-1930s,

> the stores are suddenly filled with hitherto unobtainable goods. The food in the dining halls becomes abundant. The whole country is in a heightened pre-holiday mood.[3]

Providing food enhanced the popularity of holiday events and helped to create a celebratory atmosphere.

Despite the fact that the Soviet Union was purportedly an egalitarian society, the Soviet leadership also used the celebration of holidays to single out and reward Soviet citizens who were particularly successful in fulfilling the ideals of the new Soviet men and women. They employed celebrations to reinforce a variety of hierarchies, such as awarding privileges to the select students (roughly one out of six) who had been accepted into the Communist Youth League (*Komsomol*), the organization open to fourteen- to twenty-eight-year olds that served as preparation for adult membership in the Communist Party. Only students in good academic standing who had the proper class (worker or peasant) background, or those whose family had Communist Party ties, were eligible for admission. The children of Communist Party members usually had privileged access not only to the best schools but also to the most attractive aspects of celebrations. Students' status was also shaped by their family's social and economic position and the proximity of their parents to the political elite. Those hailing from families associated with the former elites of tsarist times stood little chance to get invited to join Party or *Komsomol* ranks. Other hierarchies included that of academic performance, as grades were public knowledge, and students sat in grade order from highest to lowest in the classroom.

A Very Busy Start to the Year

The Soviet holiday calendar began on the very first day of the year, January 1, 1937, with New Year's Day. While some elite high schools and *Komsomol* organizations at universities might have had the resources to organize New Year's masquerade balls and carnivals for their students, the New Year's holiday was mostly geared to younger students. New Year's Day was a joyous holiday for children, celebrated with singing and dancing around the *yolka* (fir tree), the Soviet nonreligious version of a Christmas tree, and the distribution of small gifts to younger students. In Lydia Chukovskaia's novella about the 1930s *Sofiia Petrovna*, the title character Sofiia organizes a *yolka* celebration at the publishing house where she works, and buys gifts such as a drum, toy soldiers, and "a pretty little trumpet with a fluffy tassel" for the children of her coworkers.[4] The naive Sofiia offends some of her coworkers when she purchases nicer gifts for the children of the Communist Party members than for their children, inadvertently laying bare the way in which even the seemingly apolitical fir tree celebration could reinforce hierarchies.

While celebrating at a masquerade ball, or dancing around the New Year's tree, might seem apolitical, the fact that there was a New Year's tree at all demonstrates a compromise between the Soviet state and its citizens. The year 1937 marked only the second holiday since the official return of the *yolka* in late 1935 (albeit now as a New Year's tree rather than a Christmas tree). As an avowedly atheist state, the Soviets rejected the Orthodox Christian holiday calendar and during the tumultuous years of Stalin's "Great Turn" from 1928 to 1932, banned Christmas trees and "unmasked" Grandfather Frost (*Ded Moroz*), the Russian version of Santa Claus, "as an ally of the priest and *kulak* (the purported class enemy among the wealthier strata of the peasantry)."[5] The introduction of the New Year's holiday as a state-sponsored celebration for children indicated the desire of Soviet authorities to return to normality after the difficult years of near-civil war between city and countryside during collectivization. Authorities also continued their efforts to displace Christmas as an Orthodox Christian holiday. By offering an engaging holiday alternative, Soviet organizers aimed to decrease the appeal of Christian holiday traditions. Yet, due to the proximity of the two holidays (January 1 and January 7[6]) some families used the return of the *yolka* to restore their Christian holiday traditions covertly.

Students likely responded to the New Year's celebrations in a variety of ways. No doubt, many enjoyed the relatively apolitical festivities that brought entertainment and fun to otherwise austere lives. In those religious families where the return of the New Year's tree offered an opportunity to restore Christmas traditions, students experienced two different versions of the holiday that could vex them. Would students embrace the Soviet definitions of the holiday and reject their parents' religious ideals, or would they celebrate the religious holiday at home? The former created the chance of generational conflict, while the latter produced a possibly dangerous situation for students in which they defied school (and state) expectations through their behavior at home, by blending Soviet and non-Soviet world views in their daily lives. Either way, Soviet students had to navigate each holiday celebration in a world that was sharply different than the one in which their parents grew up and in which expectations of family life had changed dramatically.

Students had to make even more complicated moral choices at the end of January of that year, in connection with public demonstrations during the second Moscow show trial of the "anti-Soviet Trotskyist Center" that ran from January 23 through January 30, 1937. The government sought out "enemies of the people," a term that echoed the Reign of Terror (1793–4) during the French Revolution. The defendants of this notorious public trial, who included prominent former Party members such as Karl Radek (1885–1939) and Yuri Piatakov (1890–1937), were tortured or tricked by the Soviet secret police (NKVD) into confessing to heinous and improbable crimes. Their supposed misdeeds included colluding with the exiled Leon Trotsky (1879–1940), the Nazis, and the Japanese to destroy the Soviet Union and restore capitalism. On the day that the trial verdicts were read, Soviet authorities organized demonstrations demanding the death penalty for the convicted. Some high school and college students were mobilized to participate in these demonstrations, carrying banners that read "Death to the Traitors" and demanding more trials of "oppositionists–vile messengers of Trotsky."[7]

Soviet officials, then, enlisted students and workers to take to the streets to demonstrate popular support for the purges. Given the atmosphere of fear that permeated both Moscow and the country at large, it would have been extremely perilous to refuse, lest the students themselves be accused of lacking "vigilance." The appearance of traitors among formerly trusted Communist officials (an earlier trial in the summer of 1936 had already seen a number convicted of treason) would likely have elicited further confusion and shock among students. These supposed threats against the very existence of the Soviet Union were frightening, as was the groundswell of whispered rumors of neighbors and friends who had been arrested in the middle of the night as traitors who masqueraded as loyal Soviet citizens. Students with doubts or confusion about these accusations most likely kept them to themselves, while some were forced to be complicit in demanding the violent end of the convicted "traitors," and in advocating for their execution. In these circumstances, one can imagine that some students found celebrating around the *yolka*, or commemorating the accomplishments of a beloved literary figure (as they would do soon after in February) much more appealing. Yet, some students may also have found the Orwellian articulation of strong support for the Soviet state and intense hatred for enemies exhilarating.

Just as students were digesting the news that they were living among traitors on all sides, on February 10, 1937 they were also called upon to participate in the most important cultural event of the year, the commemoration of the hundredth anniversary of the death of the greatest Russian poet and founder of the Russian literary language, Alexander Sergeevich Pushkin (1799–1837). In honor of the Pushkin Centennial, every Soviet school was expected to highlight the works of Pushkin in its literature curriculum. The government sponsored the publication of more than 13 million books by and about Pushkin. Theaters performed Pushkin's works, and museums organized Pushkin exhibits. There were Pushkin "carnivals, costume balls, ice sculptures, jokes, crossword puzzles ... and even ... Pushkin cakes."[8] Almost every urban student would have been involved in some aspect of this Centennial. Luckier students might have attended costume parties based on Pushkin's characters, or be taken on field trips to "Pushkin places," such as his apartment in Leningrad at Moika 12, where he died after fighting a duel, the Lycée where he studied in Detskoe Selo (the former Tsarskoe Selo), or his country estate Mikhailovskoe in Pskov province. They might also have attended a play, ballet, or opera based on his works. Even with very limited financial resources, teachers could focus on Pushkin's work in the classroom and organize "Pushkin evenings" with poetry recitations and dramatic readings by students.

Like celebrations around the *yolka*, many Pushkin festivities will have appealed to students as apolitical fun. Despite the fact that Pushkin had been a serf-owning nobleman, and therefore an unlikely Soviet hero, he was lionized for his role in the creation of Russian literature, while much was made of his youthful support of the 1825 Decembrist revolt, the first modern revolutionary stirring in tsarist Russia. Pushkin was extremely appealing to a broad audience as a dashing, handsome, and romantic figure, and as a versatile creative genius who wrote across numerous literary genres. In the Pushkin Centennial, there was something for everyone, it seemed. Some ignored politics and were attracted to Pushkin purely as a brilliant writer. Others fashioned Pushkin as a seeker of freedom through literature amidst the political constraints of tsarism, and saw him as a model for artists and intelligentsia in a time of political censorship and repression. The Soviet central press, on the other hand, fully Sovietized Pushkin; an article published in the ubiquitous newspaper *Pravda* on the anniversary of his death even claimed that Pushkin would applaud the "destruction of the exploiting classes" like the "counter-revolutionary bourgeois exploiters" and "Trotskyite bandits" just convicted at the January show trial.[9]

The emphasis on Pushkin as a great *Russian* poet was meanwhile symptomatic of the transformation of Soviet nationality policy in the 1930s. It had begun to de-emphasize the egalitarian relationships of the eleven Soviet republics that had been previously stressed and elevated the Russian nation as the "first among equals." The Pushkin Centennial led to a flurry of translations of Pushkin's works into the languages of the non-Russian Soviet republics as "the whole Soviet Union" was supposed to be reading Pushkin. Reading the works of this particular Russian poet allegedly united the Soviet Union. One can imagine that what was likely a satisfying and exciting demonstration of Russian national pride among students in the Russian Republic might not have hard to swallow for some in Kiev or Minsk (or Yerevan or Tashkent), for Pushkin was elevated above the republics' native poets and authors. Nevertheless, millions of students across the Soviet Union experienced the festivities surrounding Pushkin as, at least to some degree, an affirmation of Soviet educational and cultural progress. In the Soviet formulation, the literature and art, which in tsarist times could only be enjoyed by the elite, now belonged to all Soviet citizens. The positive nature of the festivities had appeal to a broad range of Soviet students, who willingly participated in the celebrations honoring Pushkin.

The Two Most Prominent Soviet Holidays

May 1 and November 7 were the two most important dates in the Soviet holiday calendar. May 1 is International Workers' Day, or Labor Day, a socialist holiday that originated in North America (ironically, as Labor Day is now celebrated in September) in the 1880s and was commemorated before the October Revolution in Russia and across the industrialized world by strikes and protests. The Soviet government turned May 1 into its first joyous national holiday in May 1918 to celebrate the workers' victory in overturning the tsarist government. The first of May coincided with the arrival of spring, an event much anticipated after long Soviet winters, and it became an extremely popular holiday. The holiday granted two days off from work and school (May 1 and 2), signaling its importance to the production-obsessed Soviet government, and contributing to its popularity. November 7, the most important Soviet holiday, marked the anniversary of the October Revolution. This holiday also included two days off from work or school, November 7 and 8.

Although there had been much experimentation and inventiveness in Soviet celebrations in the 1920s, during the Stalin years, the holidays on May 1 and November 7 had settled into a predictable, and not very spontaneous, pattern.[10] Usually, on the eve of the holiday, local officials would organize mass meetings at which leaders gave (ideally) inspirational speeches about the meaning of the holiday in relation to current events, including both the international situation and progress in the fulfillment of Soviet production plans. Local officials, Party secretaries, and educational leaders often used these events to single out and reward outstanding students or workers who, like the famed miner Alexei Stakhanov (1906–77) in 1935, had set records in fulfilling their production quotas.[11] Sometimes officials awarded these successful "New Soviet Men and Women" coveted prizes such as bicycles or record players. These official ceremonies were usually followed by entertainment, food, and alcohol (in adult milieus). While students might not have been so eager to listen to official speeches, they might have found satisfaction in seeing friends win a prize (or winning one themselves), and they likely enjoyed the music, dancing, and refreshments that accompanied such meetings.

These celebratory meetings were followed by holiday demonstrations on the mornings of May 1 and November 7. Every city and town prepared a reviewing stand from which the local Party leaders viewed the parade. The holiday parades marked new Soviet geographies and denoted new centers of power at the locations where the Party leaders viewed the parade.[12] Students in towns across the Soviet Union would have thus routinely taken part in a "walking tour" of the most important Soviet places in their towns, physically reimagining and remapping the city as a Soviet rather than a tsarist city. The most important demonstration in the country took place in Moscow's Red Square, with Stalin viewing the parade from atop Lenin's Mausoleum. Although Red Square was a centuries-old meeting place, alert Moscow students would have noticed other drastic changes to the site in addition to the Mausoleum's appearance. Recently, Moscow Party boss Lazar Kaganovich (1893–1991) had ordered the destruction of several old churches at the entrances to the square, so that "the demonstration processions from the six districts of Moscow should all pour into Red Square at the same time."[13] The free entrance of the marchers into Red Square symbolized the Soviet victory over Orthodox Christianity and the affirmation of Lenin's tomb as a venerated site of pilgrimage.

Holiday parades were also deeply hierarchical events, with the order of the procession determined by the relative importance of the participants. In 1937 in Moscow, organizers deemed the military to be the most important sector of Soviet life, and the well-organized male soldiers marched first. Next came the industrial workers, then students, and finally the agricultural workers from Moscow province. By their placement in the parade, students understood that by studying they outranked agricultural laborers in the Soviet social hierarchy, but that they were not as important as the exclusively soldiers, or the primarily male workers who carried out heavy industrial labor, the most important form of Soviet labor. The internal organization of each column was hierarchical as well, and based on the fulfillment of the yearly production plan: The most productive districts of the city marched closest to the Mausoleum. The most productive factory in the district carried the district banner; individual workshops marched in the order of their success in fulfilling the plan; and the best Stakhanovites and shock workers led their workshops.

Likewise, the parade revealed students' status in public. The best students and most successful classes held the schools' banners and marched first. The parade could thus be an affirmation of individual success for the top students and groups of students, or the public display of failure for those marching farthest from Lenin's Mausoleum and at the tail end of the parade.

Once the students marching in the demonstration passed the reviewing stand, the official portions of the holiday were over for them, and they were free to celebrate in more personal ways. Students could take advantage of additional concerts and firework displays provided by Soviet authorities or they could enjoy free time. Since May 2 and November 8 were rare days off from work, the evenings of May 1 and November 7 offered significant opportunities for socializing in both formal and informal ways. Some of the personal festivities reinforced students' identities as good Soviet citizens, while others, such as drunkenness, rowdiness, and the incorporation of prerevolutionary celebratory elements, would have contradicted Soviet norms and created a space for reinforcing identities that were not particularly Soviet, or in direct conflict with Soviet norms.

Informal celebrations on May 2, 1937, were particularly fraught for Soviet authorities because Orthodox Easter happened to fall on that very day. This coincidence created a tension for families even greater than the one between Christmas and New Year's Day. Easter was the most important Orthodox holiday, and the day off from work allowed families the time to attend religious services and processions, prepare special holiday foods permitted after the fasting of Lent, and organize traditional picnics at relatives' graves in remembrance, including departed family in the celebration of Christ's resurrection. Given the tense political atmosphere in 1937, it is not clear how many urban families overtly participated in Easter celebrations, yet it is likely that at least some students took part in some elements of the Easter celebration during May 1 and 2, 1937. It is also likely that a portion of these students felt conflicted about their participation in non-Soviet activities, while others were more comfortable with a syncretic approach that blended the two holidays. The celebration of the May Day holiday, like other holidays, presented students with a series of opportunities to demonstrate loyalty to the Soviet project, and they could take those opportunities, or they could decline them in subtle or not-so-subtle ways.

In the year 1937, the anniversary of the October Revolution took on special significance because it was the twentieth anniversary of the event, and therefore the celebrations were supposed to be both more memorable and more politically significant than those of previous years. Organizers sought to differentiate the celebration of the twentieth anniversary from the usual celebratory routine. P. M. Kerzhentsev (1881–1940), the Chairman of the State Committee on the Arts, proclaimed the deep significance of the October events as follows: "the celebration of the jubilee is not just some kind of ceremonial meeting but a great political campaign, which not only celebrates our achievements after twenty years but simultaneously strikes a blow against our enemies ... and strengthens the masses' consciousness of the correctness of the Lenin-Stalin line."[14] Kerzhentsev pointed out further that the country was celebrating "the twentieth anniversary of the greatest revolution in the history of humanity" and that, "A new historical epoch in the life of humanity has begun."[15] These grandiose visions of the meaning of the holiday led to a lot of pressure on holiday organizers to produce memorable holiday commemorations and art, literature, theater, and music that celebrated the remarkable transformation of "a backward peasant country" into "a country of powerful advanced industry."[16]

Unfortunately, for the organizers of the celebration, the atmosphere of terror created by Stalin's purges profoundly interfered with preparations for this grand celebration. The mass arrests hit Communist Party cadres particularly hard, including the artists, writers, and organizers of celebrations, who were usually senior Party members. When major figures among Soviet cultural personnel were arrested, work was disrupted and the coworkers of those arrested themselves fell under suspicion for failing to be vigilant enough to recognize a traitor in their midst. While creating celebrations that followed the correct political line was always difficult, under the conditions of the purges it was almost impossible. Irrespective of the purges, there were many reversals of previous Soviet ideology in the mid-1930s (e.g., the rehabilitation of previously rejected tsars such as Peter the Great and Ivan the Terrible as heroic and exemplary figures), and it was extremely difficult for the authors of celebration to keep track of the many zigzags in the official line. Because of the purges themselves, a revolutionary hero could become a villain overnight, and so the story of the revolution constantly had to be revised to omit, or discredit, disgraced figures, the most notable of whom, of course, was Leon Trotsky. Under these difficult conditions both paralysis and hypervigilance set in as editors and writers determined that it was safer not to produce anything at all than to produce something that could be considered traitorous.

How, then, might students have experienced this anniversary in the middle of such turmoil? Under these difficult conditions, celebration organizers were likely to be on edge and more controlling of the behavior of participants and the messages on the signs and placards that they carried. Students may have had to assemble earlier for demonstrations and were likely expected to behave in a more orderly fashion during all the festivities. While the celebrations in honor of the twentieth anniversary of the Revolution did occur from November 6 to 8 as planned, they were not particularly different from earlier celebrations. It is difficult to know the extent to which the rhetoric about the momentousness of the occasion had raised expectations for the holiday. If students' expectations were raised, then the holiday itself was likely to be disappointing, for the holiday generally conformed to the familiar patterns that they had come to expect of such festivities. If one of the goals of the celebration was to engage in heightened political education to raise the consciousness of the population, then the celebration likely fell far short of this goal, too, as well-crafted artistic works and political speeches did not materialize. During this jubilee year of the Revolution, students were probably more strictly controlled and less skillfully engaged during the proceedings. In these circumstances, it seems unlikely that Soviet authorities could effectively convey the essence of the "greatest revolution" and humanity's "new epoch," to use Kerzhentsev's terms. This relatively lackluster nature of the festivities had the potential to raise questions in participants' minds about the true nature of Soviet achievements.

The Year Ends with a Celebration of Politics

Although not strictly speaking a celebration, the year 1937 ended with a large-scale civic event that was similar to a celebration: the elections to the Supreme Soviet that took place on December 12, 1937. With great fanfare, the Soviet Union had ratified the new "Stalin Constitution" on December 5, 1936, and, in July 1937, the government promulgated new election laws that this set of basic laws mandated. Although the elections to the Supreme Soviet were originally supposed to have multiple candidates on the ballot for each district, in October, the Central Committee of the Communist Party announced there would only be one candidate on the ballot per district. The December 12 elections thus became elaborate political theater in which all eligible Soviet citizens (without exception) were supposed to go to the polls to approve the candidate preselected for their district by the highest Party bodies. Students eighteen and older joined the voters and cast ballots in this celebration of Soviet democracy. Younger students might have been involved in encouraging their parents and neighbors to vote. Older teens who could not yet vote were sometimes called upon to help make sure that everyone in their precinct had voted. Precinct officials exhorted and then badgered citizens to take part in this event, since the government sought universal turnout to prove the population's approval of Stalin and the Soviet government. Each student, therefore, either took part in the elections or witnessed family members taking part in them.

Like the Pushkin Centennial at the beginning of the year, learning about the significance of the Stalin Constitution and the electoral system became a mandatory element of the school curriculum. Thus, Soviet students learned about universal, direct, equal, and secret suffrage, and about how all Soviet citizens were guaranteed rights such as the freedom of speech, freedom of religion, and freedom of the press. The distance between the principles enshrined in the constitution and realities of Soviet life caused confusion among students who dutifully studied this document at school. Many of the lessons were too complex for younger students who did not gain a firm grasp of the issues involved. Older students peppered their teachers with reasonable (but dangerous) questions like, "How can we have freedom of the press if there is censorship?"[17] The *Komsomol* organization in one eighth-grade class got into significant trouble for writing a "class constitution" on the model of the Stalin Constitution.[18] The class's "right to labor" clause stated that "the teacher does not have the right to give more work than is customary."[19] These students clearly paid careful attention to the content of the Stalin Constitution and were fully engaged in its discussion of rights. The students' careful study of the document revealed its contradictions and encouraged students to think about their own rights in potentially subversive ways. Like the other holidays in 1937, the political campaign surrounding the elections to the Supreme Soviet sought to promote students' participation in Soviet political life. Unlike the other holidays, if students became too engaged in this process, they could undermine Soviet intentions by demanding rights that the Soviet government had no intention of giving them.

This journey through the 1937 holiday calendar has focused on the major celebratory events of that fateful year. The political turmoil of the year 1937 shaped holidays in significant ways and made them distinct from the holiday celebrations that came before or after. Celebration participants were called upon to endorse the death penalty for traitors to the Soviet Union, while the poet Pushkin, though he had been a nobleman himself, was still imagined to be in favor of the "destruction of the exploiting classes." The violence of 1937 that was enacted in NKVD prisons and the camps of the *Gulag* was thus also visible in the rhetoric of celebration culture that year. This violence also shaped the organization of celebrations that year. Soviet officials at all levels were terrified of being punished for making trivial mistakes, as even simple grammatical or spelling errors in posters and placards could be perceived as sabotage. By November of 1937, the organizers of October 1917's celebration were too paralyzed by the purges to produce a triumphant celebration worthy of the jubilee anniversary. And around the same time, the highest Soviet authorities cancelled contested elections in December because of fear of the population's response to government policies.

This essay has considered many of the most significant celebrations in the 1937 Soviet holiday calendar. Yet, it is important to remember that there were numerous other celebrated dates including the anniversary of Lenin's death on January 24, Red Army Day on February 23, International Women's Day on March 8, International Youth Day in early September, and Harvest Day (primarily a rural celebration) in mid-October, among others.[20] At very frequent intervals throughout the year, the organizers of celebrations invited Soviet students to engage with Soviet ideals and norms. Holiday events almost always combined political education and the modeling of normative Soviet identities with material rewards, light-hearted entertainment, sports, food, and alcohol. These events varied in their proportions of ideology and fun, and could be, by turns, extremely attractive to young people, extremely dull and routine, a convenient cover for celebrating religious and folk traditions that the government frowned upon, or even an opportunity to criticize Soviet life.

Whether Soviet holidays were entertaining or dull, they were a significant and virtually unavoidable feature of Soviet everyday life. Soviet students navigated these holidays in a wide variety of ways from enthusiastic engagement to passive acceptance, to passive avoidance, to subversion. The celebration of holidays was an important aspect of Soviet students' daily lives and offered them myriad ways to connect with and learn about Soviet ideology, drawing them in to Soviet culture and the Soviet worldview. It also offered them opportunities for making individual choices that could either reinforce or undermine their Soviet identities.

The Soviet holiday calendar was critically important to the delivery of civic and political education to Soviet students, and to the creation of Soviet role models for them to follow, but holidays did not influence all Soviet students in the same way. Geography, nationality, economic conditions, social status, Party or *Komsomol* status, age, education level, level of academic success, political ambitions, gender, and religious beliefs all shaped how students participated in and perceived celebrations. This account has tried to emphasize the numerous factors that caused variations in how students engaged with Soviet holidays in the year 1937, and the range of individual choices (however narrow at times) for Soviet students who lived through this tumultuous era.

Notes

1 On Stalinist celebrations, see Karen Petrone, *Life Has Become More Joyous, Comrades: Celebrations in the Time of Stalin*, Bloomington: Indiana University Press, 2000; Malte Rolf, *Soviet Mass Festivals, 1917–1991*, Pittsburgh, PA: University of Pittsburgh Press, 2013; and, for postwar celebrations, see Serhy Yekelchyk, *Stalin's Citizens: Everyday Politics in the Wake of Total War*, New York: Oxford University Press, 2014.

2 Descriptions of the organization of demonstrations come from Valentina Bogdan, *Mimikriia v SSSR*, Frankfurt: Polyglott-Druck GmbH, n.d., 179–80; and from Party discussions in Moscow's Sokol'nicheskii District (*Tsentral'nyi arkhiv obshchestvenno-politicheskoi istorii Moskvy* [Central Archive of the social and political history of Moscow; from here: TsAOPIM], f. 85, op. 1, d. 1207, l. 17 [1937]).

3 H. G. Friese, "Student Life in a Soviet University," in George Kline, ed., *Soviet Education*, New York: Columbia University Press, 1957, 62.

4 Lydia Chukovskaya, *Sofia Petrovna*, trans. Aline Werth, Evanston, IL: Northwestern University Press, 1988, 29–30.

5 Richard Stites, *Revolutionary Dreams: Utopian Vision and Experimental Life in the Russian Revolution*, New York: Oxford University Press, 1989, 230.

6 The Russian Orthodox Church continued to follow the Julian calendar; Christmas thus began thirteen days later than in the Western churches during the twentieth century.

7   *New York Times*, January 31, 1937.

8   Petrone, *Life Has Become More Joyous*, 113.

9   *Pravda*, February 10, 1937.

10 See Stites, *Revolutionary Dreams*, 228.

11 See Lewis H. Siegelbaum, *Stakhanovism and the Politics of Productivity in the U.S.S.R, 1935–1941*, Cambridge: Cambridge University Press, 1988.

12 Rolf, *Soviet Mass Festivals*, 78–83.

13 Stites, *Revolutionary Dreams*, 243.

14 Petrone, *Life Has Become More Joyous*, 149, 151, 154.

15 Ibid.

16 Ibid.

17 Petrone, *Life Has Become More Joyous*, 197, 200.

18 Ibid.

19 Ibid.

20 See Choi Chatterjee, *Celebrating Women: Gender, Festival Culture, and Bolshevik Ideology, 1910–1939*, Pittsburgh, PA: Pittsburgh University Press, 2002.

11

Soviet People's Informal Interactions with Officials of the Stalin-Era Party-State

James Heinzen

In the time of Stalin, what was the role of the Soviet Party-state in people's everyday lives? Or to put it another way, how did ordinary people and the officials serving in the enormous Soviet state bureaucracy tend to interact with each other? Under Stalin, the regime was concerned with protecting the property of the state. Officials were in the position of protecting these very resources from theft and misappropriation, even amid famine and mass shortages. Yet, it is a major paradox of Soviet history that the Party-state had trouble maintaining discipline among those same officials.[1]

In the modern world, people come into contact with representatives of the state more often than in premodern societies, as governments have created large state bureaucracies to handle vast varieties of administrative functions. States like the Soviet Union with grand aspirations to "modernize" their populations and overcome their "backwardness" aimed to reach even more deeply into the everyday lives of individuals and families.[2] The USSR's leaders sought to reshape and remold social life, family life, and inner spiritual life and values.

In any social system, people interact with state administrations (governments) in both formal and informal ways. In most cases, people follow the rules, as bureaucracies move at their own, often very slow, pace. In other cases, however, people find ways to skirt the formal rules, relying instead on informal practices or arrangements to get things done. This chapter focuses on the latter, describing the important ways that people *informally* negotiated with bureaucrats in attempts to circumvent the often irrational, draconian, or inefficient rules, laws, and structures of the Stalinist dictatorship.[3] Sometimes, this "wheeling and dealing" was done at the initiative of a local official, while other times a petitioner forced the issue.

The state bureaucracy under Stalin was massive and ever expanding.[4] As the economy grew during the Stalin's collectivization and industrialization drives in the late 1920s and 1930s, the state that managed and supervised it exploded in size. After the war, it grew still further. The number of state functionaries in the Soviet Union grew almost without interruption from 1917 until the death of Stalin in 1953. The blossoming of government administrations, offices, and agencies of all kinds all over the country was encouraged by the breakneck growth of the economy, the nonstop creation of new industrial sites and even entire new cities, the planning for national defense and war, the extreme centralization of economic planning and decision-making in the "command economy," and the explosion of social welfare policies.

As a consequence of its mission to be recognized as the leading force in every aspect of people's lives, the Communist Party created hundreds of thousands of "primary Party organizations," commonly known as Party cells, in every factory, office, collective farm, cultural institution, school, and all other significant organizations in the country. Party cells were responsible for mobilizing popular support for central policies at the grass roots at every possible turn. The Communist Party in its "vanguard" role aspired to connect with the daily lives of all Soviet subjects.

In its attempts to achieve this, the Party ordered state agencies to monitor the actions and political attitudes of Soviet people, to guide and educate them, and to look after their well-being. The Party-state expected that people would internalize "Soviet" values and strictures. In essence, the Party-state aimed to achieve unlimited reach into the population's activities, beliefs, and worldview. Whether at the workplace or inside families, in public or the private spaces, the Stalinist Party-state insisted on playing the leading role. In urban areas, authorities to a larger degree succeeded at making the Party-state a major presence. In other places, especially in the countryside, the limitations of infrastructure and geography across this immense territory made the goal much more difficult to achieve.

The Party-state was never able to reach this ambitious goal of a state apparatus acting in perfect harmony with the worldview of ordinary people, in part because officials themselves did not live up to the state's expectations for them. In its attempts to create "New Soviet People," the Stalin regime tried to train a huge cohort of a new type of honest, hard-working government official. In the vision of the Party, these officials were to be the opposite of the stereotypically corrupt and lazy officials who served in tsarist administrations, and who featured prominently in the classic literature of prerevolutionary Russia. Officials should be shining examples of the "New Soviet Person." They should be pure, selfless, and fully dedicated to "the people" and the mission of the Party. These were to be absolutely incorruptible people. Ultimately, they should rise to become Party officials and Soviet administrators. The Party put its faith in these New People. But the Party's idealized hopes fell short in a number of ways.

In Soviet ideology, it was the injustices and inequalities of *capitalism* that produced the conditions in which a selfish, venal officialdom could thrive. In the capitalist world, wealthy elites would pay officials to do their bidding, from the top to the bottom of the hierarchy, in the capitals and in the provinces. For Party ideologists, capitalism was synonymous with corruption. An unresponsive and thieving civil service was not just a prominent feature of capitalism; it was absolutely *essential* to it. Once the socialist revolution triumphed in October 1917, Party leaders believed that the vices and pathologies associated with capitalism, including a greedy bureaucracy that was unresponsive to "the people," would quickly disappear.

It turned out, however, that many Soviet officials were poorly trained and educated. They lacked the kind of service ethos that Party leaders were attempting to inculcate in new civil servants. In October 1921, Lenin himself had warned about the "arrogance" of those new officials who had let their power go straight to their heads. Some of them treated the population they were supposed to serve with the same kind of contempt and incompetence that the long-disparaged tsarist-era bureaucrats had done. The Revolution was supposed to have wiped such bureaucrats—and their mercenary, unprincipled ways—from the face of the earth, or at least from the territory of Russia. But many new officials understood little about the Communist Party's mission or aspirations, choosing to exploit their positions for purely self-serving aims.

Party authorities themselves also were of two minds about the army of bureaucrats they needed to run the country. Party leaders often saw officialdom every bit as negatively as the population did. Newspaper stories savaged individual bureaucrats for their incompetence or greed. Officially produced films and fiction did the same, caricaturing them in cartoons that depicted the indignities of these interactions. The thieving or bribe-taking low- or mid-level official was a prominent fixture of the cartoons that appeared in the extremely popular satirical journal *Krokodil* (*The Crocodile*). Self-satisfied officials in fancy suits were ridiculed as fat, smug, and happy receiving poorly clothed and humble petitioners in their offices, decorated with upscale furniture in the latest style.

Official discourse made sure to label such bureaucrats as just a few leftover "bad apples," the last of a dying breed, and the final embarrassing vestiges of a quickly dying capitalist past. Yet it is telling that cartoons and literature portraying officials were almost always negative. Rarely can one find representations of the generous, wise, or effective civil servant.

Official statements declared that, indeed, there were a few self-serving bureaucrats who were holdovers from capitalist society. Their "capitalist mentalities" had not yet fully faded from their minds even as the regime claimed that a superior type of social and economic system—which Stalin called "socialism"—was being built in the 1930s and 1940s. As late as 1953, more than thirty-five years after the Revolution, the regime continued to use this language, blaming the poor performance of a handful of incompetent officials on the stubborn persistence of habits and ways of thinking inherited from the pre-Revolutionary world. As time went on, such explanations were more difficult to justify, especially a generation or two after the fall of the Romanov dynasty. And Soviet people could and did compare the arbitrariness of the bureaucrats they knew with those legendarily corrupt tsarist officials, about whom they read in prerevolutionary literature. The *chinovnik*s they encountered in such books seemed much less foreign than they were supposed to be.

Tsarist Russia was a place where certain well-established traditions of "self-interested giving" among officials and petitioners had flourished. Some of them gained new life in the Soviet Union. One of the most common of these traditional practices was *podnoshenie*, or "the bringing of gifts." The practice of *podnoshenie* meant that lower-level officials would make payments up the hierarchy to their superiors in the administrative pyramid. Bosses would expect regular "gifts" from their employees; those at the top of the pyramid stood to benefit the most. At the lower levels of the bureaucracy, petty officials often found the money for the payments to their superiors by skimming it from the local population, in a second practice known as *kormlenie*, using one's position to "feed" from the population. Officials would supplement their small salaries by demanding payment in money or in kind for services that they were supposed to provide for free as part of their duties. These interlocking bureaucratic practices of "feeding" and "bringing gifts" easily made the transition across the revolutionary divide of 1917. They found fertile ground in many Soviet workplaces in conditions of widespread shortage, a large and swelling bureaucracy, and poor salaries for bureaucrats.

The historian Elena Zubkova has emphasized that Soviet people regarded the Party-state at the national level to be a distant entity, cut off from the daily lives of average people.[5] Despite the Party's claim to represent the interests of all citizens, many people thought of the central government structures in Moscow as a faraway, abstract thing that had little meaningful connection to their day-to-day lives. Although it was the leadership in Moscow that failed to keep the Party's promises of abundance and equality that had been made to the population, people normally directed their resentment at *local* officials occupying positions in social, economic, and political administrations.

Locally, Soviet people interacted with the growing bureaucracy in a number of ways. Popular accounts are full of cases in which people describe unpleasant interactions they have had with rude, foolish, or lazy bureaucrats. Frustrating encounters with arbitrary and callous officials was part of the everyday experience of Soviet people. One can get a sense of their complaints from the enormous quantity of indignant letters—sometimes anonymous, but often signed—that the population fired off to institutions of every possible type. Letters alleging some kind of malfeasance by local officials poured into prosecutors' offices and courts of law, to housing and health agencies of every stripe, and to regional and national newspapers. Most of these letters were never published, of course, because of the heavy censorship that prevailed throughout the country. Letter writers typically blamed local officials for the hardships they were enduring, rather than pointing the finger at central policies or Party leaders in Moscow. They often claimed (usually wrongly) that incompetent or corrupt local bureaucrats were failing to carry out Moscow's beneficent central directives. Had local officials only properly followed Moscow's instructions, they believed, their lives would be greatly improved.

The fact that the government often failed to provide accurate information heightened this problem. Into the vacuum of reliable evidence flowed every kind of rumor. These rumors, which often spread like wildfire, typically reinforced the supposition that local officials were lying to the population, hiding critical information, and hoarding supplies for themselves that were supposed to go to ordinary people. Such anecdotes could cast doubt on—and sometimes undercut the legitimacy of—local power structures.

In spite of popular stereotypes, most low-level officials were not able really to enrich themselves at the expense of local populations. Most officials did not live in opulence. They eked out a marginal existence, often struggling to find sufficient food and decent clothing, like the rest of the population. Surprisingly, perhaps, most low-level officials were paid little more than the average wage of most factory workers. As a result of their low salaries, petty bureaucrats often believed that they had to earn a little something extra on the side in order to lift themselves from subsistence living. Yet, despite their rank and poor salaries, local officials had a great deal of power over essential aspects of people's lives.

Yet there was a stratum of Party members at the top of both central and local hierarchies who *did* earn more than most other people in Soviet society. Popular resentment of the privileges enjoyed by well-to-do officials was by all accounts great, inspiring anger and envy. Letters from the population are full of complaints about what ordinary people saw as the unfair perks of the elites. They bitterly decried high officials' access to cars, their large and well-furnished apartments, their power to build nice *dachas* (cottages) for themselves, their trips to fine resorts for family vacations, and their ability to gain entrance to secret "special stores" that were well-stocked with scarce and high-quality goods that most people could never get their hands on. Some people even began to question the legitimacy of the "workers' state" in light of the obvious structural inequalities that they witnessed firsthand.

Furthermore, in the absence of private property and private markets, Party and state bureaucrats were charged with many economic management functions and controlled access to natural resources and the nation's wealth. Indeed, a key reality of Soviet political and social life was that state bureaucrats controlled people's access to nearly all essential goods and services, including those that were in short supply (known colloquially as *defitsitnye* goods). The responsibilities of many officials had this critical access and supply function at their heart. State officials rather than private businesses were the purveyors of necessities and luxuries alike, including food. The 1930s saw persistent shortages of food, due to the negative consequences of collectivization, poor harvests, and the 1932–3 famine. The war and postwar period experienced more catastrophic food problems, including another famine in 1946–7. Those who had access to food or the ability to distribute it through the trade network, therefore, were powerful people in any setting, whether urban, rural, or military.

Living under an oppressive regime, where the formal channels for getting things done often simply did not work; Soviet people sought out and found ways to obtain what they needed. They found avenues—legal, semilegal, and illegal—to advance their interests. Many people learned to use state agents as vehicles to meet their needs and even to get ahead. People, in general, seek out informal ways to get around the formal rules in all types of states and societies, of course. Yet, the Stalin-era USSR posed particular challenges for citizens and officials alike, challenges that created remarkable possibilities for deal-making. Under these circumstances, ordinary Soviet people became quite adept at maneuvering through the labyrinthine bureaucracies that they encountered at every turn. Indeed, they had no choice. People usually wanted to make the bureaucracy live up to the promises that the Party had made to the Soviet population. They expected the state and its officials to furnish them with the kind of life that Stalin described to them as their birthright in a socialist society. And government bureaucrats also became quite skilled at taking advantage of the challenges and frustrations that ordinary people faced in obtaining things in short supply. Officials themselves often created those obstacles artificially with obscure rules and procedures, with the purpose of forcing petitioners to make a deal to overcome them.

One way in which officials and ordinary people came into contact was through a type of relationship known colloquially as "*blat*." Unlike a bribe, which is a payment to an official to do something illegally, *blat* is defined as the mutual exchange of favors based on acquaintanceship. If one had friends in the right places (known as "having *blat*,") one might be able to acquire certain hard-to-find things quite a bit more easily. A person could help their friends—and be helped in return. A butcher might set aside a nice cut of meat for their acquaintance, the plumber, who in turn would repay the favor by working after hours on the butcher's broken sink. Officials who knew each other might trade some help with admission to a university in exchange for a spot at the top of a long waiting list for an upgraded apartment or for a document granting permission to live in a city. *Blat* did not involve money, and was not considered to be strictly illegal. It is nicely illustrated by the popular Russian saying, "Don't have a hundred rubles, have a hundred friends." It was the rare person, however, who had useful contacts in *every* area of life where they might need help. A person who lacked those *blat* connections might have to resort to a cash payment to an official to get what he/she needed—that is, a bribe.

Thus, some bureaucrats were willing to negotiate under the table with petitioners for these goods and services. Illicit negotiations in the shadows that resulted in illegal deals between ordinary people and officials were a common way of getting things done.

At many points in their lives, Soviet people needed the assistance of state bureaucrats for a number of vital things: to gain admittance to higher education, to acquire or change jobs, to live in the city, to acquire pensions, and to obtain medical care and housing. And opportunities to make deals abounded. The Soviet Union was a society on the move, in a literal sense. In the Stalin years, Soviet people migrated from the countryside to the growing towns and industrial cities in extraordinary numbers. All cities, both new and old, were populated not only by industrial workers and recently relocated rural people, but by armies of state officials in charge of managing the population's labor and needs. These local officials had a great deal of control over what and how much people consumed, where they lived, how their medical care and legal problems were handled, where and how they worked and went to school, and whether they received their pensions and benefits.

Travel on the railroads was another area in which common citizens frequently came into contact with state employees looking to earn something extra on the side. Sales staff and conductors could demand illicit "bonuses" when they sold tickets to travelers or collected them, or they could make side deals so that people without a ticket could land a spot on the train. Barter was common in these situations. A bottle of alcohol, a jar of honey, or a nice cut of meat might be enough to "grease the wheels" and land a person a seat on a crowded train. Considering the vast amount of rail travel people needed to undertake in these years of upheaval as people moved to the cities, migrated from one part of the country to another, or took part in wartime evacuations, these spontaneous barter economies were commonly seen on the railways.

In Soviet people's contacts with officialdom, one gains insight into the challenges of everyday life under Stalinism, as people struggled to take care of themselves and their families, often in extreme conditions. A significant part of everyday life involved fulfilling the responsibilities required of them by the state, some of which were nearly impossible without the help of an office holder. These involved obtaining myriad permissions, verifications, and other documents.

In memoirs and letters, people marvel at the mountains of paperwork with which they constantly had to cope. Paperwork meant signatures and official stamps, and signatures meant finding bureaucrats with the authority—and willingness—to sign. Sometimes they would expedite documents only in exchange for cash. Other times, officials would fill out the proper registrations only if they received a favor or "gift" in exchange. In the absence of a payment, they could force people to wait in long lines, or purposely slow the movement of paperwork to a crawl.

Cradle-to-grave bureaucracy, often part and parcel of the Soviet Union's grand vision of universal social welfare provided by the state, meant that people needed to get hold of voluminous quantities of documents at every stage in their lives. To live in the city, to find a new apartment, or to change jobs, one needed stacks of paperwork. If one found oneself in trouble with the police or had a legal problem, one had better have all the necessary identity papers and other proper certifications. In nearly every transaction with the state, people had to show their internal passports, which were like gold. If a person were unlucky enough to lose their passport, or if it was destroyed in the wartime chaos or some other catastrophe, people would have to replace it, often at huge effort and at a hefty price.

In the Soviet Union, many people hoped to achieve a semblance of upward mobility, to find new and skilled work that offered better pay or status. They understood that the best work opportunities were normally to be found in the larger cities, and especially in Moscow and Leningrad. Many millions of people moved to the big cities, either from rural areas or from the USSR's thousands of towns and smaller cities. Living in most Soviet cities required permission, and the documents that gave such authorization were controlled by city officials who regulated in-migration and labor. To obtain permission to move to the big city, one typically had to interact with officials in several agencies. Informal deals often had to be struck, and these deals could cost money or other valuable "gifts." Interactions with the state officials who could smooth the path to upward mobility thus could exact a steep price from migrants.

The Second World War caused an apocalyptic destruction of lives, property and infrastructure, including the vast destruction of important personal papers and essential documents of all types. Large swaths of the population, especially (but not only) those who lived in territories that had been occupied by the Nazis, had to replace these papers. This situation gave bureaucrats more opportunity to sell their services illegally by demanding money for services they should have carried out for free.

Officials who worked in the country's enormous network of housing administrations were also in an excellent position to make deals for access to apartments. Given the country's shortage of housing stock, officials could ask for extra money to move up in waiting lists. This was true both amid the great growth of the urban population during the 1930s and after the extensive damage to millions of apartments during the war. Housing officials could ask for under-the-table payments to guarantee good apartments, or to secure a place to live in a desirable part of town. After the war, people returning from Siberian or Central Asian evacuation to the western part of the country often found themselves having to negotiate with municipal housing officials just to regain access to the apartments they had inhabited before the war.

Certain professionals were in position to trade services for cash. Doctors are an excellent example. In the absence of private medical practices doctors were state employees. Physicians were in a vital position in the Soviet administration, because besides providing health care, it was also the responsibility of doctors to supply certain key documentation. In the course of their lives, Soviet people frequently needed to obtain crucial paperwork from medical personnel. Letters from doctors attested to a person's physical ability to perform certain jobs. They also provided excuses explaining why people missed work or could not do certain types of heavy labor for medical reasons. As such, doctors could ask for illicit payments to produce such paperwork, whether legally, to document a truly existing injury or disability, for example, or illegally, to falsely attest that a person was unfit to serve in the military, for example, or that they could not be transferred to a job in a region that was considered undesirable. In the wake of Stalin's draconian labor laws in the 1930s, one could be imprisoned for missing work, or if one came to work late without a medical excuse. In such circumstances, a doctor's excuse could mean the difference between freedom and imprisonment. Given this outsized influence, doctors were in a position to ask for myriad "gifts" in exchange for documents that citizens absolutely had to have.

Those people who somehow managed to get access to an automobile often encountered various types of inspectors or traffic policemen (known as GAI). Sometimes they shook drivers down, looking to make a few rubles on the road. Inspectors could threaten to impound a vehicle if the driver did not pay or offer an appropriate gift. If drivers' documents were not in order, unscrupulous traffic police could force them to pay a hefty "fine," which often went directly into the policeman's pocket (with a share going to their boss as *podnoshenie*). Officials responsible for issuing and checking auto registrations could do the same. One can think of these illegal "fees" as akin to a kind of unofficial "tax" on automobile ownership, enforced in an ad hoc way by those officials who had the power to take away people's right to drive.

In sum, Soviet administrations bore no semblance to the ideal, professionalized bureaucracy that the Party leadership had hoped to create. Rather, the incentives in the Stalinist system were for officials to dodge the rules, to wheel and deal, and to sell access for things in short supply. Although this involved a great deal of risk, many officials created what were essentially small businesses inside the bureaucracy. Bureaucrats sold access to people who were willing to pay to get the scarce necessities of everyday life or to increase their standard of living. A type of entrepreneurial spirit flourished among these bureaucrats, who were willing to barter with the citizens whom they served in principle.

For their part, the Soviet citizens who made these deals quite often believed that they had no choice but to make deals with officials in the shadows in order to survive, or to achieve a decent standard of living. While they sometimes felt some shame or embarrassment about making payments under the table, especially if the authorities caught them, it also seems that people usually were able to justify their actions morally, at least to themselves. They rationalized these illicit behaviors as something that was forced on them by circumstances. They believed that they were made desperate by officials who failed to assist them or denied them what they were due. As had been the case in Imperial Russia, the secret deal-making with bureaucrats was considered by many people as a necessary skill amid the privations and uncertainties of everyday life.

Notes

1 As has been noted elsewhere, many Western scholars use the term "Party-state," to describe the hybrid government of the Soviet Union, in which at all levels the Communist Party was entangled with the government. Usually, key decisions were made in Party bodies, and then ratified or formalized by the state administration (the legislative soviets and their executive organs).

2 See, among others, James C. Scott, *Seeing Like a State: How Certain Schemes to Improve the Human Condition Have Failed*, New Haven, CT: Yale University Press, 1998. For continuity (or not) in this regard with the Russian Empire, see Eric Lohr, *Russian Citizenship: from Empire to Soviet Union*,

Cambridge, MA: Harvard University Press, 2012; and Joshua Sanborn, *Drafting the Russian Nation: Military Conscription, Total war and Mass Politics, 1905–1925*, DeKalb: Northern Illinois University Press, 2011.

3 Apart from J. Heinzen, *The Art of The Bribe: Corruption under Stalin, 1943–1953*, New Haven, CT: Yale University Press, 2016; and J. Heinzen, *Inventing a Soviet Countryside: State Power and the Transformation of Rural Russia, 1917–1929*, Pittsburgh, PA: University of Pittsburgh Press, 2004. See also Serhy Yekelchyk, *Stalin's Citizens: Everyday Politics in the Wake of Total War*, Oxford: Oxford University Press, 2014; E. Cohn, *The High Title of a Communist: Postwar Party Discipline and the Values of the Soviet Regime*, DeKalb: Northern Illinois University Press, 2015; and, for a later period, A. V. Ledeneva, *Russia's Economy of Favours: Blat, Networking and Informal Exchange*, Cambridge: Cambridge University Press, 1998.

4 For more, see several of the works in the bibliography as well as some of the other contributions to this collection.

5 See Elena Zubkova, *Russia after the War: Hopes, Illusions and Disappointments, 1945–1957*, Armonk, NY: M. E. Sharpe, 1998.

12

The Religious Front: Militant Atheists and Militant Believers

Gregory L. Freeze

Traditionally, the standard narratives of Soviet history gave short shrift to religion. That neglect reflected the presumptions of the "totalitarian" school, which accepted at face value the regime's own propaganda—its claim to control every facet of its citizens' life, including the spiritual. Given all the unbridled attacks in anti-religious *agitprop* (agitation and propaganda), given the disestablishment of the Orthodox Church and decimation of its clergy, it seemed entirely credible that believers were a small and dwindling minority, limited mainly to the elderly and rural population. Such a decline also matched the expectations of Western scholars, who saw "secularization" as a universal paradigm that made religion an inevitable casualty of modernization. The demise of the Church in Russia seemed perfectly normal, perhaps accelerated by the brutal anti-religious methods of Stalinism in the 1930s.

Recently, however, historians have come to reject that narrative of inevitable and ubiquitous dechristianization.[1] With the collapse of the Soviet Union, it became possible to access previously closed archives and gain a new picture of religious life in the Soviet era. We now know that the regime could destroy churches but not belief, that Orthodoxy not only survived but thrived, and that the believers repeatedly forced the regime to retreat and compromise. Neither I. V. Stalin nor his successors ceased trying to dechristianize, and anti-religious policies (of varying intensity) persisted to the end of the Soviet regime. But to no avail: once the regime imploded in 1991, the number of self-professed believers soared—typically, 70 percent or more self-identifying as Orthodox, with only a tiny minority professing to be atheist or agnostic.[2] This chapter examines the secularizing project and seeks to shed light on why it failed.

Religious NEP and Religious Revival

When the Bolsheviks came to power in October 1917, they were determined to make war on religion and, especially, the Russian Orthodox Church (to which more than two-thirds of the population adhered). In addition to their Marxist views (which castigated religion as the "opium of the proletariat"—superstition that made a benighted folk docile), the Bolsheviks regarded the Orthodox Church as a bastion of counterrevolution, its clergy—in their view—allied with the regime and propertied elites. Hence the Bolsheviks hastened to nationalize Church property, to deny the Church any legal rights, to confiscate parish schools and secularize education, and to subject the clergy to discrimination and repression. With a tenuous hold on power, however, the Bolsheviks were loath to offend the mass of believers. Their tactic was to disestablish the "Church" (the institution) but to empower the "church" (parish), giving parishioners total control over their local church and clergy. That was the key premise of the famous "Decree on the Separation of Church from State" (January 23, 1918); the tactic promised to neutralize the counterrevolutionary "Church" but without antagonizing believers. Indeed, before 1917 parishioners had increasingly clamored for greater autonomy and power, and the Decree served to realize their aspirations. In the Bolsheviks' calculus, this was a temporary concession: modernization would inevitably eliminate "superstition," with religion fading away on its own.

To the Bolsheviks' dismay, their clever tactic led to the revival, not extinction, of popular Orthodoxy. The key dynamic was empowerment of parishioners, who reshaped religious practice to fit their needs (regardless of ancient canons and episcopal directives). The laity also reconstituted the parish clergy, driving off unpopular priests and choosing new ones—more inclined to serve their wishes and, increasingly, coming from the modest ranks of the common folk. That led to a social revolution in the clergy, replacing the hereditary clerical caste with men from the lower classes—and with closer ties to the culture and interests of the parishioners. Believers also became the "owner" of the parish, using its funds to meet local needs, not the demands of a distant bishop. In 1922, the Bolsheviks bolstered this parish "proprietary mentality" when they decided to expropriate church valuables (gold, silver, and precious stones), ostensibly to alleviate suffering caused by famine on the Volga, but also aimed at unmasking the avarice of the "counterrevolutionary" clergy. In fact, however, the squads sent to confiscate church valuables encountered a firestorm of opposition from parishioners, who fought to defend *their* church and *their* valuables. By early 1923, the regime retreated to a "religious NEP," which lay the emphasis on suasion instead of force in combatting religion. The regime did not abandon its goal of dechristianization, but intended to rely on anti-religious propaganda and on youthful unbelievers (in a newly established League of Atheists) to enlighten the benighted masses.

That *agitprop* proved wholly ineffective, and party officials were horrified to see a revival, not decline, of religiosity. Local functionaries sent lurid reports about the occurrence of "miracles" (which drew huge throngs of pilgrims) and about a surge in religious observance (i.e., a rising rate of baptisms, weddings, and other church rites). Even the attempt to close parish churches ran aground: despite efforts by local authorities and clamor in the press, the number of parish churches actually *increased* by 10.5 percent during 1926–8. It was not only peasants but also workers—like those in Vladimir province east of Moscow—who demanded that a church be opened.[3] The League of Atheists existed mainly on paper. In May 1929, its chairman, Emelian Iaroslavskii (1878–1943), conceded that believers comprised 80 percent of the population. The revival also bore a political subtext, since it seemed to enhance the influence of clergy and *kulaks*, that is, exploiters and counterrevolutionaries in Communist eyes. The press played up the political threat, with reports about "a young priest" as purportedly active, "gathering women and holding talks with them that castigate the Soviet order."[4] The secret police noted such activism and warned about the need for vigilance to prevent "a unification of all counter-revolutionary forces around the anti-Soviet activists of the clergy and church people."[5] By the late 1920s, the party concluded that "religious NEP"—like the NEP (New Economic Policy) more generally—was a disaster and that it must make a radical policy shift.

From the Great Turn to the Great Terror (1929–39)

Amidst rising anti-religious rhetoric, on April 8, 1929, the government promulgated a decree on "religious associations." The most important legislative act since the Decree on the Separation of the Church from the State in 1918, this law set strict limits on the activities of religious communities and, in effect, extended the disestablishment of the national "Church" to the parish "church." It also mandated a systematic reregistration of existing parishes, thereby providing an opportunity for the mass closing of parishes. Coming amidst a crescendo of anti-religious *agitprop*, the decree marked the onset of "mass secularization" (*sploshniaia sekuliarizatsiia*).

The assault on the parish was indeed an integral part of "mass collectivization" (*sploshniaia kollektivizatsiia*). The connection was no accident; breaking with NEP's soft line on the peasantry, the regime had no reason to mollycoddle believers in the village. The link between collectivization and assault on the parish explicit,

Simultaneous with the transition to new collective forms of the economy in areas of mass collectivization, underway as well is the process of an accelerated excoriation of religious ideology—expressed in the mass movement to close churches ... , the burning of icons, a refusal to celebrate religious holidays.[6]

Authorities added "militant" to the name of its anti-religious organization (henceforth: "League of Militant Atheists") and drastically increased its membership (from 138,000 in 1927 to 3.5 million in 1930, and then to 5.7 million in 1932).[7] Its slogans for an anti-Easter campaign were revealing:

Anyone who is for Easter is against socialism...
    We shall wipe off the face of the earth the church and sectarian organizations—the bastion of kulaks and nepmen.[8]

Gone too was the facile assumption of automatic secularization: "It is impossible to think that religion will disappear by itself."[9]

This assault, however, relied not on militant *agitprop* but on repression and church closings. Extralegal arrests in the 1920s had been relatively limited (e.g., 832 in 1926), but these now rose dramatically: 5,475 in 1929 and 13,354 in 1930.[10] Significantly, this time the police arrested not only clergy but also lay believers, whom they now labeled as "church people" (*tserkovniki*). Clergy and "church people" were specifically targeted in dekulakization; for instance, a regional report in March 1930 included 388 clergy (7 percent of those arrested).[11] The new assault also took aim at the parish church itself. Encouraged by anticlerical rhetoric from above, local officials deployed various tactics to close churches: imposing absurdly high insurance fees and taxes, inspections that condemned a church to be in disrepair or health threat, or convening a faux-parish assembly (comprised of nonbelievers) asking that the parish church be turned into a club or school. Altogether, by 1933, authorities had closed 19 percent of the Orthodox parishes in the Russian Soviet Federative Socialist Republic (RSFSR), a radical reversal to the growth in the 1920s.

The onslaught provoked courageous resistance from clergy and believers. The ranking prelate, Metropolitan Sergii (Stragorodskii, 1867–1944), filed a protest denouncing the new measures (such as exorbitant taxes) as a tactic to force the collectivized, destitute parishioners to abandon their church "voluntarily." He also denounced the subterfuge of a sham "parish assembly" as a clear violation of believers' rights. The real parishioners also fought back. They filed petitions and appeals, emphasizing that they had paid all taxes and that they needed the church.[12] They were hardly prepared to be defenseless lambs sent to slaughter. As the NKVD itself emphasized, if some wavering believers had agreed to close their church, resistance steadily stiffened, and by early 1930 "reports from many places tell of middle peasants fleeing from collective farms, accompanied by a substantial movement to reopen churches, recover confiscated church bells, and release cult servitors from exile."[13] In 1930, believers filed appeals against local authorities, such formal complaints increasing 336 percent over the previous year (see Figure 12.1). The clergy and activist laity conducted agitation, as in one village, where they urged others "to cease work on collectivization" and to "free the church and clergy from taxes."[14] The pious were not always peaceful: in 1930 (a year marked by violent protests against collectivization), church closings accounted for 11 percent of all disorders.[15] This account of villagers' ferocious defense of their church is typical:

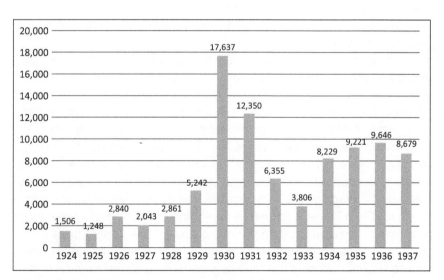

FIGURE 12.1 *Believers protests against church closings, 1924–37*
Note: The years 1924–34 include only the RSFSR; data for 1936–7 include all republics in the USSR.
Sources: GARF, f. 5263, op. 1, d. 32, ll. 56–57; Iu.N. Makarov, Russkaia pravoslavnaia tserkov' v usloviiakh sovetskoi deistvitel'nosti (1917 g.-konets 1930-kh gg.), Krasnodar: N.p., 2005, 286.

Local anti-Soviet elements in the village used this [church closing] for their own purposes. When the tocsin was sounded, up to 200 women (who had also supported keeping the church at the last village meeting) charged as a group, hurling sticks and stones at the members of the village soviet, and as a result the commission [sent to close the church] had to flee.[16]

Protests and resistance caused Moscow to retreat, just as it did in the collectivization drive in general. The exorbitant taxes on clergy, the chief official in the anti-religious apparatus pointed out, "are shifted to the shoulders of the masses, who are still benighted by religion."[17] As ever, party leaders put the blame on overzealous local officials, accusing them of "distortions in party policy."[18] The shift in policy was striking. The Leningrad party, for example, issued an order to "cease the forcible liquidation of religious associations and objects (under the cover of a fictive wish of the population)" and "under no circumstances permit derisive insults toward the religious feelings of the peasantry."[19] The arrest of clergy and "church people" also dropped sharply (from 13,354 in 1930 to 899 in 1934). Moscow not only denounced the forcible closing of churches but also reversed some closings as illegal. Efforts to mobilize the anti-religious also disappeared; membership in the League of Militant Atheists plunged from 3.5 million in 1930 to a tenth that by 1934. The result, a report noted in 1937, was "almost a complete breakdown both in the organizational work of the League as well as the dissemination of anti-religious propaganda."[20]

However, the retreat of 1931–4 (as in the case of collectivization) was temporary: the government thereupon resumed its assault on the "Church and church," that is, on the clergy and believers. While the renewed attack reflected the more radical temper of the mid-1930s, it was also due to the rising activism of priests and parishioners. The secret police kept churches under surveillance and filed reports about the discontent among believers (who complained, for example, that "at the present time it is very difficult for churches to exist because Soviet authorities take large taxes").[21] The audacity of "church people" was not only inspired by their apparent victory during the Great Turn, but also by the impending "Stalin Constitution," with its guarantee of religious freedom.[22] In the public discussion prior to its formal adoption in 1936, believers seized the opportunity to press their demands, a view reflected in letters to the Party newspaper for peasants (as summarized in a report to the Communist Party): "Give all citizens complete freedom [of religion], do not oppress any nation or confession, open all Orthodox churches and other chapels, free the Orthodox priests and other people who were sent into exile."[23] In October 1936, the NKVD reported that religious activists were appealing to the believers to "make use of the new Constitution and organize so as to ensure the easier advancement of [their] people to the leadership."[24]

The police arrested a priest for insisting that "we must make use of the new Constitution and quickly open the church ... [w]hoever does not campaign for a church will be damned."[25] The Soviet press openly reported "the extraordinary intensification of the activity of church people in urban and rural areas."[26] The Party's accusations were not unfounded: the sheer number of protests was enormous, amounting to 27,546 for the years 1935–7. Even the "Great Terror" did not deter believers. In 1938, for example, authorities in Iaroslavl' sent Stalin a report about a disorder that involved 500 to 600 "church people" and unveiled threats: "We shall not permit the removal of our church bells, and if they dare to attempt to do so by using force, we'll resort to violence."[27] Apart from reports that parishioners were seeking to elect priests to the Supreme Soviet, the regime was confronted with the shocking results of the 1937 census, in which 57 percent of the population—despite twenty years of atheist *agitprop* and repression, despite the specter of persecution—dared to profess that they were believers. The police also reported "a noticeable growth of fanatical devotion to the church, which is expressed in an increase in the number of pre-Christmas services in churches, in an increase in the revenues of churches, and in the manifestation of animosity because a number of churches have been closed and church people arrested."[28]

That religiosity—and resistance—impelled the Communist Party to launch an all-out war on the Church. The Party pressed the young to join the League of Militant Atheists (its membership reaching 2.0 million by 1938) and raised the volume on anti-religious *agitprop*. But the main thrust was repression and coercion, now indeed unleashed at an unprecedented level. As a result, the regime closed most Orthodox churches (Figure 12.2). The RSFSR, for example, had just 1,700 parishes in 1939, a tiny fraction of the 34,091 reported in 1928. And of these just a few hundred parishes were still functioning in the RSFSR by the time Nazi Germany invaded on June 22, 1941. A diocese like Ufa, for example, went from 393 churches in 1929 to just 3 in 1941, and none of these even had a priest. Local authorities were so busy closing churches that in many cases they did not even have the time, or resources, to renovate them for use as clubs, libraries, or schools; the buildings stood there, empty and idle, a provocative insult to believers.

The closings, so massive and coercive, provoked fierce resistance from believers. As a central commission observed in 1936, many local functionaries resorted to arbitrariness and coercion in their zeal to de-church their province. In contrast to the early 1930s, however, this time authorities in Moscow turned a blind eye to administrative abuse, declining either to reverse illegal closings or to reprimand local soviets.

All this unfolded against the background of the "Great Religious Terror" of 1937 and 1938. Precise numbers are lacking, but both the Church and the church, both clergy and parishioners, paid dearly for their piety and politics. One

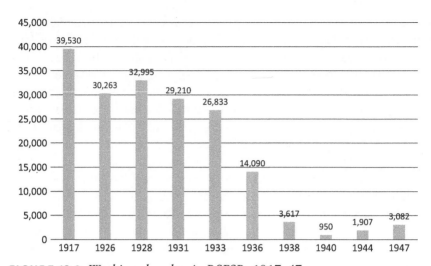

FIGURE 12.2 *Working churches in RSFSR, 1917–47*
Source: M. I. Odintsov, "Religioznye organizatsii v SSSR nakanune i v pervye gódy
Velikoi Otechestvennoi voiny (1938–1943 gg.)," Otechestvennye arkhivy 2, 1995,
37–67: 44–5.

widely cited source reports that religious activism accounts for the repression of 168,000 citizens in 1937 and 1938, of whom 106,000 were executed.[29] Altogether, clergy and church people represented 5–6 percent of those subjected to repression in 1937–8.[30] Many were victims of Order No. 00447, the infamous decree of July 30, 1937, that set purge quotas for each province and specifically listed "church people" among the targets. Significantly, lay activists, not just clergy, were a target of repression and sometimes even a primary victim.

The church closings and repression, however, had an important unintended consequence: it drove religious life underground. The "catacomb" church first emerged in the 1920s as an anti-Soviet movement, most famously among those who rejected the Metropolitan Sergii's "Declaration" of 1927 affirming political loyalty to the Soviet government. By the late 1930s, however, the underground Church assumed a far greater magnitude: the mass closing of churches made unregistered communities the only outlet for believers. The mass closings also unleashed an army of ex-clergy, unemployed and ready to provide religious services at makeshift sites. The largest all-Soviet newspaper, *Pravda*, cited the example of Ivanovo *oblast'*, "where, after the closing of churches, under the influence of priestly agitation, the underground performance of religious rites began."[31] The catacomb church even organized a clandestine "church council" in 1937 in Ust'-Kut (a small town in Irkutsk *oblast'*), which reaffirmed Patriarch Tikhon's anathema on the Communist regime and admonished believers not to receive rites from "clergy who have been legalized by the anti-Christian government."[32]

Ironically, the anti-religious campaign weakened the regime's capacity to monitor the religious sphere. That is, by disestablishing the (institutional) "Church" and the (parish) "church", the government lost the capacity to count, much less control, believers. That is why the 1937 census (along with believers' bold response to the 1936 constitution) took authorities by surprise. At a critical plenum in February 1937, A. A. Zhdanov (1896–1948) expressed a concern common among his colleagues in the Politburo:

> Priests of various ranks and tendencies are now developing a very animated activity. There is a significant number of applications from a series of regions and oblasts to reopen closed churches. It is known that the priests have now submitted a draft law to the Central Executive Committee of the USSR that, in a clerical spirit, expands a certain point in the constitution regarding freedom of conscience. They want to "concretize" the law and propose to offer their assistance in this concretization.[33]

Thus, the regime had eliminated virtually all sites of institutionalized religion, but not communities of believers. In other words, the hard line resulted not in mass dechristianization but in mass religious dissent of various stripes, such as the Truly Orthodox Christians (which was resolutely anti-Soviet and often apocalyptical).[34] As one metropolitan explained in a memorandum to German occupiers in November 1941, the official "Church" was no more, but the catacomb Church was flourishing.[35]

War, Concessions, Containment: 1939–53

When war broke out in Europe in September 1939, the Soviet government did not initially reverse religious policy on territories it ruled before the expansion triggered by the Molotov-Ribbentrop Pact: repression and closings continued, if at a slower pace. Indeed, "de-churching" was virtually complete: the number of Orthodox churches shrank from 1,750 in 1939 to a few hundred by June 1941. In some areas the de-churching was total; twenty-five *oblasts* did not have a single working church.[36] Repression also dropped partly because of the cessation of the Great Terror but also because of a party directive of November 11, 1939: "Recognize as inexpedient henceforth the practice of the NKVD organs regarding the arrest of the clergy and believers of the Russian Orthodox Church."[37] However, while repression was reduced, it was hardly negligible: 2,231 religious activists were arrested in 1940 (1.7 percent of the total 132,958) and 3,098 in 1941 (2.3 percent of the 133,740).[38] The regime did intensify anti-religious propaganda, and membership in the League of Militant Atheists increased (from 2 million in 1938 to 3.5 million in 1940).[39] The propaganda campaign, as before, elicited scant support among over-tasked Party functionaries and had little impact, eliciting a ritualized complaint from central authorities: "The negligent attitude of Party organizations toward anti-religious propaganda is leading to increased activism of church people and sectarians."[40] In September 1939, the head of *agitprop* in Leningrad compiled a digest of reports about the "subversive activity of church people," emphasizing not only their political danger but also the high level of religiosity.[41] On the eve of war, the Leningrad branch of the League of Militant Atheists confirmed that "we atheists still have much work to do for overcoming religious traditions."[42]

However, the government *did* adopt a soft line in its religious policy for territories annexed in the wake of the Molotov-Ribbentrop Pact. These territories included several million believers (variously estimated at 6–7.5 million), 64 monasteries (with 5,100 monks and nuns), and 3,350 parishes (including 1,278 in Ukraine).[43] The government refrained from persecution here, doubtlessly hoping to facilitate assimilation and to minimize resistance. That motive was transparent in the deliberations of a Party commission in 1940, which warned that the closing churches and repression would only drive believers into the arms of counterrevolutionaries.[44] Thus, the government continued closings and repression in the interior, but not in the newly acquired areas.

The German invasion of June 22, 1941, led the regime to extend the soft line to interior regions as well.[45] Repression virtually ceased (arrests of religious activists, for example, dropped to 106 in 1942, that is 0.06 percent of the total 190,957).[46] Church closings not only ceased but entered a phase of reversal, with churches reopened, first in areas occupied by German forces, then in territories under Soviet control as well. The Germans sought to mobilize popular support against the "godless communists," but the Soviet government had more complex motives for this retreat. Apart from seeking to minimize discontent among believers, the government was eager to take advantage of patriotic support of the war by the Church. Metropolitan Sergii appealed to believers to defend the motherland on the first day of the war (twelve days *before* Stalin's famous radio address) and issued numerous patriotic pronouncements during the war.[47] Strikingly, the League of Militant Atheists publicly affirmed that the many clergymen were true patriots.[48] The Church provided not only moral but also material support: it enjoined believers to purchase war bonds and to support Church fundraising for the Red Army (including the forty T-34s in the Church's "Dmitrii Donskoi Tank Column").[49] In January 1943, Stalin personally authorized the Church to open a bank account to collect such donations, recognizing the Church as a legal entity for the first time since the October Revolution.[50] The most sensational demonstration of the new policy was the widely reported meeting of Stalin and three ranking prelates on September 4, 1943. That encounter was a watershed in church-state relations: Stalin gave permission to reestablish the patriarchate (vacant since Patriarch Tikhon's death in 1925) and agreed to help the Church reestablish its administration, seminaries, and parishes.[51] In short, the state was eager to promote Orthodox patriotism, even at the risk of religious revival.

That shift in policy also served to appease Western Allies and tamp down their criticism of Soviet religious repression. This motive inspired the Soviet propaganda campaign abroad, evident in the publication of a book by leading prelates that claimed religious liberty in the Soviet Union (entitled *The Truth about Religion in Russia* and translated into several foreign languages).[52] The government also encouraged direct meetings between Orthodox and Western clergy.[53] Toward the end of the war, the government hoped that the patriarchate would exercise a beneficial influence in the liberated Orthodox countries of the Balkans and perhaps elsewhere in liberated Europe. The Church's role in foreign policy continued after the war. In 1946, for example, the patriarchate received thirteen delegations of foreign clergy, established ties with the Anglican Church, and participated in international ecumenical activities.[54]

German religious policy also was a factor: the German forces reopened 2,150 churches in occupied territories, such as Kursk, Orel, and Voronezh provinces (332, 108, and 116 churches, respectively).[55] The Crimean diocese, which had a single church on the eve of war, expanded to eighty-two under German occupation.[56] It was hardly feasible to undo immediately or quickly what the Nazi occupiers had done. The Orthodox Church was especially strong in Ukraine; by 1945 it had nearly 7,000 churches, including 1,300 in newly annexed areas and 5,400 in prewar Soviet *oblasts*.

To control the "Church and churches," the government established a new administrative organ, the Council on the Affairs of the Russian Orthodox Church (CAROC). Its chairman, G. G. Karpov (1898–1967), an employee of the secret police, dealt directly with the patriarch and had a network of local plenipotentiaries. CAROC was not only to monitor the Church but also to compile data on the churches, clergy, budgets, and religious observance (e.g., numbers of baptisms and size of crowds on high holidays like Easter). Although its data were neither complete nor exact, it provided the first regular reports on religion since the Revolution.[57] CAROC also oversaw the opening of new churches, a process initiated by believers but requiring approval by state authorities. The government approved many applications, but denied many more: of the applications to reopen 5,184 churches (mostly in 1946), it approved a mere 1,270 (20.9 percent).[58]

Nevertheless, the reopenings, both during the war under German occupation and (on a lesser scale) on Soviet-held territories and after the war under the

CAROC, created a network of parishes. According to a report of August 27, 1946, the Russian Orthodox Church had 13,215 functioning churches, with the majority in Ukraine (8,550), and 2,866 in the much larger RSFSR, with the balance scattered among other Soviet republics.[59] But the Church had hardly reestablished its scale before the Great Turn, much less the October Revolution. While the increase in the RSFSR was substantial (from a few hundred in 1941), those 2,866 churches represented just 8.4 percent of the 34,091 reported in 1928. And within the RSFSR, the distribution of parishes was uneven, their number tending to be much smaller in areas that were never under German occupation, such as Gor'kii and Tambov provinces (with thirty-four and thirty-five churches, respectively). Given that the RSFSR was underchurched (it had over half of the Soviet population, but only 22 percent of all churches in the USSR), it is hardly surprising that 96 percent of all applications to reopen churches came from the RSFSR, with Riazan *oblast'* ranking first.[60] In these underchurched areas, believers had limited opportunities to worship legally and perforce relied on the "catacomb" church and unofficial clergy.

The CAROC also monitored the activities of prelates, priests, and parishes. A few days after the Stalin meeting of September 1943, a convocation of bishops elected Metropolitan Sergii as patriarch and, after his death, a Church Council convened in early 1945 and chose Metropolitan Aleksii (Simanskii, 1877–1970) of Leningrad as his successor, a position he was to occupy for twenty-five years. The Church hastily restaffed the episcopate, partly by obtaining the release of seventeen bishops from the *Gulag* camps and by consecrating another thirty-six, so that by January 1946 the Church could govern through sixty-one hierarchs, a massive increase from the four prelates on the eve of war. Georgii Karpov, the chair of CAROC, developed a good working relationship with patriarchs Sergii and Aleksii but found some bishops intractable. Famously independent was the archbishop of Tambov, Luka (Voino-lasenetskii, 1877–1961), who had a medical degree and earned fame as a military surgeon (for which he even received a Stalin Prize in 1946). Archbishop Luka was not shy about demonstrating his faith publicly, to the great irritation of the police (who nicknamed him "the obscurantist" [*mrakobes*]).

But not all went smoothly for the Church: it proved even harder to staff a church than to open it. The government had closed all the seminaries during the first years of Soviet power, and young priests had very little education (57 percent of postwar priests had only an elementary schooling). At best, the Church could appoint elderly clergy (educated and ordained before the Revolution), and indeed most "new" priests were graybeards (76 percent being over age fifty-one), at best a temporary stopgap solution. The patriarch was adamant about reestablishing the Church's educational system and by 1947 had managed to reopen two academies (elite tertiary institutions) and eight seminaries (secondary schools).

By 1947, however, the regime was shifting toward a more restrictive religious policy. The shift was partly due to evidence of a surge in popular religiosity.[61] During the war, Party *apparatchiks* were already warning about the "the growth of religious influence among the toilers of Leningrad."[62] That piety was evident in the proliferation of miracle-working icons and springs, which attracted huge throngs of pilgrims, public demonstrations of religiosity utterly anathema to Party ideologues.[63] The fact-gathering CAROC also gathered evidence of an increase in religious observance; the cathedral in Kuibyshev, for example, reported that church weddings rose from 139 (1940) to 867 (1945), and then jumped to 1,258 the following year.[64] That caused some functionaries of CAROC to submit reports like this:

> In the over-flowing building of the church there was a chaotic jostling of crowds of believers and non-believers—one boy was carried about because it was impossible to move [and the multitude was so great that many could not fit into the church and] at least 2,000 believers stood outside the doors of the cathedral.[65]

Party stalwarts had accepted wartime concessions to the Church as a tactical necessity, but complained increasingly about the threat posed by religious "fanatics."[66]

By 1947, amidst a general campaign to reassert Party preeminence or Party-mindedness (expressed in the slogan of *partiinost'*), anti-religious ideologues gained growing influence and demanded a harder line. The result was a cautious policy of containment: fewer new approvals, a modest number of closings. As a result, from 1947 to 1953 the number of parish churches dropped by 2.4 percent (see Figure 12.3). Even so, the government avoided coercion and at most resorted to legal tactics, especially higher levies. At times, inordinately so; in Ufa province, for example, state levies took 81 percent of parish revenues in 1948.[67] Authorities also suppressed public displays of religiosity, such as miracle sites and pilgrimages.[68] The press did ramp up anti-religious rhetoric in the state-controlled media and emphasized the magnitude, and threat, of religious fervor.[69] The following letter in *Pravda* was typical: "All of Riazan is going to church to bless the Easter cakes and *kulich*: old men and old women, but also youth."[70]

Despite the more conservative tone in the religious policy, believers persisted in efforts to reopen the local church. In petitions (submitted multiple times, affixed with mass signatures, sometimes sent directly to Stalin and other leaders), parishioners employed diverse rhetorical strategies. They usually emphasized their patriotism and wartime sacrifices, explaining that they "experience a feeling of grief and insult from being deprived of a public and open memorial service for their fathers and grandfathers, who created

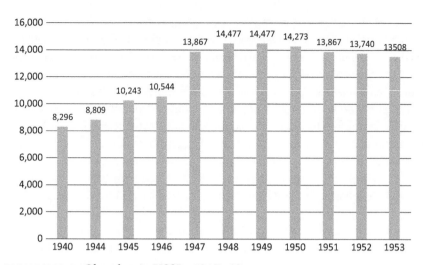

FIGURE 12.3 *Churches in USSR, 1917–40*
Source: Shkarovskii, Russkaia Pravoslavnaia Tserkov', *398.*

the power and glory of our motherland, and especially religious services to honor our sons and brothers, who fell recently on the field of battle for our dear motherland."[71] Some parishioners stressed that Orthodoxy was patriotic and loyal and hence the best defense against the alien sectarianism that the Party had come to regard as especially opprobrious. Believers occasionally recycled the regime's peace rhetoric, portraying Orthodoxy as a bulwark against Western and especially papal militarism: "The Vatican supports those who instigate war [;we] need to pray for peace in the entire world".[72] Sly parishioners also updated the traditional "distance" argument (no church was nearby) by invoking the goal of socialist construction and arguing that believers lost much valuable production time when traveling to a remote church.[73] The militant abjured clever rhetoric and simply threatened to strike: "In our country they only speak and write about freedom of religion, but in fact there is none [, but i]f we are not given our church, we will stop working on the kolkhoz."[74]

CAROC, despite the shift in political winds, acted as an advocate for the Church, not just as its monitor. It argued that unregistered religious organizations were uncontrolled and that in such cases it had no information about revenues, clergy, believers, or religious observance.[75] Therefore, it warned, the mass rejection of applications created an opportunity for self-appointed proselytizers of unknown origin and status:

In districts where there are no working churches or these are in short supply, there is a quite widespread performance of religious rights and services outside of churches by unregistered priests, and sometimes by people who do not belong to the clergy. [to which it added in 1948 in a reiteration of its opposition to a blanket ban on new churches] ... , since this will result in having the illegal performance of religious rites and services, mostly by various dark and anti-soviet forces."[76]

Underground religious life was no rarity and "in a series of places such services bears a mass character."[77] Indeed, unregistered parishes far outnumbered the registered ones. In Riazan, for example, the *oblast'* had several-fold more unregistered than registered churches.[78] In Gor'ky, similarly, *oblast'* reported 47 registered churches, but 242 unregistered ones.[79] The proliferation of unregistered parishes, however, was not necessarily due to obstruction by anti-religious *apparatchiks*: some believers preferred to remain unregistered and to enjoy certain advantages, above all, freedom from external control and onerous state levies.[80]

In Stalin's last years, however, policy remained contradictory and conflicted in religious matters, as it was in many other spheres. But the wartime concessions remained largely intact, with a reestablished Church, thousands of registered parishes, and untold number of unregistered communities in the catacomb Church. Stalin's heirs would inherit this trinity of Church, church, and catacomb: all became the target of Khrushchev's anti-religious campaign from 1958 to 1964. All nonetheless survived until the fall of the Soviet Union, and all have thrived in post-Soviet Russia.

Notes

This research was supported by grant N 15-18-00119 from the Russian Science Foundation.

1　G. L. Freeze, "Confessions in the Soviet Era: Analytical Overview of the Historiography," *Russian History* 1, 2016, 1–25.

2　G. L. Freeze, "From Dechristianization to Laicization: State, Church, and Believers in Russia," *Canadian Slavonic Papers* 1–2, 2015, 6–34.

3　P. Bliakhin, *Kto i zachem stroit tserkvi*, Moscow: Priboi, 1929.

4　A. Berelovich and V. P. Danilov, *Sovetskaia derevnia glazami VChK-OGPU-NKVD, 1918–1939*, 4 vols, Moscow: Rosspen, 1998–2012, vol. 2: 822.

5　Ibid.

6　*State Archive of the Russian Federation* (GARF), *fond* 5407, *opis'* 1, *delo* 26, *list* 11.

7　E. Iaroslavkii, "O zadachakh antireligioznoi propagandy v period sotsialistichekogo nastupleniia," *Pod znamenem marksizma* 3, 1931, 36–55, 50; M. V. Shkarovskii, *Russkaia Pravoslavnaia Tserkov' pri Staline i Khrushcheve*, Moscow: Krutitskoe patriarshee podvor'e, 1999, 97.

8　GARF, f. 5407, op. 1, d. 43, l. 77.

9 Iaroslavskii, "O zadachakh," 48.

10 O. B. Mozokhin, *Pravo na repressii. Vnesudebnye polnomochiia organov gosudarstvennoi bezopasnosti*, Moscow: Kuchkovo pole, 2011, 379, 399, 406.

11 Berelovich and Danilov, *Sovetskaia derevnia*, vol. 3, part 1: 130.

12 GARF, f. 4570, op. 1, d. 292, l. 18.

13 M. I. Odintsov, "Purgatory," *Russian Studies in History* 2, 1993, 53–81, 66.

14 Ibid.

15 L. Viola, *Peasant Rebels under Stalin: Collectivization and the Culture of Peasant Resistance*, Oxford: Oxford University Press, 1996, 137.

16 Smolensk Party Archive (US National Archives), T87/20/155.

17 Iu.P. Bardileva, "Predat' sudu, vsekh lits, ulichennykh v izdevatel'skikhy vykhodkakh po otnosheniiu k veruiushchim," *Noveishaia istoriia Rossii* 1, 2011, 216–27, 218.

18 Ibid.

19 Ibid.

20 Central State Archive, St. Petersburg (TsGA SPB), f. 25, op. 8, d. 88, l. 101.

21 Ibid.; TsGA SPB, f. 7384, op. 2, d. 54, l. 32 ob.

22 A. K. Sokolov, "Konstitutsiia 1936 goda i kul'turnoe nasledie stalinskogo sotsializma," *Sotsial'naia istoriia: ezhegodnik*, 2008, 137–63, 149–50.

23 V. Danilov et al., eds., *Tragediia sovetskoi derevni*, 5 vols, Moscow: Rosspen, 1999–2006, vol. 4: 822.

24 F. Corley, *Religion in the Soviet Union; an Archival Reader*, New York: New York University Press, 1996, 107.

25 Ibid., 108.

26 V. Aleksandrov, "Dat' otpor agitatsii tserkovnikov," *Vlast' sovetov* 10, 1937, 22.

27 Russian State Archive of Modern History (RGANI), f. 89, per. 49, d. 24, ll. 1–3.

28 TsGA SPB, f. 7584, op. 2, d. 54.

29 A. N. Iakovlev, *A Century of Violence in Soviet Russia*, New Haven, CT: Yale University Press, 2002, 94–5. A tabulation by the NKVD for 1937 and 1938 cites a lower figure (50,769). See R. Binner and M. Junge, "Vernichtung der orthodoxen Geistlichen in der Sowjetunion in den Massenoperationen des Großen Terrors 1937–1938," *Jahrbücher für Geschichte Osteuropas* 52, 2004, 515–33, 523. For a case study of Leningrad, see M. I. Shkarovskii, *Repressii pravoslavnogo dukhovenstva Leningrada i oblasti v 1930-e gg.*, St. Petersburg: Kniaz' Vladimirskii sobor, 2010.

30 N. E. Emel'ianov, "K voprosu o chisle novomuchenikov i ispovednikov russkoi pravoslavnoi tserkvi v XX veke," *Ezhegodnaia bogoslovskaia konferentsiia Pravoslavnogo Sviato-Tikhonovskogo Instituta* 15, 2005, 265–71, 269.

31 N. Semashko, "Odna iz zadach izbiratel'noi kampanii," *Vlast' sovetov* 10, 1938, 21.

32 A. A. Tupitsyn, "Pomestnye sobory XX veka kak fenomen dukhovnoi zhizni: na primere Ust'-Kutskogo sobora Katakombnoi tserkvi 1937 g.," available at: http://publishing-vak.ru/file/archive-history-2013-1/4-tupitsin-aleksei-anatolevich.pdf, accessed December 12, 2017.

33 "Materialy fevral'sko-martovskogo plenum TsK VKP(b) 1937 g. 26 fevralia 1937 g.," *Voprosy istorii* 5, 1993, 3–14, 4–5.

34 I. I. Osipova, " *O, Premiloserdyĭ – budi s nami neotstupno –*": vospominaniia veruiushchikh Istinno-Pravoslavnoĭ (Katakombnoĭ) tserkvi, St. Petersburg: Kifa, 2011; W. C. Fletcher, *The Russian Orthodox Church Underground, 1917–1970*, New York: Oxford University Press, 1971, 180–229.

35 Shkarovskii, *Russkaia pravoslavnaia tserkov'*, 100.

36 Ibid., 116–17.

37 F. Oleshchuk, "Kommizm i religiia," *Bol'shevik* 8, 1940, 85.

38 Mozokhin, *Pravo*, 477, 484.

39 E. Iaroslavskii, "Zadachi antireligioznoi propagandy," *Antireligioznik* 5, 1941, 1–8, 1; Shkarovskii, *Russkaia pravoslavnaia tserkov'*, 97.

40 Kh. Kessler and G. E. Kornilov, eds., *Kolkhoznaia zhizn' na Urale, 1935–1953*, Moscow: Rosspen, 2006, 166.

41 TsGA SPB, f. 25, op. 20, d. 152, ll. 1–2.

42 TsGA SPB, f. 25, op. 10, d. 279, l. 14.

43 Shkarovskii, *Russkaia pravoslavnaia tserkov'*, 101–2.

44 Ibid., 110.

45 O.Iu. Vasil'eva et al., comp., *Russkaia pravoslavnaia tserkov' v gody Velikoi Otechestvennoi voiny 1941–1945 gg.*, Moscow: izd-vo Krutitskogo podvor'ia, 2009; M. I. Odintsov and A. S. Kochetova, comp., *Konfessional'naia politika v Sovetskom Soiuze v gody Velikoi Otechestvennoi voiny 1941–1945 gg.*, Moscow: Rosspen, 2014; and M. I. Odintsov and T. A. Chumachenko, *Sovet po delam Russkoi Pravoslavnoi Tserkvi pri SNK (SM) SSSR i Moskovskaia patriarkhiia: epokha vzaimodeistviia i protivostoianiia, 1943–1965 gg.*, St. Petersburg: ROII, 2013.

46 Mozokhin, *Pravo*, 493.

47 See the texts in Sergii, Russkaia pravoslavnaia tserkov' i Velikaia Otechestvennaia Voina; Sbornik tserkovnykh dokumentov, Moscow, 1944.

48 Shkarovskii, *Russkaia pravoslavnaia tserkov'*, 121.

49 Ibid., 138.

50 T. A. Chumachenko, "Pravovaia baza gosudarstvenno-tserkovnykh otnosheniiu v 1940-e – pervoi polovine 1960-kh godov," *Vestnik Cheliabinskogo gosudarstvennogo universiteta* 24, 138–49, 139–40.

51 M. I. Odintsov, *Russkie patriarkhi*, Moscow: RAGS, 1999, 283–91.

52 *Pravda o religii v Rossii*, Moscow, 1942.

53 See, for example, the reports to Stalin in 1945 and 1946 about the exchange of church delegations in M. I. Odintsov, "Russkaia pravoslavnaia tserkov' stala na pravil'nyi put'," *Istoricheskii arkhiv* 4, 1994, 90–112, 97–102.

54 M. I. Odintsov and T. A. Chumachenko, "Rabota Soveta po delam RPTs nosila politicheskii kharakter," *Svoboda sovesti v Rossii* 2, Moscow, 2005, 455–87.

55 Shkarovskii, *Russkaia Pravoslavnaia Tserkov'*, 170.

56 N. Donenko et al., comp., *Krymskaia eparkhiia v dokumentakh Sviatitelia Luki (Voino-Iasenetskogo) i nadziraiushchikh organov 1946–1961*, Simferopol': Orianda, 2015, 233.

57 Shkarovskii, *Russkaia Pravoslavnaia Tserkov'*, 18–20.

58 Chumachenko, "Pravovaia," 141.

59 Odintsov, "Russkaia pravoslavnaia tserkov'," 102–12.

60 Iu.V. Geras'kin, "Podacha khodataistv ob otkrytii khramov v 1940-1950-e gody kak sposob otstaivaniia konstitutsionnogo prava na svobode ispovedaniia," *Vestnik Cheliabinskogo gosudarstvennogo universiteta* 24, 2008, 132–8, 133.

61 D. Peris, " 'God Is Now on Our Side': The Religious Revival on Unoccupied Soviet Territory during World War II," *Kritika* 1, 2000, 97–118.

62 TsGA SPB, f. 25, op. 5, d. 196, ll. 49–51).

63 U. Huhn, *Glaube und Eigensinn. Volksfrömmigkeit zwischen Orthodoxer Kirche und sowjetischem Staat*, Wiesbaden: Harrassowitz, 2014.

64 E. Zubkova, *Russia after the War*, Armonk, NY: M. E. Sharpe, 1998, 69.

65 Iu.V. Geras'kin, *Vzaimootnosheniia Russkoi Pravoslavnoi Tserkvi, obshchestvo i vlasti v kontse-1930-kh – 1991 gg.*, Moscow: MGPU, 2008, 134–5.

66 E. Zubkova et al., eds., *Sovetskaia zhizn' 1945–1953*, Moscow: Rosspen, 2003, 639.

67 N. T. Abdulov, "Ufimskaia eparkhiia v sisteme gosudarstvenno-tserkovnykh otnoshenii 1917–1991 gg.," kand. dissertatsiia, avtoreferat, University of Ufa, 2006, 18. The tax burden was the principal issue in appeals; see E. I. Maliukov and T. A. Chumachenko, "Deiatel'nost' upolnomochennogo SDRPTs po cheliabinskoi oblasti v period pozdnego Stalinizma, 1948–1953 gg.," *Central Russian Journal of Social Sciences* 10, 2015, 236–46, 240.

68 Iu.V. Geras'kin, *Russkaia pravoslavnaia tserkov', veruiushchie, vlast' (konets 30-kh – 70-e gody XX veka)*, Riazan: Riazanskii gos. universitet, 2007, 82–94; Huhn, *Glaube*, 214–48.

69 N. V. Shabalin, *Russkaia Pravoslavnaia Tserkov' i sovetskoe gosudarstvo v seredine sorokovykh-piatidesiatye gody XX veka*. Kirov: n.p, 2004, 29–30.

70 Geras'kin, *Vzaimootnosheniia*, 135.

71 A.Iu. Mikhailovskii, "Khodataistva veruiushchikh ob otkrytii khramov kak kanal vzaimodeistviia s vlast'iu v sfere religioznoi politiki (1943–1958 gg., na materialakh riazanskoi oblasti)," *Vestnik Tambovskogo universiteta* 3, 2010, 360–5: 361; Zubkova, *Sovetskaia zhizn'*, 648.

72 Geras'kin, "Podacha," 134.

73 A. G. Podmaritsyn, "Khodataistva ob otkrytii khramov v Kuibyshevskoi oblasti (1943–1961)," *Vestnik Samarskogo gosudarstvennogo universiteta* 8, 2012, 80–4, 82.

74 E.Iu. Zubkova, *Poslevoennoe sovetskoe obshchestvo: politika i povsednevnost' 1945–1953*, Moscow: Rosspen, 2000, 105.

75 Kessler and Kornilov, *Kolkhoznaia zhizn'*, 166.

76 Mikhailovskii, "Khodataistva," 361.

77 M. I. Odintsov, "Gosudarstvo i tserkov' v gody voiny," *Istoricheskii arkhiv* 3, 1995, 117–35, 120.

78 O. Sibireva, "Pravoslavnaia religioznost' v pozdnem SSSR: Primer Shatskogo raiona Riazanskoi oblasti," *Neprikosnovennyi zapas* 5, 2010, available at: http://magazines.russ.ru/nz/2010/5/si9-pr.html, accessed December 12, 2017.

79 Miakinin, "Polozhenie," 238.

80 Ibid., 235.

Further Reading

Translated Primary Sources

Abramov, Fyodor. *The New Life: A Day on a Collective Farm*. New York: Grove Press, 1963.

Alexievich, Svetlana. *The Unwomanly Face of War: An Oral History of Women in World War II*. New York: Random House, 2017.

Babel, Isaac. *Red Cavalry and Other Stories*. Edited by Efraim Sicher. Translated by David McDuff. New York: Penguin, 2006.

Bidlack, Richard, and Nikita Lomagin, eds. *The Leningrad Blockade, 1941–1944: A New Documentary History from the Soviet Archives*. Translated by Marian Schwartz. New Haven, CT: Yale University Press, 2012.

Bittner, Stephen. *The Kremlin's Scholar: A Memoir of Soviet Politics under Stalin and Khrushchev*. New Haven, CT: Yale University Press, 2007.

Bulgakov, Mikhail. *The Master and Margarita*. Translated by Diana Burgin and Katherine Tiernan O'Connor. New York: Vintage, 1996.

Chistyakov, Ivan. *The Day Will Pass Away: The Diary of a Gulag Prison Guard*. London: Pegasus Books, 2017.

Chuikov, Vasily. *The End of the Third Reich*. Translated by Ruth Kisch. London: MacGibbon, 1967.

Chukovsky, Kornei. *Diary: 1901–1969*. New Haven, CT: Yale University Press. 2005.

Dimitrov, Georgi. *The Diary of Georgi Dimitrov*. Translated by Jane T. Hedges, Timothy D. Sergay, and Irina Faion. Edited by Ivo Banac. New Haven, CT: Yale University Press, 2003.

Garros, Veronique et al., eds. *Intimacy and Terror: Soviet Diaries of the 1930s*. New York: Free Press, 1997.

Geldern, James von, and Richard Stites, eds. *Mass Culture in Soviet Russia: Tales, Poems, Songs, Movies, Plays and Folklore, 1917–1953*. Bloomington: Indiana University Press, 1995.

Getty, J. Arch, and Oleg V. Naumov. *The Road to Terror: Stalin and the Self-Destruction of the Bolsheviks, 1932–1939*. Translated by Benjamin Sher. 2nd ed. New Haven, CT: Yale University Press, 2010.

Ginzburg, Evgeniia. *Journey into the Whirlwind*. Translated by Paul Stevenson and Max Hayward. New York: Harcourt, 1967.

Grossman, Vasily. *Life and Fate*. Translated by Robert Chandler. New York: New York Review Books, 2006.

Grossman, Vasily. *A Writer at War: A Soviet Journalist with the Red Army, 1941–1945*. Edited and translated by Antony Beevor and Luba Vinogradova. New York: Vintage, 2007.

History of the All-Union Communist Party (Bolsheviks): Short Course.
London: Greenwood Press, 1976.

Khlevniuk, Oleg. *The History of the Gulag: From Collectivization to the Great Terror.* Translated by Vadim A. Staklo. New Haven, CT: Yale University Press, 2004.

Khrushchev, Nikita Sergeevich. *Memoirs of Nikita Khrushchev.* Edited by S. N. Khrushchev. 3 vols. University Park, PA: Pennsylvania State University Press, 2013.

Kopelev, Lev. *To Be Preserved Forever.* Edited and translated by Anthony Austin. New York: Lippincott, 1977.

Lugovskaya, Nina. *The Diary of a Soviet Schoolgirl, 1932–1937.* Moscow: Glas, 2003.

Lugovskaya, Nina. *I Want to Live: The Diary of a Young Girl in Stalin's Russia.* New York: Houghton Mifflin, 2006.

Mandelshtam, Nadezhda. *Hope against Hope: A Memoir.* Translated by Max Hayward. New York: Atheneum, 1970.

Meretskov, K. A. *Serving the People.* Translated by David Fidlon. Moscow: Progress, 1971.

Mucholsky, F. V. *Gulag Boss: A Soviet Memoir.* Oxford: Oxford University Press, 2010.

Petrone, Karen, and Kenneth Slepyan. *The Soviet Union and Russia, 1939–2015: A History in Documents.* Oxford: Oxford University Press, 2016.

Scott, John. *Behind the Urals: An American Worker in Russia's City of Steel.* Bloomington, IN: Indiana University Press, 1989.

Shalamov, Varlam. *Kolyma Tales.* Translated by John Glad. New York: Penguin, 1995.

Shearer, David, and Vladimir Khaustov. *Stalin and the Lubianka: A Documentary History of the Political Police and Security Organs in the Soviet Union, 1922–1953.* New Haven, CT: Yale University Press, 2015.

Siegelbaum, Lewis, and Andrei Sokolov, eds. *Stalinism as a Way of Life: A Narrative in Documents.* New Haven, CT: Yale University Press, 2000.

Solzhenitsyn, Aleksandr I. *In the First Circle.* Translated by Harry T. Willetts. New York: Harper Collins, 2009.

Solzhenitsyn, Aleksandr I. *The Gulag Archipelago, 1918–1956.* Translated by Thomas P. Whitney. 3 vols. New York: Harper & Row, 1974, 1978.

Stalin, Joseph. *The Stalin-Kaganovich Correspondence, 1931–36.* Translated by Steven Shabad. Edited by R. W. Davies et al. New Haven, CT: Yale University Press, 2003.

Stalin, Joseph. *Stalin's Letters to Molotov, 1925–1936.* Translated by Catherine A. Fitzpatrick. Edited by Lars T. Lih, Oleg V. Naumov, and Oleg V. Khlevniuk. New Haven, CT: Yale University Press, 1995.

Suny, Ronald G. *The Structure of Soviet History: Essays and Documents.* 2nd ed. Oxford; Oxford University Press, 2013.

Trotsky, Leon. *My Life: An Attempt at an Autobiography.* Translation of *Moia Zhizn'.* New York: Pathfinder, 1970.

Viola, Lynne, et al., eds. *The War against the Peasantry, 1927–1930: The Tragedy of the Soviet Countryside.* Vol. 1. New Haven, CT: Yale University Press, 2005.

Zamyatin, Yevgeny. *We.* Translated by Mirra Ginsburg. New York: Harper, 2001.

Scholarly Literature

Adler, Nanci. *The Gulag Survivor: Beyond the Soviet System*. London: Routledge, 2001.

Adler, Nanci. *Keeping Faith with the Party: Communist Believers Return from the Gulag*. Bloomington: Indiana University Press, 2012.

Adler, Nanci. *Victims of Soviet Terror: The Story of the Memorial Movement*. Westport, CT: Praeger 1993.

Alexopoulos, Golfo. *Illness and Inhumanity in Stalin's Gulag*. New Haven, CT: Yale University Press, 2017.

Alexopoulos, Golfo. *Stalin's Outcasts: Aliens, Citizens and the Soviet State, 1926–1936*. Ithaca, NY: Cornell University Press, 2003.

Barnes, Steven A. *Death and Redemption: The Gulag and the Shaping of Soviet Society*. Princeton, NJ: Princeton University Press, 2011.

Berkhoff, Karel. *The Harvest of Despair: Life and Death in Ukraine under Nazi Rule*. Cambridge, MA: Belknap, 2008.

Berkhoff, Karel. *Motherland in Danger: Soviet Propaganda during World War II*. Cambridge, MA: Harvard University Press, 2012.

Bernstein, Frances. *The Dictatorship of Sex: Lifestyle Advice for the Soviet Masses*. DeKalb, IL: Northern Illinois University Press, 2011.

Blackwell, Martin J. *Kyiv as a Regime City: The Return of Soviet Power after Nazi Occupation*. Rochester, NY: University of Rochester Press, 2016.

Boterbloem, Kees. *Life and Death under Stalin: Kalinin Province, 1945–1953*. Montreal: McGill Queen's University Press, 1999.

Boterbloem, Kees. *The Life and Times of Andrei Zhdanov, 1896–1948*. Montreal: McGill Queen's University Press, 1999.

Brandenberger, David. *National Bolshevism: Stalinist Mass Culture and the Formation of Modern Russian National Identity, 1931–1956*. Cambridge, MA: Harvard University Press, 2002.

Brandenberger, David. *Propaganda State in Crisis: Soviet Ideology, Indoctrination, and Terror under Stalin, 1927–1941*. New Haven, CT: Yale University Press, 2012.

Broekmeyer, Marius. *Stalin, the Russians and Their War: 1941–1945*. Madison, WI: University of Madison Press, 2000.

Chatterjee, Choi. *Celebrating Women: Gender Festival Culture and Bolshevik Ideology, 1910–1939*. Pittsburgh, PA: University of Pittsburgh Press, 2002.

Cohen, Laurie R. *Smolensk under Nazi Rule: Everyday Life in Occupied Russia*. Rochester, NY: University of Rochester Press, 2013.

Cohn, Edward. *The High Title of a Communist: Postwar Party Discipline and the Values of the Soviet Regime*. DeKalb: Northern Illinois University Press, 2015.

Conquest, Robert. *The Harvest of Sorrow: Soviet Collectivization and the Terror-Famine*. New York: Oxford University Press, 1987.

Davies, R. W., and Stephen G. Wheatcroft. *The Years of Hunger: Soviet Agriculture, 1931–1933*. Houndsmills: Palgrave Macmillan, 2004.

Davies, Sarah. *Popular Opinion in Stalin's Russia: Terror, Propaganda and Diseent, 1934–1941*. Cambridge: Cambridge University Press, 1997.

Davies, Sarah and James Harris. *Stalin's World: Dictating the Soviet Order*. New Haven, CT: Yale University Press, 2014.

DeHaan, Heather D. *Stalinist City Planning: Professionals, Performance, and Power in 1930s Nizhnii Novgorod.* Toronto: University of Toronto Press, 2013.

Edele, Mark. *Stalinist Society, 1928–1953.* Oxford, Oxford University Press, 2011.

Edele, Mark. *Soviet Veterans of World War Two: A Popular Movement in an Authoritarian Society, 1941–1991.* New York: Oxford University Press, 2009.

Edgar, Adrienne. *Tribal Nation: The Making of Soviet Turkmenistan.* Princeton, NJ: Princeton University Press, 2006.

Erickson, John. *The Road to Berlin: Stalin's War with Germany.* Vol. 2. London: Cassell, 2004.

Erickson, John. *The Road to Stalingrad: Stalin's War with Germany.* Vol. 1. New Haven, CT: Yale University Press, 1999.

Ewing, E. Thomas. *The Teachers of Stalinism.* New York: Peter Lang, 2002.

Fainsod, Merle. *Smolensk under Soviet Rule.* Cambridge, MA: Harvard University Press, 1958.

Filtzer, Donald. *The Hazards of Urban Life in Late Stalinist Russia: Health, Hygiene and Living Standards, 1943–1953.* Cambridge: Cambridge University Press, 2010.

Fitzpatrick, Sheila. *The Cultural Front: Power and Culture in Revolutionary Russia.* Ithaca, NY: Cornell University Press, 1992.

Fitzpatrick, Sheila. *Everyday Stalinism: Ordinary Life in Extraordinary Times: Soviet Russia in the 1930s.* Oxford: Oxford University Press, 1992.

Fitzpatrick, Sheila. *Stalin's Peasants: Resistance and Survival in the Russian Village after Collectivization.* Oxford: Oxford University Press, 1996.

Fitzpatrick, S., and Y. Slezkine, eds. *In the Shadow of Revolution: Life Stories of Russian Women from 1917 to the Second World War.* Princeton, NJ: Princeton University Press, 2000.

Getty, J. Arch. *Practicing Stalinism: Bolsheviks, Boyars and the Persistence of Tradition.* New Haven, CT: Yale University Press, 2013.

Glantz, David. *The Battle for Leningrad, 1941–1944.* Lawrence: University Press of Kansas, 2002.

Glantz, David. *Colossus Reborn: The Red Army at War, 1941–1943.* Lawrence: University Press of Kansas, 2005.

Glantz, David. *Stumbling Colossus: The Red Army on the Eve of World War.* Lawrence: University Press of Kansas, 2011.

Gorodetsky, Gabriel. *Grand Delusion: Stalin and the German Invasion of Russia.* New Haven, CT: Yale University Press, 2001.

Graziosi, Andrea et al., eds. *After the Holomodor: The Enduring Impact of Great Famine on Ukraine.* Cambridge, MA: Harvard Ukrainian Research Institute, 2014.

Gross, Jan T. *Revolution from Abroad: The Soviet Conquest of Poland's Western Ukraine and Western Belorussia.* Princeton, NJ: Princeton University Press, 2002.

Halfin, Igal. *From Darkness to Light: Class, Consciousness and Salvation in Revolutionary Russia.* Pittsburgh, PA: University of Pittsburgh Press, 2002.

Halfin, Igal. *Stalinist Confessions: Messianism and Terror at the Leningrad Communist University.* Pittsburgh, PA: University of Pittsburgh Press, 2009.

Hagenloh, Paul. *Stalin's Police: Public Order and Mass Repression in the USSR, 1926–1941.* Baltimore, MD: Johns Hopkins University Press, 2009.

Harris, James. *The Great Fear: Stalin's Terror of the 1930s*. Oxford: Oxford University Press, 2016.

Harris, James. *The Great Urals: Regionalism and the Evolution of the Soviet System*. Ithaca, NY: Cornell University Press, 1999.

Healey, Dan. *Bolshevik Sexual Forensics: Diagnosing Disorder in the Clinic and the Courtroom, 1917–1939*. DeKalb: Northern Illinois University Press, 2009.

Healey, Dan. *Homosexual Desire in Revolutionary Russia: The Regulation of Sexual and Gender Dissent*. Chicago, IL: University of Chicago Press, 2001.

Heinzen, James. *The Art of the Bribe: Corruption under Stalin, 1943–1953*. New Haven, CT: Yale University Press, 2016.

Heinzen, James. *Inventing a Soviet Countryside: State Power and the Transformation of Rural Russia, 1917–1929*. Pittsburgh, PA: University of Pittsburgh Press, 2004.

Hellbeck, Jochen. *Revolution on My Mind: Writing a Diary under Stalin*. Cambridge, MA: Harvard University Press, 2009.

Hessler, Julie. *A Social History of Soviet Trade: Trade Policy, Retail Practices, and Consumption, 1917–1953*. Princeton, NJ: Princeton University Press, 2004.

Hirsch, Francine. *Empire of Nations: Ethnographic Knowledge and the Making of the Soviet Union*. Ithaca, NY: Cornell University Press, 2005.

Hoffmann, David. *Peasant Metropolis: Social Identities in Moscow, 1929–1941*. Ithaca, NY: Cornell University Press, 2000.

Holloway, David. *Stalin and the Bomb*. New Haven, CT: Yale University Press, 1994.

Holmes, Larry E. *The Kremlin and the Schoolhouse: Reforming Education in Soviet Russia, 1917-1931*. Bloomington: Indiana University Press, 1991.

Holmes, Larry E. *Stalin's School: Moscow's Model School No. 25, 1931–1937*. Pittsburgh, PA: University of Pittsburgh Press, 1999.

Holmes, Larry E. *Stalin's World War II Evacuations: Triumph and Troubles in Kirov*. Lawrence: University of Kansas Press, 2017

Hosking, Geoffrey. *Rulers and Victims: The Russians in the Soviet Union*. Cambridge, MA: Harvard University Press, 2009.

Inkeles A., and R. Bauer. *The Soviet Citizen: Daily Life in a Totalitarian Society*. Cambridge, MA: Harvard University Press, 1959.

Jones, Jeffrey W. *Everyday Life and the Reconstruction of Soviet Russia during and after the Great Patriotic War, 1943–1948*. Bloomington, IN: Slavica, 2008.

Junge, Marc. *Stalin's Mass Repression and the Cold War Paradigm*. N.p.: Amazon, 2016.

Kassymbekova, Botakoz. *Despite Cultures: Early Soviet Rule in Tajikistan*. Pittsburgh, PA: University of Pittsburgh Press, 2016.

Keller, Shoshana. *To Moscow, Not Mecca: The Soviet Campaign against Islam in Central Asia, 1917–1941*. New York: Praeger, 2001.

Kenez, Peter. *The Birth of the Propaganda State: Soviet Methods of Mass Mobilization, 1917–1929*. Cambridge: Cambridge University Press, 1985.

Khalid, Adeeb. *Making Uzbekistan: Nation, Empire, and Revolution in the Early USSR*. Ithaca, NY: Cornell University Press, 2015.

Khlevniuk, Oleg. *Master of the House: Stalin and His Inner Circle*. New Haven, CT: Yale University Press, 2008.

Khlevniuk, Oleg. *Stalin: New Biography of a Dictator*. New Haven: Yale University Press, 2016.

Khlevniuk, Oleg, and Yoram Gorlizki. *Cold Peace: Stalin and the Soviet Ruling Circle, 1945–1953*. Oxford: Oxford University Press, 2005.

Kiaer, Christina, and Eric Naiman, eds. *Everyday Life in Early Soviet Russia: Taking the Revolution Inside*. Bloomington, IN: Indiana University Press, 2005.

Kirschenbaum, Lisa. *The Legacy of the Siege of Leningrad, 1941–1995: Myth, Memories and Monuments*. Cambridge: Cambridge University Press, 2006.

Kostyrchenko, Gennadi. *Out of the Red Shadows: Anti-Semitism in Stalin's Russia*. Amherst, NY: Prometheus, 1995.

Kotkin, Stephen. *Magnetic Mountain: Stalinism as a Civilization*. Berkeley: University of California Press, 1997.

Kotkin, Stephen. *Stalin: Paradoxes of Power, 1878–1928*. New York: Penguin, 2015.

Kotkin, Stephen. *Stalin: Waiting for Hitler, 1929–1941*. New York: Penguin, 2017.

Krementsov, Nikolai. *The Cure: A Story of Cancer and Politics from the Annals of the Cold War*. Chicago: University of Chicago Press, 2002.

Krementsov, Nikolai. *Stalinist Science*. Princeton, NJ: Princeton University Press, 1997.

Kuromiya, Hiroaki. *Freedom and Terror in the Donbas: A Ukrainian-Russian Borderland, 1870s–1990s*. Cambridge: Cambridge University Press, 2003.

Kuromiya, Hiroaki. *Stalin: Profiles in Power*. New York: Longman, 2005.

Kuromiya, Hiroaki. *Voices of the Dead: Stalin's Great Terror in the 1930s*. New Haven, CT: Yale University Press, 2007.

Kuznetsov, Anatoli. *Babi Yar: A Document in the Form of a Novel*. New York: Farrar, Straus and Giroux, 1970.

Ledeneva, A.V. *Russia's Economy of Favours: Blat, Networking and Informal Exchange*. Cambridge: Cambridge University Press, 1998.

Lenoe, Matthew E. *The Kirov Murder and Soviet History*. New Haven, CT: Yale University Press, 2010.

Lewin, Moshe. *The Making of the Soviet System: Essays in the Social History of Interwar Russia*. New York: New Press, 1985.

Lewin, Moshe. *Lenin's Last Struggle*. Ann Arbor: University of Michigan Press, 2005.

Lohr, Eric. *Nationalizing the Russian Empire: The Campaign against Enemy Aliens during World War One*. Cambridge, MA: Harvard University Press, 2003.

Marshall, Alex. *The Caucasus under Soviet Rule*. New York: Routledge, 2010.

Martin, Terry. *An Affirmative Action Empire: Nations and Nationalism in the Soviet Union, 1923–1939*. Ithaca, NY: Cornell University Press, 2001.

McDonald, Tracy. *Face to the Village: The Riazan Countryside under Soviet Rule, 1921–1930*. Toronto: University of Toronto Press, 2016.

Merridale, Catherine. *Ivan's War: Life and Death in the Red Army, 1939–1945*. New York: Picador, 2007.

Merridale, Catherine. *Night of Stone: Death and Memory in Twentieth-Century Russia*. London: Granta, 1999.

Nekrich, Aleksander. *The Punished Peoples: The Deportation and Fate of Soviet Minorities at the End of the Second World War*. New York: Norton, 1981.

Osokina, Elena. *Our Daily Bread: Socialist Distribution and the Art of Survival in Stalin's Russia, 1927–1941*. Armonk, NY: M. E. Sharpe, 2001.

Petrone, Karen. *The Great War in Russian Memory*. Bloomington, IN: Indiana University Press, 2011.

Petrone, Karen. *Life Has Become More Joyous, Comrades: Celebrations in the Time of Stalin*. Bloomington: Indiana University Press, 2000.

Petrov, Nikita, and Marc Jansen. *Stalin's Loyal Executioner: People's Commissar Nikolai Ezhov, 1895–1940*. Stanford, CA: Hoover Institution Press, 2002.

Plamper, Jan. *The Stalin Cult: A Study in the Alcheny of Power*. New Haven, CT: Yale University Press, 2012.

Pipes, Richard. *Russia under the Bolshevik Regime*. New York: Vintage, 1995.

Polonsky, Rachel. *Molotov's Magic Lantern: A Journey in Russian History*. New York: Faber and Faber, 2011.

Polyan, Pavel. *Against Their Will: The History and Geography of Forced Migrations in the USSR*. Budapest: Central European University Press, 2003.

Pons, Silvio. *Stalin and the Inevitable War, 1936–1941*. New York: Routledge, 2002.

Priestland, David. *Stalinism and the Politics of Mobilisation*. Oxford: Oxford University Press, 2007.

Raleigh, Donald J. *Provincial Landscapes: Local Dimensions of Soviet Power, 1917–1953*. Pittsburgh, PA: University of Pittsburgh Press, 2001.

Randall, Amy E. *The Soviet Dream World of Retail Trade and Consumption in the 1930s*. Houndsmills: Palgrave Macmillan, 2008.

Ree, Erik van. *The Political Thought of Joseph Stalin: A Study in Twentieth-Century Revolutionary Patriotism*. New York: Routledge, 2002.

Robinson, Paul. *The White Russian Army in Exile, 1920–1941*. New York: Oxford University Press, 2002.

Rolf, Malte. *Soviet Mass Festivals, 1917–1991*. Pittsburgh, PA: University of Pittsburgh Press, 2013.

Rossman, Jeffrey J. *Worker Resistance under Stalin: Class and Revolution on the Shop Floor*. Cambridge, MA: Harvard University Press, 2005.

Service, Robert. *Lenin: A Biography*. Cambridge, MA: Harvard University Press, 2000.

Service, Robert. *Stalin: A Biography*. Cambridge, MA: Belknap, 2005.

Service, Robert. *Trotsky*. Cambridge, MA: Belknap, 2009.

Shearer, David R. *Industry, State, and Society in Stalin's Russia, 1926–1934*. Ithaca, NY: Cornell University Press, 1996.

Shearer, David R. *Policing Stalin's Socialism: Repression and Social Order in the Soviet Union, 1924–1953*. New Haven, CT: Yale University Press, 2009.

Shearer, David R. "Wheeling and Dealing in Soviet Industry: Syndicates, Trade, and Political Economy at the End of the 1920s." *Cahiers du Monde Russe* 36 (1995): 139–60.

Siegelbaum, Lewis H. *Borders of Socialism: Private Spheres of Soviet Russia*. Basingstoke: Palgrave, 2006.

Siegelbaum, Lewis H. *Stakhanovism and the Politics of Productivity in the USSR, 1935–1941*. Cambridge: Cambridge University Press, 1988.

Slepyan, Kenneth. *Stalin's Guerillas: Soviet Partisans in World War II*. Lawrence: University Press of Kansas, 2006.

Snyder, Timothy. *Bloodlands: Europe between Hitler and Stalin*. New York: Basic Books, 2012.

Solomon, Peter H. *Soviet Criminal Justice under Stalin*. Cambridge: Cambridge University Press, 1996.

Stites, Richard. *Revolutionary Dreams: Utopian Vision and Experimental Life in the Russian Revolution*. Oxford: Oxford University Press, 1991.

Stone, David R. *Hammer and Rifle: The Militarization of the Soviet Union, 1926–1933*. Lawrence: University Press of Kansas, 2000.

Stone, David R., ed. *The Soviet Union at War, 1941–1945*. Barnsley: Pen and Sword, 2010.

Veidlinger, Jeffrey. *The Moscow State Yiddish Theater: Jewish Culture on the Soviet Stage*. Bloomington, IN: Indiana University Press, 2006.

Viola, Lynne. *Peasant Rebels under Stalin: Collectivization and the Culture of Peasant Resistance*. Oxford: Oxford University Press, 1999.

Viola, Lynne. *Stalinist Perpetrators on Trial: Scenes from the Great Terror in Soviet Ukraine*. Oxford: Oxford University Press, 2017

Viola, Lynne. *The Unknown Gulag: The Lost World of Stalin's Special Settlements*. Oxford: Oxford University Press, 2007.

Voslensky, Michael. *Nomenklatura: Anatomy of the Soviet Ruling Class*. London: Bodley Head, 1984.

Watson, Derek. *Molotov: A Biography*. Houndsmills: Palgrave Macmillan, 2005.

Weiner, Amir. *Making Sense of War: The Second World War and the Fate of the Bolshevik Revolution*. Princeton, NJ: Princeton University Press, 2002.

Weiner, Douglas. *A Little Corner of Freedom: Russian Nature Protection from Stalin to Gorbachev*. Berkeley: University of California Press, 2002.

Weiner, Douglas. *Models of Nature: Ecology, Conservation and the Cultural Revolution in Soviet Russia*. Pittsburgh, PA: University of Pittsburgh Press, 2000.

Werth, Alexander. *Russia at War, 1941–1945*. New York: Dutton, 1964.

Werth, Nicolas. *Cannibal Island: Death in a Siberian Gulag*. Princeton, NJ: Princeton University Press, 2007.

Wood, Elizabeth. *The Baba and the Comrade: Gender and Politics in Revolutionary Russia*. Bloomington: Indiana University Press, 2000.

Yekelchyk, Serhy. *Stalin's Empire of Memory: Russian-Ukrainian Relations in the Soviet Historical Imagination*. Toronto: University of Toronto Press, 2004.

Yekelchyk, Serhy. *Stalin's Citizens: Everyday Politics in the Wake of Total War*. Oxford: Oxford University Press, 2014.

Zubkova, Elena. *Russia after the War: Hopes, Illusions and Disappointments, 1945–1957*. Armonk, NY: M. E. Sharpe, 1998.

Zubok, Vladislav M. *A Failed Empire: The Soviet Union in the Cold War from Stalin to Gorbachev*. Chapel Hill: University of North Carolina Press, 2008.

Zubok, Vladislav M., and Constantine Pleshakov. *Inside the Kremlin's Cold War: From Stalin to Khrushchev*. Cambridge, MA: Harvard University Press, 1997.

Index